淮南市博物馆藏镜

Bronze Mirrors Collected at Huainan Museum

淮南市博物馆 编著
Edited by Huainan Museum

文物出版社

目　录　Contents

淮南市博物馆藏镜概述

　　铜镜，从新石器时代晚期出现到近代被玻璃镜所取代，在我国流行、使用了四千多年，是我国古代使用最普遍、延续时间最长的一种生活日用铜器。它既是实用器，又是精美的艺术品，正面光可鉴人，是古代照面饰容和整理衣冠不可缺少的日常用具；背面大多装饰着精美的纹饰或刻工精巧的铭文，反映出当时的政治、经济、文化特征和社会风尚，因而具有重要的研究价值。

　　"以铜为镜，可以正衣冠；以古为镜，可以知兴替；以人为镜，可以明得失。"唐太宗李世民从铜镜的实用功能引喻出对社会发展轨迹的思想认知，予后人以深刻启示。透过一面面小小的铜镜，可以从中窥探中国古代历史文化演化的大千世界。

一

　　《轩辕黄帝传》记载，黄帝"因铸镜以像之，为十五面，神镜宝镜也"。考古发现也证明铜镜在新石器时代晚期即已出现。20世纪70年代，在距今四千多年前的齐家文化墓葬中出土两面铜镜，证明我国是最早铸造和使用铜镜的国家之一。

　　商周是我国青铜工艺发展的鼎盛时期，出土的青铜器数以万计，但出土的商周铜镜，到目前为止，屈指数来也不过30面，且主要出土于黄河上游地区，中下游出土较少。因此，人们一般认为中国铜镜产生于黄河上游的甘肃、青海地区。相比较于青铜时代灿烂辉煌、种类繁多的青铜器，铜镜从诞生之初到战国早期长达1800多年的历史中发展滞缓，造型、纹饰等远远落后于一般青铜器。究其原因，早期铜镜的生产制作与中原地区的青铜器生产制作是两个系统，铜镜没有形成自身的体系，使用范围十分狭窄，是达官贵人的珍稀之物。

　　春秋晚期至战国早期，随着西北游牧民族向中原地区迁徙，铜镜在中原地区开始流行并广泛使用。进入中原后，它首先被贵族阶层认同，到战国中晚期才进入社会各阶层，从此铜镜的铸造和使用兴盛起来，并形成一门独特的工艺体系。秦汉以后铜镜成为百姓生活中广泛使用的日用器，铜镜的质量、数量大幅度提高。汉唐时期的铜镜百花争艳，尤其是唐代铜镜制作，达到了中国古代铜镜制作水平的高峰，种类繁多、式样新颖，新工艺、新造型、新纹饰不断涌现。五代、宋以后，虽然铜镜逐渐式微，但仍是人们必备的生活日用品。

　　铜镜的成像效果，是由原料中铜、锡、铅等合金的配比成分所决定的。战国时，铜镜的原料比例已基本成熟和稳定，这种含铅的高锡青铜配比较为符合照面需求，并且稳定地发展到后代。唐代，由于锡含量适当增加，铜镜的使用达到了最佳效果。《周礼·考工记·六齐》中说："金锡半，谓之鉴燧之齐。"郑玄注："鉴，亦镜也。"通过对历代铜镜标本所做的化验结果看，"金锡半"是指锡的比例约占铜含量的一半，而不是各占一半。古代工匠通过不断的实践，发现了最为合理的配方。《淮南子·修务训》中记载："明镜始下型，朦然未见形……及其粉以玄锡，摩以白旃，须眉微毫可得而察。"所谓"玄锡"是指锡汞，当指以锡汞摩擦镜子，使其光亮鉴人。在使用中，如果年深日久不磨，就正如唐元稹《谕宝诗》所言"莫邪无人淬，两刃幽壤铁。秦镜无人磨，一片埋雾月"了。

东晋顾恺之《女史箴图》中，有当时用镜照面梳妆的场面。右侧仕女席地侧身而坐，左手执镜，右手梳发，镜中有影像；左侧仕女面对悬镜而坐，身后立一仕女为其梳理云鬓。从画面判断，执镜圆形有柄，便于手执；悬镜置于镜架之上，直径较大，镜背飘有丝带，当是用丝织类带子系于架上。这是我们见到的最早使用铜镜的完整场景，也是所见最早的有柄铜镜资料。

从已掌握的考古资料看，古人用镜有手执、悬挂、置于案台和随身携带等四种使用方法。战国、汉代的铜镜出土时，镜面上常附着有漆器或丝织品的残留物，可能是盛放或包裹铜镜的物品。湖北九连墩战国楚墓出土有盛放铜镜的漆质梳妆盒。唐代瓷器中有专用于盛放铜镜的瓷镜盒，唐代寿州窑瓷器中发现有烧制十分讲究的蜡黄釉镜盒，越窑、长沙窑等也有此类产品，说明古人对铜镜是十分珍爱的。古人对铜镜的珍视还表现在墓葬中常常随葬铜镜，这是"视死如生"思想的体现，要在阴间继续使用生前爱物。

在古人的意识中，铜镜除理容的实用功能外，其本身还是一件通灵宝物，具有辟邪庇佑的功能。汉镜铭文中常有"辟不祥"、"长保二亲"等字句，正如今人将玻璃镜置于门头、梁脊之上一样，有驱邪镇妖的寓意。而墓葬中出土的铜镜，其造型、纹饰、铭文等时代特征鲜明，考古工作者据此能够判断出墓葬的大致时代，从而成为考古断代的标尺，备受考古工作者的重视和喜爱。

二

淮南市博物馆馆藏铜镜的特点，与淮南地区历史发展、建制沿革、地下遗存埋藏等密切相关。

淮南地区水网密布，土地肥沃，气候宜人，历史遗存积淀深厚。在市境内沿淮河及其支流东淝河、西淝河、窑河、泥河、黑河、瓦埠湖及舜耕山南北两侧，共发现古文化遗址 34 处。其中新石器时代遗址 10 处、商周遗址 9 处、汉唐遗址 15 处，（另有历代古墓葬 133 座（群）），主要分布于淮河两岸和舜耕山南麓。众多的古文化遗址反映出自古以来这里就是人类聚居生活的地方。

新石器时代晚期直至春秋早期，东夷中的淮夷人活跃在淮河两岸。《孟子·离娄下》记载："舜，东夷人。……耕于历山下。"一说，历山即淮南舜耕山，相传舜帝南巡在此教民稼穑。《后汉书·东夷传》记载，商武乙时，东夷人有过一次大规模的向南迁徙过程，"分徙淮岱，渐居中土"，在淮河定居的一支东夷人就被称为淮夷，于西周时在此建立了州来国，成为淮河中下游地区的一个重要方国。

春秋末期，楚国东渐，蔡楚交恶，蔡国南下寻求吴国庇护，迁都至州来，改州来为下蔡。其都城在今淮南市境西三公里处寿县县城一带，其统治时间从公元前 493 年至公元前 447 年，共 46 年，历经昭侯、成侯、声侯、元侯和侯齐五世，后被楚灭。1955 年在寿县西门内发现蔡昭侯墓，1959 年在淮南蔡家岗发现蔡声侯墓，验证了这段史实。公元前 241 年，即楚考烈王二十二年，楚国迁都寿春（今淮南西寿县），改寿春为郢，淮南成为楚的京畿之地，历经考烈王、幽王、哀王、负刍四代。至公元前 223 年，秦国大将王翦攻破郢都寿春，楚国灭亡。1933 年，在淮南市杨公镇朱家集李三孤堆发现楚幽王大墓，震惊了国人，引发了学术界研究楚文化的热潮。近年来，考古工作者在李三孤堆、武王墩大墓周围也探测到多个大型车马坑。而在其周边，现仍保留有黄歇墓、大古堆、小古堆、王八古堆、白泥古堆、尖古堆、闫氏古堆等十几座有大型封土的古墓葬，证明此地是一处先秦时期分布密集、保存完整、规格等级高的贵族墓葬群。2005 年以来，配合合（肥）淮（南）阜（阳）、淮（南）蚌（埠）高速公路和合（肥）淮（南）蚌（埠）高速铁路等基本建设项目，在此发掘的战国至唐宋时期的古墓葬多达 1000 余座。

西汉初年，汉高祖刘邦首置淮南国，都寿春（今寿县），辖郡包括九江、庐江、衡山、豫章四郡，领地跨越江淮。汉文帝十六年（公元前 164 年），刘安继为淮南王。刘安在八公山下招贤纳士，致门客数千，撰书炼丹，使淮南地区政治、经济、文化高度发展。东汉时期淮南地区的建制仍沿用西汉建制，汉末，袁术据寿春改设淮南郡。从淮南地区两汉墓葬资料看，此期社会相对安定，墓葬中的随葬品较秦及以前显著增多。

墓葬形制更加多样化，从先秦时期单一的土坑墓，演化到土坑木椁墓、土坑石椁墓、石室墓、多室砖室墓和为数众多的小型砖室墓，几乎每一形制的墓葬都出土有铜镜。从其纹饰风格看，有中原镜，也有吴地鄂州镜、绍兴镜，充分反映出淮南是南北文化的交汇区域，通过淮河、大运河汇集了长江、黄河两岸的各式铜镜。

唐代，淮南地区进入了经济繁荣时期，自南北朝中晚期创烧的寿州窑，至晚唐窑火绵延了四百多年。淮河水道不仅将寿州窑的各种产品行销到江淮地区和长江中下游地区，也将各地优质商品带回淮南。本地区出土的各地唐镜能够折射出当时社会安定、商贸繁荣的景象。

北宋统一后，设置淮南路，市境为寿州辖。北宋末年，市境分属寿春府和下蔡县。宋金对峙的初期，市域仍属寿春、下蔡二县。后宋金以淮河为界，淮河以北为金国所辖，金国在下蔡置寿州，淮河以南为南宋统治。淮河地区成为各种政权争夺的战场，干戈不息，政权交替频繁，淮南失去了汉唐时期的政治、经济、文化区域中心的区位优势。反映在墓葬上，在淮南地区发现的五代以后的古墓葬总量不多，分布特征不明显。

三

淮南地区自春秋战国开始，成为本地区的政治、经济、文化中心，出土的铜镜即从这一时段开始。

本书辑录淮南市博物馆藏战国铜镜 17 面，装饰纹样包括素地镜、纯地纹镜、羽状纹地四叶纹镜、龙纹镜、龙纹菱纹镜、连弧龙纹镜、四山镜、变形兽纹镜、菱形纹镜等。

1972 年淮南市谢家集区红卫轮窑厂 M4 出土的单线连弧纹镜，是本地区发现的铜镜铸造时代最早的一面。其连弧纹的装饰形式是在素地上以小三弦钮为中心，用单线隆起十一个内向连弧纹，装饰手法非常简洁。这种单线形式的连弧纹镜到战国后期演化成宽带状连弧纹和以云雷纹、蟠螭纹、涡纹做地的七弧和八弧不等的形式。馆藏铜镜中还有一件形制、纹饰与之相同的素地单线连弧纹镜，但镜体稍厚，尺寸也稍大。这两面铜镜有早期楚镜风格，说明在楚国迁都寿春之前，楚文化因素已浸润淮河流域。

云雷地纹铜镜，时代稍晚，三弦钮，小圆钮座，以圆涡纹及两个底边相对的双线三角纹相间排列，满布镜背。纹饰有横穿的范线，可知该镜由两块陶范拼接而成；地纹比较疏朗，与战国晚期以失腊法铸造的细密地纹有明显区别。较湖南长沙年佳湖 896 号楚墓出土的云雷地纹镜直径更要小些，钮座所占比例也小一些。

羽状纹地四叶镜 4 面，均出土于市域西部的唐山、李郢孜镇一带。其中圆钮座 3 面，方钮座 1 面；山字纹四叶 1 面，蟠桃形四叶 3 面。羽状纹地蟠桃形四叶纹铜镜时代较早，出现在战国中晚期之交，在湖南、湖北楚墓中出土较多。2010 年 8 月，在淮南市谢家集区李郢孜镇谢家集小区 21 号楼工地出土的战国四叶纹镜，羽状地纹非常精细，但其镜体已明显增厚，镜缘宽大，放置手中感觉沉重，已经没有楚镜小巧轻薄的感觉，说明这种羽状纹地四叶镜延续时间很长，一直到战国末期还在流行。

1957 年在淮南市唐山公社邱家岗和 1987 年在淮南市谢家集红卫轮窑厂出土的 2 面四山纹铜镜是战国楚镜中的代表作品。邱家岗出土的是八叶四花朵四山纹镜，直径 13.7 厘米，厚 0.4 厘米，方钮座，山字底边与方钮座平行布置。山字间置四朵四桃叶形花，方钮座的四角和四个山字右侧凹处各伸一片桃形花叶，以绞索形花枝将花朵与花叶联系。左旋山字与细密的羽状纹地构成均匀、细腻、富丽、繁缛的动感画面。与此镜纹饰、尺寸相同的一面铜镜出土于湖南长沙楚墓，编号 M1554 ：7，直径 13.8 厘米，厚 0.4 厘米，分类为Ⅰ类Ⅵ式，为战国晚期中段，与邱家岗这面形制、尺寸基本相同，时间大约在公元前 277 年至公元前 250 年，即在楚国迁都寿春之前。这两面铜镜尺寸、纹饰的布局安排，尤其是山字笔画的粗细十分相近，这在众多的四山镜中是比较罕见的，应为同一时段、同一区域铸造。长沙是当时楚镜的铸造中心，仅《长沙楚墓》就收录了 49 面，淮南邱家岗出土的这面铜镜当来自长沙。

羽状纹地四山四鹿纹镜，1987 年 12 月出土于淮南市谢家集区红卫轮窑厂，是一面比较罕见的山字纹镜。三弦钮，方钮座，镜背满铺细密的羽状地纹，四山纹间以四兽，兽为回首翘尾的鹿形。国内已知带鹿纹的四山镜仅见于上海博物馆，装饰手法十分相近，唯钮座略有区别，一圆一方。上博藏镜上的四鹿与淮南市博物馆藏镜的形态相同，但制模时是将鹿形及周边做成不规则的四方形，后在羽状地纹上抠出同样形状，镶嵌其中，从而造成羽状地断裂，形成了一个清晰的轮廓，廓内成为素地；而淮南镜的四鹿是以鹿身为廓，嵌入羽状地纹中，使羽状地纹相互连接而丝毫不断。也有可能是四鹿与羽状地纹一次制模，使镜面纹饰非常完美和谐。从其制范工艺上看，淮南这面铜镜技艺更显精湛、纯熟一些。这种山字纹间以兽纹的铜镜发现极少，另有一件三山三鹿镜藏于法国巴黎，鹿纹也是回首翘尾，鹿形的装饰手法与国内这两面非常相近。贺刚先生在《说山字纹镜》中说："三山镜仅见一件，附饰鹿纹。安徽淮南所见一件装饰鹿纹的四山镜有明确的出土地点，其奔鹿与前者以及上海馆藏的一面四山镜的鹿纹完全一样。这类奔鹿纹的山字镜直径都比较大，地纹甚其细密，时代风格相近，鉴于出土山字纹铜镜数量最多的湖南地区至今未发现过类似的鹿纹镜，推测其产于淮南的可能性要大一些。"这一推测是有事实依据的，从淮南地区及六安、蚌埠、合肥、阜阳及周边地区发现的大量战国楚镜看，除湖北荆州、湖南长沙等地外，本地出土的楚镜数量要远远高于其他地区。所以在战国晚期，作为楚国都城京畿地区的淮南很有可能是当时的铸镜中心。

龙纹类镜，计7面，其中有3面为蟠螭龙菱纹，均来源于市域西部与寿县接壤的地区，如唐山镇、李郢孜镇、杨公镇一带。蟠螭纹镜，又称龙纹镜、蟠虺纹镜，是由盘曲的龙和蛇纹组成主纹饰，区别较难，称谓多不统一，一般多称之为蟠螭纹。淮南地区所见蟠螭纹镜，尺寸大小不一，小的7~12厘米，大的16~23厘米。其中尺寸最大的一面出土于一座汉初墓葬中，为三弦钮，圆钮座，钮座上以绞索纹为廓，以满铺的云雷纹为地，三条龙均匀分布于镜面。三只龙首靠近圆钮座。造型十分生动，为四分之三侧面像，两只圆目十分清晰，大口中上、下各有三齿，龙角向前弯曲，龙身作腾飞状，勾曲伸展，羽状形小翅布满身躯。外区饰以一道弦纹、一道绞索纹。蟠螭纹镜中的龙首，常见一目，该镜为二目，且十分形象逼真。该镜虽出土于汉初墓葬中，但其整体风格属晚期楚式镜，应该是战国末期的蟠螭镜了。本馆旧藏中有一件羽状纹地变形兽纹镜，三弦钮，圆钮座，主体纹饰十分特别，似兽也似几何纹，兽的首部为曲尺形，尾部为如意云头，躯体呈"C"形弯曲，几乎看不到兽纹的任何特征。同类镜出土很少，已知有湖南常德楚墓出土的一件，比淮南这件稍大。有学者称其为变形兽纹，尚待更多的资料进行证实。若确为兽纹，为何楚国铸镜工匠要将兽纹变形得如此夸张？其原因十分耐人寻味。

汉代铜镜是馆藏铜镜中的大宗，约占总数的百分之四十。本书辑录的76面汉代铜镜，装饰纹样包括蟠螭纹、连弧纹、铭文圈带、草叶纹、星云纹、博局纹、四乳或多乳禽兽花鸟纹、龙虎纹、神兽画像纹等。从淮南馆藏铜镜看，汉代早期的装饰风格从战国繁缛神秘的纹样中解脱出来，以道家清静无为的理念为基础；中晚期后，受儒家思想影响，纹饰透露着规范、浑厚的世俗性和宗教色彩。大量的镜铭是两汉时期各种思想学说和世俗文化的折射，铭文内容涉及吉祥祝福语、表达相思感情、赞美铜镜质量以及体现神仙、阴阳五行思想等，铭文间常夹有"⊙"或"而"。

1957年淮南市谢家集区赖山公社出土的蟠螭纹镜，三弦钮，伏螭座，座外有一周铭文："愁思以悲，愿君毋说，相思愿毋绝"，外环两周弦纹、两周绞索纹。主纹为蟠螭纹，还保留着战国风格，纹饰以三线勾勒，满布镜背，是典型的西汉早期铜镜。另三面四叶蟠螭纹镜，均是三弦钮，伏螭钮座，座外有四重绞索纹，内环铭"大乐贵富，千秋万岁，宜酒食"，以一鱼纹结句。四镜主纹皆以火焰状花叶间隔蟠螭纹，蟠螭小首，圆目，尖嘴，身躯流转弯曲，舒展自如，装饰方法十分相近。这种以三线并行勾勒纹饰的装饰方法对模范技术要求很高，到武帝时在早期的博局镜上还有使用，此后就十分少见了。

本书收录博局类铜镜16面。博局纹间填以蟠螭、四神鸟兽羽人、四神、四乳四神鸟兽、四乳八鸟、四乳四神、六乳神兽、八乳神兽、八乳卷云、卷云、几何纹等，构成丰富多彩的博局纹镜。

博局镜，又称规矩镜，因国家博物馆藏新莽时期的"善铜四神博局镜"自名"博局"，后统一称谓此类镜为博局镜。汉代盛行博戏，《说文解字》云："局戏也，六箸十二本也。"博局棋上有六黑六白十二个棋子，二人对博。在汉代，上至王公、下到百姓均乐此不疲。但博局还可用作祭神仪式，将博局与四神、羽人、瑞兽交汇在一起，传达的是阴阳五行和神仙思想，这可能是博局镜普遍流行的重要因素。博局镜一般为圆钮座或四叶纹（又称柿蒂纹）钮座，座外饰双线大方格，方格内有纹饰或铭文。主区博局纹间以四神、羽人、鸟兽或填以几何纹。最早的博局镜见于武帝时期，但主要流行于西汉晚期至东汉早期。成熟的博局镜纹饰细腻、制作精良，尤其是王莽时期的博局镜，如同当时的铸币，达到了很高的水准。东汉中晚期，博局纹及其相间的纹饰趋向简化，制作粗糙，到魏晋之初博局镜就逐渐消失了。

1987 年 7 月在淮南市谢家集区唐山乡双古堆 M11 土坑石椁墓中出土的博局镜，直径 21 厘米，厚 0.8 厘米，镜铭"大乐贵富，得所好，千秋万岁，延年益寿"，与河北满城汉窦绾墓出土的"大乐富贵博局蟠螭纹镜"在尺寸、纹饰、铭文上基本相同。窦绾墓是汉代诸侯王级大墓，下葬于武帝太初元年（公元前 104 年），而 M11 的墓口长 4.45 米，宽 2.84 米，深 1.6 米，形制不是很大，墓中伴出印章，上有鸟虫篆书"周安"两字，可知墓主应是汉淮南国的高级官吏。这面博局镜也是本地区发现的时代最早的此类铜镜。

2006 年 6 月和 2010 年 8 月，在淮南市谢家集区出土了两面十分精美的八乳四神羽人鸟兽纹博局镜。这两面铜镜的制范相当精细，其纹饰清晰秀丽，博局纹见棱见角，四神及羽人、鸟兽的细线纹华丽细腻。谢家集新村镜为圆钮，圆钮座，座外环八小乳，间以小花草纹，主区四神较写实，有趣的是在其宽缘上也装饰了拉长变形的四神图案。主纹与镜缘同时装饰四神图案的博局铜镜比较少见，在广州东汉前期墓中出土过一面，比淮南这面略小，制范技术也稍差。赖山窑厂镜为圆钮，方钮座，座外环列十二小乳，间以十二辰铭，主区纹饰外有一周铭文"上大山兮，见仙人，食玉英，饮澧泉，驾交龙兮，乘浮云，宜官秩，保子孙"，中区与外区间隔以栉齿纹和锯齿纹。这面铜镜最具特色的也是镜缘部分，宽镜缘上饰一周流云纹，极为精美，可与国家博物馆藏新莽时期的善铜四神博局镜相媲美，甚至更显规整。由此看来，赖山窑厂镜铸造时间大致在王莽时期，或在其前后不远的时间段内。

本书收录草叶纹镜 2 面，均为内向十六连弧八叶（单层），配四组花叶和桃形花苞，铭文右旋读"见日之光，天下大明"。草叶纹镜流行的时间大约在西汉早期到西汉中期，草叶纹的寓意是汉初清静无为思想的具体表现，尤其是文景时期，社会稳定，人们安居乐业，崇尚自然，以花草图案和"见日之光"来表达对现实生活的理解。

星云纹铜镜是西汉中期继草叶纹镜后开始流行的，它的钮与博山炉很近似，镜背上的星云纹反映了汉代人对宇宙星象的理解。1958 年出土于淮南市唐山公社的星云纹铜镜，连峰式钮（或称博山炉式钮），钮座外环绕内向十六连弧纹，主区纹饰以四乳分区，每区间以五个小乳钉。如果从分区的四个乳钉算起，正好每组为七星。内向十六连弧缘。星云纹铜镜流行时间不长，大约始于武帝时，在昭宣时比较流行，以后迅速衰落。

日光镜和昭明镜是西汉中期到东汉早期十分流行的铜镜，在淮南地区发现较多。本书收录日光镜 6 面，昭明镜 7 面。淮南地区发现的日光镜直径多在 6~10 厘米，半球钮，圆钮座，座外环绕连弧纹，主纹为日光铭文圈带，夹于两周栉齿纹之间。宽素缘。大多制作粗糙。有学者认为这种直径较小、制作粗糙的铜镜可能是专门用于随葬的冥镜。本地区出土的昭明镜较日光镜形制要大一些，制作也比较规整。一般是半球钮，圆钮座，座外环一周内向连弧纹或联珠纹，主纹为铭文圈带，除座外环联珠纹的铜镜有两周铭文圈带外，其余是一周铭文，夹于两周栉齿纹之间。皆宽素缘。昭明镜出现在昭宣时期，较日光镜稍晚一些。两种铜镜的铭文字体，早期为篆体，比较方正，以后逐渐隶化，到晚期时隶化已十分明显。2010 年 9 月淮南市谢家集公安分局移交的一面铜镜，直径 10.7 厘米，主区铭"内清质以昭明，光辉象夫日月，心忽愿忠然而不泄"，内区铭"见日之光，长毋相忘"，将常见的昭明镜铭文和日光镜铭文合于一镜，比较少见，其制作比较规范，比常见的日光镜形制要大，应该是一件实用器。

龙虎纹铜镜，一般是指龙虎对峙的高浮雕盘龙镜，是神兽画像镜的雏形。本书收录龙虎镜 5 面，在市域东部上窑镇和西部谢家集区皆有发现。其中龙虎纹 3 面，龙纹 2 面，均半球钮，主纹为龙虎纹环绕半球钮，作对峙状。龙纹的布局与龙虎纹基本相似，只是将身体占据全部镜面。从淮南这5面龙虎纹镜看，单龙纹的铜镜制作远不如龙虎纹对峙镜，其时代可能要晚至三国六朝时期。

本书收录画像镜4面，重列式布局的三段、四段、五段各1面，对置式1面。其中三段式建安二十年（公元215年）铭文镜，主纹第一段为东王公、西王母，第二、三段各为二神人，镜面一侧为左青龙、右白虎。镜缘上铭文为"吾作明镜，幽涷三商，官克□虎，天皇五帝，伯牙弹琴，吉羊□白虎青龙，建安二十年"。五段式画像镜，每段列坐神人，靠镜缘处，每段均布置神兽、禽鸟。第四段中央有"宜官"铭文，镜缘有一周铭文"吾作明镜□□□五帝至天皇，伯牙弹琴，黄帝除凶，朱昌玄武，白虎青龙，更宜高官□□□"，此镜与《中国铜镜图典》收录的建安十年重列式神兽镜基本相同，应当是同一时期的作品。

神人画像镜是东汉中晚期到三国六朝时期最具特色的新式纹样铜镜。这种铜镜是以高浮雕的东王公、西王母、伍子胥以及青龙、白虎等神兽形象为主区纹饰，极富立体感，是一幅幅惟妙惟肖的立体画卷，成为中国美术史上的一朵奇葩。神人画像镜的产地，主要在吴地的会稽和鄂城。大约在东汉末年建安年间会稽山阴（今绍兴）成为铸镜中心，湖北鄂城（今鄂州市）稍晚于会稽，两地均铸有这类铜镜。神人画像镜主要流行在长江两岸，淮河以北鲜见。而淮南地区自春秋晚期开始，就与吴地往来频繁，吴越青铜器在此屡有发现。在商贸、文化相互交融的东汉末年，淮南地区出土了大量吴越文化的瓷器和铜器，其间自然包括吴地铜镜。

唐代是中国封建社会的全盛时期。这一时期，国家统一，社会稳定，人民安居乐业，经济和文化空前繁荣，也促进了铜镜制作技术和艺术的大幅度提高，并使其产生了划时代的变革。唐镜以浑厚凝重的镜体、式样新颖的造型、丰富多样的题材和富丽繁盛的豪迈风格，将中国铜镜艺术推向了高峰。

淮南地区在隋唐时期迎来了本地区有史以来的经济、文化发展的繁荣时期。创烧于南北朝中晚期的寿州窑，在盛唐时烧制出了令人喜爱的黄釉产品，使其在四百多年间的烧造历史中达到了顶峰。便利的淮河水道将一船船的寿州窑瓷器运往各地，也将各地的优秀文化产品带回。新中国成立以来，在除北部地区以外的市域内相继发现了一批唐代墓葬，出土有唐镜和寿州窑黄釉瓷器，热烈喜人的瓷器与熠熠生辉泛着银光的唐镜交相辉映，向我们昭示了大唐盛世的辉煌。

1957年在淮南市田家庵区黑泥乡（现安城镇）发现的一座砖室墓中，出土了9件铜器、3件银器和1件寿州窑瓷壶。该墓出土的折枝花镜，直径21.8厘米，缘厚0.4厘米，镜钮边环饰三朵小折枝花，间以三只飞跃的小鸟，主区饰大折枝花两种各三朵，相间环绕。镜面布局饱满，十分华丽，一派茂盛景象，是一面盛唐时期的铜镜。同墓出土的寿州窑黄釉翻唇口瓷壶，通高39.4厘米，腹径27.5厘米，厚唇外卷，溜肩，鼓腹，肩上饰四个双股系，施黄釉至唇下。此墓出土的唐镜与寿州窑瓷器相互印证，反映出在盛唐时期寿州窑黄釉瓷器同折枝花铜镜一样，受到当时人们的喜爱并随葬其墓中。

本书收录有淮南地区发现的唐代铜镜22面。形制有圆形、菱花形、葵花形等，装饰纹样包括瑞兽纹、瑞兽葡萄纹、瑞兽鸾鸟纹、禽鸟纹、盘龙纹、双鸾衔绶纹、交枝花鸟纹、折枝花纹、宝相花纹等。

淮南地区发现的唐镜中，以花卉纹类镜和瑞兽禽鸟镜居多。花卉图案是整个唐代装饰纹样中的一个重要主题，是唐代人热爱生活、享受太平的真实反映。其中的宝相花镜始出现于隋代，有浓郁的佛教色彩，唐代时十分盛行，并将其造型、组合发展到极致。淮南发现的花卉类镜中有交枝花鸟镜、四花枝镜、六花枝镜、散点宝相花镜等。本书收录的7面花枝类铜镜的装饰造型均枝叶并茂，布局上舒展自如，纹饰生动饱满。有的在大花中间以小花朵或飞跃的小鸟，构成一幅幅美丽的画面。

唐代铜镜纹饰常见的瑞兽禽鸟主要有：狻猊（狮子）、麒麟、龙凤、孔雀、仙鹤、鸳鸯、鹦鹉等，其中一些是传统纹样，如龙纹。一些是从国外传入并加以改造的新式纹样，如狮子与葡萄纹等。本书收录的14面瑞兽禽鸟类铜镜，装饰纹样有双鸾瑞兽、双鸾双鸟、双鸾飞鸟云纹、瑞兽纹、瑞兽葡萄纹等，镜面的形制有圆形、菱形、葵形等。

　　1960年淮南市唐山公社出土的双鸾双瑞兽铜镜，镜面主区纹饰呈上下布局。下部瑞兽为狻猊（狮子），上部瑞兽与下部瑞兽看似相像，但其头上有一角，似为独角兽。二瑞兽右向飞奔，双鸾面对镜钮做振翅状。镜面纹饰布置十分均匀美观，瑞兽形体硕壮，应为唐高宗至德宗时期制镜高峰时期的作品。2010年9月，淮南市谢家集公安分局移交的八出菱花形双鸾双瑞兽镜，是此类镜中的代表作品。八出菱花廓内饰如意形小花朵或小蜂蝶，相间排列，环绕镜缘，主区纹饰以双鸾双瑞兽间以小折枝花，绕硕大伏兽钮布置，镜面布局错落有致、繁而不乱，一派欣欣向荣的景象。镜中的鸾鸟与折枝花表达的正是白居易诗中所言："在天愿作比翼鸟，在地愿为连理枝"的生动景象。

　　瑞兽葡萄镜，又作海兽葡萄镜，它的产生与3世纪中叶在波斯萨珊王朝兴起的摩尼教有关。海兽在摩尼教中被视为力量的象征，葡萄自汉武帝时张骞出使西域带入中国后，被演化赋予为多子的象征，瑞兽代表武士。在唐武则天时摩尼教传入中国，有文献记载摩尼教徒觐见女皇，武则天喜好其说，令其留京授经。而在敦煌也曾发现其教经残卷。此后，葡萄和瑞兽这种纹饰在唐镜中很快被广泛应用，成为最具代表性的唐镜风格，推动唐镜达到了中国铜镜史的顶峰期。瑞兽葡萄镜纹饰繁缛神秘，雍容富丽，又有"多谜之镜"一说。淮南发现的瑞兽葡萄镜，以瑞兽和葡萄蔓枝构成主区纹饰，内区四只瑞兽呈伏卧状，外区绕以葡萄蔓枝叶、果实、飞禽相间，镜缘内有一周小联珠纹为栏，镜面装饰富丽饱满。两面葡萄纹镜虽有锈蚀，但仍能窥见此类铜镜的艺术特色。

　　盘龙镜，又称单龙镜，这种纹饰在战国时期和汉代已经装饰在镜面上，汉代螭龙以双线勾勒，属平面图案式造型，魏晋时龙纹开始凸起，到唐代，龙的身躯造型已高高隆起，成为十分具象的写实形象。这种盘曲飞腾的龙，古人称之为盘龙。李白有"美人赠此盘龙之宝镜，烛我金缕之罗衣"的诗句，就明确称其为盘龙镜，在当时此镜还有"天子镜"的称呼，较盘龙镜的称呼更为普遍。淮南发现的这面盘龙镜，葵形，纹饰不分区，一条腾空的龙绕钮作"C"形盘曲，回首、张口、露牙、大口作吞珠之状。龙体伸肢露爪，鳞片满身，精健强壮，神态轩昂，四周云纹缭绕，灵活飞动。纹饰造型敦实，刻画精细，气势夺人，显示出唐代铜镜制造的高超技艺。

　　唐亡后，中国进入五代十国的分裂时期。两宋时，北宋和辽、夏并立，南宋和金对峙，呈现出动乱复杂的政治局面。战争的频繁导致铜料匮乏，制镜业从此一蹶不振。文献记载，当时铜镜虽可民铸，但须官方查验，市面交易，按量计价。宋湖州镜铭上常见"炼铜照子每两六十文"、"无比炼铜每两一百文"等铭文，反映出铜的价格昂贵，这使得铜镜的厚度变薄，铜镜手工业发展受到严重制约。一直到明清两代，铜镜的制作，不再追求华美，只注重实用，浮雕式铜镜急剧减少，几乎完全被平面图案化纹饰所取代，且轻薄少纹或简纹者多。

　　本书收录宋、金时的铜镜18面，纹饰和铭文涉及湖州铭文镜、人物故事镜、人物山水镜、菊花纹镜、几何纹镜等。

　　本书收录的湖州铭文镜3面，形制有六出菱花形和盾形两种。铭文有"湖州石十五郎炼铜照子"、"湖州石家法炼青铜照子"等。湖州镜大约始于北宋晚期，盛行于南宋初期到中期。北宋末年，北方人口大举南迁，经济重心南移，手工业也随即发展起来，当时的湖州、饶州、临安府、平安府等地铸镜闻名全国。湖州镜上几乎都没有花纹，仅铸有作坊主姓名或价格等，往往在名号上冠以"真"、或"真正"，以表明正宗，防止假冒。当时的铸镜有官作，也有私作，本书收录的3面湖州镜工艺一般，略显粗糙，应当是私家作坊铸镜。

　　南宋时，宋金政权以淮河为界对峙，因而在市境淮河两岸的文化遗存中，还有一批金代铜镜。这也是位居淮河岸边的淮南地区，兼有南北方文化面貌的一个重要特征。金朝是女真人建立的北方政权，反映在铜镜艺术上呈现了多元的文化面貌，以其民族习俗和社会风尚的粗犷厚重融入铜镜艺术，镜面的风格与湖州镜纹样区别很大。本书收录的6面金代铜镜，均为传统人物故事和花草纹样，装饰特点是粗线条、大块面造型，简化，甚至忽略细节，但别有一番韵味。馆藏的许由巢父故事镜与河北保定发现的一面同类镜十分相似，尤其是镜面上方有一个空白的长方形方框，内无铭。《中国铜镜图典》收录的同样镜上，框内有铭"许由洗耳，巢父饮牛"。这种方框内的铭文，早期是官府检验记铭或刻铭。金代有铜禁制度，"私铸铜器，法当徒"，这两面铜镜有可能是以官镜为本私铸。本书收录的童子骑马镜与1958年5月河北省完县出土的"镜子局造骑马镜"十分相近,弓形小钮,花式钮座,主区饰浮雕八童子骑马,同向环绕。在镜面的一侧有一方框,内铸"镜子局官"。两镜尺寸、纹饰布局相似,惜淮南这面锈蚀较重。

明清制镜业较两宋时期的制镜业有所改观,曾有大量仿汉式铜镜,镜体有所增厚。但总的情况是铜镜用料少,冶铸工艺水平不高,一般铜镜的质地黄中闪白,多显粗糙,纹饰也不甚清晰。到西方玻璃镜传入中国后,传统铜镜逐渐失去了照容的功能,只保留了铜镜的形式,成为辟邪的吉祥物用作悬挂装饰了。

本书收录有明清铜镜19面。其中人物杂宝镜5面、鱼纹镜1面、八卦镜1面、铭文镜9面、仿汉镜3面、有柄花草纹镜2面。

明代人物杂宝镜,是明代铜镜具有代表性的典型器。明代较宋元时期的制镜业有所发展,铜镜生产数量增多,不少铜镜装饰富有新意。明代铜镜一般比宋元时形制大一些,镜体也厚重些。整体上看,明代铜镜的质量有所提高,是铜镜衰落期的回光返照。纹样中常见"八宝",分别是轮、螺、伞、盖、花、罐、鱼、肠,又称法轮、法螺、宝伞、白盖、莲花、宝罐、金鱼、盘肠。本是佛教庙宇中的供器,也称其为八吉祥。在铜镜上用作装饰图案,就不限于八宝了,增加了钱文、祥云、灵芝、卷轴书画、银锭、元宝、犀角、方胜、珊瑚、磬、鹿、梅花等,成为"杂宝"或"多宝"镜了。这些杂宝寓意吉祥如意、福禄双全、平安长寿等。淮南发现的5面人物杂宝镜中,有一面属于明代杂宝镜中的精品,其直径达40厘米,厚1.4厘米,外区饰人物14位,以一周凸弦纹为栏,主区以"富贵双全"四字带框铭为主题纹饰,镜面满布动物、花卉、云朵等杂宝图案,构成了一幅富贵平安、热闹喜庆的生动画面。该镜的铜质优良,纹饰清晰,模铸规范,不是一般私家作坊所能够制作的,可能是明代官作之镜。另4面铜镜有3面圆形,1面方形,属常见的明代铜镜,制作工艺、纹样装饰较前述大铜镜要逊色多了。

铜镜发展到清代已全面衰落,不仅铜料质量低下,并且纹饰简单,工艺粗糙,质量较明代又相差甚远,数量也大为减少。本书收录的2面清代有柄铜镜,是同期铜镜中具有代表意义的作品。馆藏锦地菱形花有柄镜,圆形,在锦地上开菱形花窗,内饰上下对称的如意形花朵纹,花朵中间有蕊,两侧伸出长细叶片。此镜工艺制作上还讲究质量,模制规范,纹饰清晰,可能是官府铸造。另一面礼字铭有柄镜,圆形,镜的主区为宽带弦纹内饰的"礼"字铭,上部有"张九锡造"四字圆押印铭,下部有"上上青铜"铭方形押印,两侧沿镜弧饰长长的折枝花,此镜纹饰布局比较讲究,但其材质、制范工艺略显粗糙,应是民间作坊铸造。

铜镜是中国传统文化的载体,铜镜虽小,但其浓缩概括的装饰图案和纹样折射出的是中国历史发展的兴衰演变,是社会生活方方面面的写照,具有强烈的艺术感染力。

纵观四千年铜镜的发展历史,我们可以从中感受其鲜明的时代特征,探寻它所凝聚的艺术内涵,见证青铜工艺水平的不断进步和演化,体会古代艺术家的丰富想象力和创造力。铜镜的传承和发展,伴随着时代的变迁,王朝的更替,在形制特征、纹饰艺术、主题表现、工艺技术等方面,都发生着重大变革。铜镜和古代其他历史文物一样,是我们中华民族的宝贵文化遗产,其神韵必将永远留在人们记忆之中。

淮南市博物馆馆长 沈汝青

2011年1月8日

Preface

The bronze mirror, as a bronze for daily use which was commonly used for the longest period of time in ancient China, had been used for more than 4,000 years by Chinese people before the introduction of the glass mirror, appearing in the late Neolithic Age. It was not only a practical commodity, but even an art treasure, including one shiny side, which serves as an indispensable tool for reflecting people's face and readjusting their appearance, and a decorative side with exquisite designs and carved inscriptions, which provides importance reference on politics, economy, cultural features and social morals at that time and has important research value.

Li Shimin, the Emperor Taizong of the Tang Dynasty (618AD — 907AD), used the practical function of the bronze mirror to describe the thought on the track of social development and said, "with bronze as a mirror, one can rectify dress; with history as a mirror, one can know dynasties changed; with person as a mirror, one can understand advantages and disadvantages", which gives later generation with deep enlightenment. Such the small bronze mirrors give us a glimpse of Chinese historical and cultural evolvement.

I

As recorded in the *Biography of the Yellow Emperor, Xuanyuan*, the Yellow Emperor cast the bronze mirrors. According to archaeological discoveries, the bronze mirror appeared in the late Neolith Age. Two bronze mirrors unearthed from the tombs of the Qijia Culture dating to 2,000 years ago in 1970s show that China is one of the earliest countries who cast and used bronze mirrors.

The Shang and Zhou Dynasties were the golden period of the bronze, with thousands of bronzed unearthed. But there are less than 30 bronze mirrors of the Shang and Zhou Dynasties found mainly in the area of the upper reaches of the Yellow River and rarely in the area of middle and lower reaches until now. So some scholars make a conclusion that the Chinese bronze mirror appeared in the area of the upper reaches of the Yellow River including Gansu and Qinghai. Compared with a great variety of splendid bronzes, the bronze mirror had grown sluggish delay for 1,800 years from its birth to the early Warring States Period, its shapes and decorations falling far behind the bronzes. The reason for this is that the bronze mirror making did not form its own procedure in the early period, separating with the bronze making in the Central Plain and the bronze mirror was only served for high officials and noble lords.

The nomad people in the northwest area migrated to the Central Plain from the late Spring and Autumn Period to the early Warring States Period and the bronze mirror prevailed and widely used in the Central Plain at the same time, which was first accepted by the nobility. The casting and use of the bronze mirrors became prosperous and formed a unique process system when it was used by all levels of the society in the middle and late Warring States Period. As the commodity for the people's daily use, the quality and number of the bronze mirror had been greatly improved since the Qin and Han Dynasties. In the Han and Tang Dynasties, the bronze mirror prospered, especially the Tang Dynasty was a peak period for the bronze mirror making in ancient time, with variety of types, new shapes, innovative technology and modern designs springing up. The bronze mirror had been innovated slowly and already become an indispensable commodity for people's daily life since the Five and Song Dynasties.

The imaging effect of the bronze mirror is decided by proportion of ingredients of the alloy containing copper, tin and leads and so on. The proportion of ingredients became mature in Warring States Period. The alloy with lead and tin in a high quantity resulted in reflecting one's image and was still in use. In the Tang Dynasty, the bronze mirror had the best image quality with tin content increasing. As recorded in *Liu Qi* of *Kao Gong Ji* of *Zhou Li*, the best mirror was cast with half proportion of copper and half tin. Analyzing the samples of the bronze mirrors through the ages, the result shows that the proportion of tin occupies half the copper content. The ancient makers obtained the best formula through constant practice. It is recorded in *Xiu Wu Xun* of *Huai Nan Zi* that the bronze mirror must be brilliant enough to reflect one's image when being polished with tin and mercury. As described in the poem *Yu Bao Shi* written by Yuan Zhen of the Tang Dynasty, the mirror will reduce the image quality without being polished for a long time.

The painting of Admonitions of the Instructress to the Palace Ladies by Gu Kaizhi in the Eastern Jin Dynasty reflects the scene of dressing and making up in front of the mirror, the lady on the right sitting on the ground, holding a mirror in the left hand and combing by the right hand, with her image in the mirror, the lady on the left sitting and facing the mirror, with a lady combing her hair and sitting behind her. According to the painting, there are two mirrors, one with handle, which is easy to hold in hand, the other with large diameter and decorative strip on the back, which was tied to the stand with the strip. The scene of the painting is the most complete scene of first using mirror that had ever been found and the earliest record of the bronze mirror with handle.

Based on the archaeological discoveries, the bronze mirror was used with holding in hands, hanging, putting on the table and keeping with people. When unearthed, the bronze mirrors of the Warring States Period and the Han Dynasty often attached fragments of lacquer or silk to its surface, which could be used to place or pack the mirror according to some scholars. A lacquer dressing box placing the bronze mirror was unearthed from the tomb of the Warring States Period at Jiuliandun, Hubei. There was a porcelain box that was used exclusively for placing the bronze mirror in the Tang Dynasty, such as exquisite wax-yellow-glazed mirror box of Shouzhou Kiln, the similar porcelains of Yue Kiln and Changsha Kiln, which show that the bronze mirror was appreciated by the ancient people. The bronze mirror was often buried with the dead, reflecting not only that it was treasured but also the idea of regarding death as a start of another birth.

In ancient China, the bronze mirror was served not only as a practical commodity of dressing and making up, but also a channeling tool which had function of warding off evil spirits. The Han mirrors were often carved with characters "*Bi Bu Xiang*" (blessing) and "*Chang Bao Er Qin*" (blessing parents), which expressed people's good wishes of expelling evil spirits and safeguarding life, like the grass mirror that are hanging on the door or the beam now. The bronze mirrors unearthed from the tombs, with distinct shapes, designs and inscriptions of the times, can become the basis for dating the times of the tombs and the standard of archaeologically dating, which catches redoubled attention by the archaeologists.

II

The features of the bronze mirrors collected at Huainan Museum are closely related with historical development, evolution of organizational system and underground remains in Huainan region.

The Huainan region has rich historical and cultural remains, with densely covered rivers, fertile soil and good climate. There are 34 sites of ancient culture, reflecting that this region have been inhabited by human being from the earliest time, along the Huai River and its branches, Dongfei River, Xifei River, Yao River, Ni River, Hei River and Wabu River, and at the south and north sides of the Shungeng Mountain in Huainan City, among which 10 sites belong to the Neolithic Age, 9 sites the Shang and Zhou Dynasties, 15 sites the Han and Tang Dynasties and 133 tombs of past ages which are located at both sides of the Huai River and the south of the Shungeng Mountain.

The Huai *Yi* of the Eastern *Yi* tribes lived at the both sides of the Huai River between the late Neolithic Age and the early Spring and Autumn Period. The *Li Lou Xia* of *Meng Tzu* says, "Shun, come from the Eastern *Yi* tribes and farmed under the Li Mountain." Some scholars think that the Li Mountain is the present-day Shungeng Mountain in Huainan City, at which, it is said, Shun cultivated the people the knowledge of farming here on his southern trip. As recorded in Biography of Eastern *Yi* in *Hou Han Shu*, the Eastern *Yi* tribes once migrated southwards on a large scale during the reign of the Emperor Wuyi of the Shang Dynasty and established the Zhoulai State, one of the important states in the area of the middle and lower reaches of the Huai River, in the Western Zhou Dynasty.

Following the expansion of the Chu State towards the east, the wars broke out between the Cai and the Chu in the late Spring and Autumn Period. The Cai was forced to move towards the south and sought refuge from the Wu State, with moving its capital to Zhoulai, renamed as Xiacai after being the capital of the Cai State, which is located in Shou County, 3 kilometers away from Huainan City towards the west. Through the reigns of the Marquis Zhao, the Marquis Cheng, the Marquis Sheng, the Marquis Yuan and the Marquis Qi, it was conquered by the Chu, lasting 46 years from 493 BC to 447 BC. The tomb of the Marquis Zhao of the Cai, which was found at the east gate of Shou County in 1955, and the tomb of the Marquis Sheng, which was found at Caijiagang, Huainan City in 1959, provide the evidence for this period of history. The Chu State moved its capital to Shouchun renamed Ying (the present-day Shou County in Huainan City) in the 22nd year of the King Kaolie of the Chu (241 AD). In 221 AD, its capital was invaded by Wang Jian, the general of the Qin State and the Chu State was extinguished, lasting the reign of four generations including the King Kaolie, the King You, the King Ai and the King Fuchu. The discovery of the tomb of the King You of the Chu at Lisangudui, zhujiaji, Yanggong Town, Huainan City in 1933, shocked in the whole country and provoked an upsurge of the research of the Chu Culture in academic circle. In recent years, several large-scaled chariot pits have been found around Lisangudu and Wuwangdun. Around these pits, there are dozens of ancient tombs with large-scaled grave mound such as Huaixie mu, Dagudui, Xiaogudui, Wangbagudui, Bainigudui, Jiangudui and Yanshigudui and so on, revealing that the area was a well-kept tombs group of the nobles with intensive distribution and high ranks in the Pre-Qin Period. Over 1,000 ancient tombs between the Warring States Period and the Tang and Song Dynasties have been unearthed during the infrastructure construction since 2005.

In the early Western Han Dynasty, Liu Bang, the Emperor Gaozu of the Han, established the Huainan State with the capital Shouchun (the present-day Shou County), covering the Jiang-Huai region and including Jiujiang, Lujiang, Hengshan and Yuzhang. Liu An was entitled the King of Huainan in the 16th year of the Emperor Wen of the Han. Liu An invited scholars as guests to his estate, boasting of thousands of hangers-on, and they wrote books and made pills of immortality together, which promoted greatly the development of the politics, economy and culture in Huainan area. The organizational system of the Western Han Dynasty had been used in the Eastern Han Dynasty. In the late Han Dynasty, Yuan Shao established Huainan Prefecture and Shouchun was under the jurisdiction of the Huainan Prefecture. The evidence of the Han tombs unearthed in Huainan area reveals that the society became stable in this period, with more funeral objects than the Qin Dynasty and various shapes such as shaft tombs with wood chamber, shaft tombs with rock chamber, rock tombs, brick-chambered tombs, numerous brick tombs, which were evolved from the shaft tombs of the Qin Dynasty. Based on the design feature, the bronze mirrors, which can be unearthed from each shape of the tombs, include the mirrors from the Central Plain, Ezhou mirrors in the Wu region and Shaoxing mirrors, reflecting that the Huainan area has been a intersection area of the culture of the North and the South and the bronze mirrors from the Yellow River and the Yangtze River come together here by the Huai River and the Grand Canal.

In the Tang Dynasty, the economy prospered in Huainan area. The Shouzhou Kiln appeared in the middle and late Southern and Northern Dynasties and ended in the late Tang Dynasty, lasting for over 400 years. Through the branches of the Huai River, the porcelain wares of the Shouzhou Kiln were transported to the Yangtze-Huai region and the goods all over the country were transported back to Huainan. The bronze mirrors from all over the country unearthed here reveal a prosperous scene of stable society and flourishing trades

In the Northern Song Dynasty, the Huainan area was under the jurisdiction of Shouzhou. In the late Northern Song Dynasty, it was under the jurisdiction of Shouchun and Xiaocai. In the early period of the wars between the Song and the Jin, it was still under the jurisdiction of Shouchun and Xiacai. Later, it is bounded by the Huai River into two areas, one under the jurisdiction of the Jin kingdom and the other under the Southern Song Dynasty. With frequent wars and power changes, the Huai River area became an important battlefield, losing gradually its superiority as the center of the politics, economy and culture in the Han and Tang Dynasties. The ancient tombs after the Five Dynasties were found in a small number in Huainan area, holding obscure feature of distribution.

III

Huainan had been the center of the politics, economy and culture in the region since the Spring and Autumn and Warring States Periods. The earliest bronze mirrors unearthed belong to this period.

In this book, there are seventeen bronze mirrors of the Warring States Period, which are collected at the Huainan Museum, including mirror with simple design, mirror with ground motif, mirror with feather-like pattern as ground motif and four-leaf design, mirror with dragon design, mirror with design of interlaced hydras and lozenge, mirror with design of interlaced hydras and linked arcs, mirror with inscription of four "Shan" characters, mirror with stylized animal pattern and mirror with lozenge design.

The mirror with design of linked arcs formed by single line, which was unearthed from the Tomb 4 of Hongwei Annular Kiln Works in Xiejiaji District, Huainan City in April, 1972, is the earliest bronze mirror found in this region. It is decorated concisely with a knob with three-string design as the center and eleven linked arcs inward formed by single line. The design of linked arcs formed by single line evolved into the design of linked arcs formed by broad band, seven or eight linked arcs with cloud and thunder design, interlaced hydras design or whorl design as the ground motif. There is another mirror with the same shape and design, but heavier body and bigger size, which is also collected at the museum. These two mirrors, with a style of the early Chu bronze mirrors, reveal that the Chu culture had spread into the Huai River area before the Chu State moved its capital to Shouchun.

The mirror with design of cloud and thunder as ground motif belongs to a later time, with a knob with three-string design on a round base. The design is in the shape of alternate arrangement of whorl pattern and two triangles formed by double lines, covering the whole back side. There is a mark line of mold crossing the decorations, showing that the mirror was jointed together with two pottery molds. The sparse ground motif is distinguished from the close ground motif of the late Warring States Period cast by the lost-wax method. Compared with the mirror unearthed from the No. 896 tomb at Nianjiahu, Changsha, Hunan, this mirror has a shorter diameter and a knob base at a smaller scale.

There are four mirrors with feather-like pattern as ground motif and four-leaf design unearthed at the area of Tangshan and Liyingzi Town west of the city, among which three mirrors has a round knob base and one a square base, one mirror is decorated with design of four *Shan*-shaped leaves and three mirrors with design of four peach-shaped leaves. The mirrors with peach-shaped leaf design, earlier than other mirrors with leaf design, appeared at the turn of the middle and late Warring States Period and were unearthed mainly from the Chu tombs in Hunan and Hubei. The mirror with four-leaf design of the Warring States Period, with delicate ground motif, heavy body and thicker rim, had lost the light and thin features of the Chu mirrors and reveals that this kind of mirror had been used until the late Warring States Period, which was unearthed from a construction site of No. 21 Building in Xiejiaji District, Huainan City in August, 2010.

The two mirrors with inscription of four "*Shan*" characters are the treasures of the Chu bonze mirrors in the Warring States Period, which were unearthed respectively at Qiujiagang, Tangshan Commune, Huainan City in 1957 and from the Kongwei Annular Kiln Works in Xiejiaji District, Huai City in 1987. The mirror with design of eight leaves and four flowers and inscription of four "*Shan*" characters unearthed at qiujiagang is 13.7cm diameter and 0.4cm thick. It has a square knob base, each side of which is in parallel with the bottom stroke of each character "*Shan*". The characters are spaced with four peach-leaf-shaped petals. A petal casts outside each corner of the square and the right side of each character. The petals and leaves are connected with the chain-shaped branches. It is an exquisite and elegant pattern composing of characters inclining to the left and ground motif. The mirror with the same design was unearthed from the Chu tomb in Changsha, Hunan, with number M1554:7, 13.7cm diameter and 0.4cm thick, which belongs to the middle period of the late Warring States Period (about 277 AD — 250 AD), Base on the similar size, designs and strokes, it is inferred that these two mirrors were cast at the same region at the same time. Changsha was the center of the Chu bronze mirror casting at that time and there are 49 bronze mirrors listed in the *Chu Tomb in Changsha*. The mirror of Qiujiagang may be cast in Changsha.

The mirror with inscription of four "*Shan*' characters, design of four deer and feather-like pattern as ground motif, as a rare treasure of the mirrors with four "*Shan*" characters, has a knob with three-string design on a square base and is decorated with feather-like pattern as ground motif and four "*Shan*" characters spaced with four deer looking back, which was unearthed from the Hongwei Annular Kiln Works in Xiejiaji Distric, Huainan City in December, 1987. The mirror with four "*Shan*" characters and deer design known at present is collected at the Shanghai Museum, with the similar decoration but a round knob base. The deer design of the mirror at the Shanghai Museum has the same shape with the mirror at the Huainan Museum, but is inlaid in the ground motif as an irregular square, distinguishing from the mirror of Huainan with the deer inlaid in the ground motif, which shows a harmony pattern. According to the technology, the mirror in Huainan was cast with more mature technology. It is rare that the mirrors with four "*Shan*" characters are decorated with animal design. Another mirror with three "*Shan*" characters and three deer is collected in Paris, France. As recorded in the *Thoughts on the Mirror with inscription of 'Shan' character* written by He Gang, "The mirror with three 'Shan' characters is the only one, with deer design. We know the unearthed site of the mirror in Huainan, which has the deer design as the same as the mirror in Shanghai and Paris. The mirrors with "*Shan*" character and deer design have a larger diameter, close ground motif and similar style. This kind of mirrors were found in Hunan in a great number but is not decorated with deer design. So it is inferred that the mirror may be cast in Huainan." This conclusion is based on the facts. Except Jingzhou of Hubei and Changsha of Hunan, the area of Huainan, Lu'an, Bengbu, Hefei and Fuyang unearthed the Chu bronze mirrors with a larger number than other area. Hence, Huainan, the capital of the Chu State in the late Warring States Period, may be the center of the bronze mirror casting.

There are seven mirrors with interlaced hydras design, among which three mirrors, unearthed at the adjoining area with Shou County such as Tangshan Town, Liyingzi Town and Yanggong Town, are decorated with interlaced hydras and lozenge. The interlaced hydras design, also called dragon design or coiled serpent design, is formed with coiling dragon and snake as the major pattern. The mirrors with interlaced hydras design unearthed in Huainan have different sizes, with the shortest diameter of 7cm to 12cm and the longest diameter of 16cm to 23cm. The mirror with the largest size, unearthed from a tomb of the early Han Dynasty, has a knob with three-string pattern on a round base surrounded with twisted rope design and is decorated with design of cloud and thunder as the ground motif and three flying dragons with rare two eyes, showing the style of the late Chu bronze mirrors. The mirror with feather-like pattern as ground motif and stylized animal pattern in museum has a knob with three-string pattern on a round base and is decorated with a unique design in the shape of geometry-shaped beast with zigzag-rule-shaped head, *Ruyi*-shaped tail and C-shaped body, which was called the stylized animal pattern by some scholars. The mirror with the same design was only unearthed from the Chu tomb in Changde, Hunan, with a bigger size. It is interesting that the makers of the Chu State cast this exaggerated design on the mirror.

There is a large amount of the Han bronze mirrors among mirrors collected at museum, occupying about forty percent. Seventy-six mirror of the Han Dynasty are listed in the book, with design of interlaced hydras, linked arc, grass leaf, nebular, gambling, four nipples, several nipples, beast, bird, flower, dragon, tiger, portrait of deities and inscription band. The mirrors collected at the Huainan Museum reveal that the decorative style of the mirror reflected the idea of Taoism in the early Han Dynasty, abandoning the exquisite and mysterious designs of the Warring States Period, and was influenced with the idea of Confucianism in the middle and late Han Dynasty, showing the standard of the time and religious content. The inscriptions, with character "*Er*", mirror the thoughts and cultures of the Han Dynasty, expressing good wishes, love, good quality of the mirror and ideas of the Schools.

The mirror with interlaced hydras design, as the representative of the early bronze mirrors of the early Western Han Dynasty, has a knob with three-string design on a hydras-dragon-shaped base and is decorated with a band of inscription "*Chou Si Yi Bei, Yuan Jun Wu Shuo, Xiang Si Yuan Wu Jue*", two bands of string pattern, two bands of twisted rope design and the interlaced hydras design formed with three lines as the major motif, showing the style of the Warring States Period, which was unearthed at Laishan Commune, Xiejiaji District, Huainan City in 1957. Other three mirrors with design of four leaves and interlaced hydras have knobs with three-string design on a hydras-dragon-shaped base and are decorated with four bands of twisted rope design, a band of inscription "*Da Le Gui Fu, Qian Qiu Wan Sui, Yi Jiu Shi*" which are spaced with a fish design and flame-shaped leaves spaced with interlaced hydras as the major motif. The design formed with three lines, requiring the technology of molding at a high degree, began to disappear since the early period of the reign of the Emperor Wu of the Han Dynasty.

There are eighteen bronze mirrors with gambling design listed in the book. The design of gambling is often spaced with interlaced hydras, deities, birds, beasts, nipples, cloud and geometric patterns, forming a well-arranged decorative pattern.

The mirror with gambling design is also called the mirror with standard design. A mirror with gambling design of the Xin Dynasty is named "*Bo Ju*" (gambling), which is collected at the National Museum, hence the name. The gambling prevailed in the Han Dynasty. As recorded in *Shuo Wen Jie Zi*, the game was played between two players with each player having six men. Some scholars thought that the gambling was also served as a ceremony sacrificing to the gods. The gambling with deities, winged men and mythical creatures express the belief in fairies, so the mirrors with gambling design were widely used. The mirror has a round knob on a four-leaf-shaped (also called kaki calyx) base, a square formed with double lines outside the base and designs and inscriptions in the square. The gambling design first appeared in the reign of the Emperor Wu of the Han Dynasty, but widely used between the late Western Han Dynasty and the early Eastern Han Dynasty. The mirror reached a peak in the reign of Wang Mang, with delicate designs, high quality and advanced technology. It began to decay in the late period of the middle Eastern Han Dynasty, with simplified pattern and rough technology, and finally disappeared in the early Wei and Jin Dynasties.

The mirror with gambling design, which was unearthed from the M11 tomb, a shaft tomb with stone chamber, at Shuanggudui, Tangshan Town, Xiejiaji District, Huainan City in July, 1987, is similar with the mirror from the tomb of Dou Wan at Mancheng, Hebei on size, decoration and inscription. Dou Wan was buried in 104 AD at a king-level burial system. The M11 tomb is in a small size with 4.45cm long, 2.84cm wide and 0,8cm deep. According to the signet with inscription "*Zhou An*" in bird and insect script, the occupant may be a high officer of the Huainan State. This mirror is the earliest mirror with gambling design found in the region.

The two mirrors with design of eight nipples, four deities, winged men, birds, beasts and gambling, with delicate mold and clear decorative pattern, were unearthed respectively in Xiejiaji District, Huainan City in June, 2006 and in August, 2010. The mirror unearthed at Xincun has a round knob on a round base surrounded with eight nipples and flower design. The major motif and the rim of the mirror are adorned with four deities, which is less common. The mirror with the same design but smaller size was unearthed from the tom of the early Eastern Han Dynasty in Guangzhou. The mirror unearthed at Laishan kiln workshop has a round knob on a square base surrounded with twelve nipples and is decorated with a band of inscription as the major motif. The mirror, which is peculiar with a band of drifting cloud on the rim, can be comparable with the mirror with gambling at the National Museum and even well-arranged. From this, the mirror may be cast around the reign of Wang Mang.

There are two mirrors with grass-leaf design in this book, which has sixteen linked arcs inward, four groups of leaves and peach-shaped bud and a band of inscription. The mirror was widely used between the early Western Han Dynasty and the middle Western Han Dynasty. The design reflects the idea for letting things taking their own course in the early Han Dynasty and represents the understanding of the life under the background of peaceful society and love for nature, especially in the reign of the Emperor Wen and the Emperor Jing of the Han.

The mirror with nebular design prevailed after the mirror with grass-leaf design in the middle Western Han Dynasty, with a

Boshan-incense-burner-shaped knob. The nebular design represents the understanding for the universe in the Han Dynasty. The mirror is decorated with sixteen linked arcs and seven stars as the major motif. The mirror first appeared in the reign of the Emperor Wu of the Han, was widely used in the reign of the Emperor Zhao and the Emperor Xuan of the Han, and began to decay after that, lasting a short period.

The mirror with inscription "*Ri Guang*" and the mirror with inscription "*Zhao Ming*" were widely used between the middle Western Han Dynasty and the early Eastern Han Dynasty and were unearthed at a great number in Huainan. There are six mirrors with inscription "*Ri Guang*" and seven mirrors with inscription "*Zhao MIng*" listed in the book. The mirrors with inscription "*Ri Guang*" unearthed in Huainan, mostly with 6cm to 10cm diameter, have a half-sphere-shaped knob on a round base and are decorated with linked arcs and the band of inscription "*Ri Guang*" as the major motif that is surrounded with two bands of fine-toothed pattern. The mirrors have a broad rim with simple design and were cast with rough technology. Some scholars thought they were only buried with the dead. The mirrors with inscription "*Zhao Ming*", with a bigger scale and well arrangement, have a half-sphere-shaped knob on a round base and are decorated with a band of continuous beads or linked arcs and the band of inscription as the major motif. The mirror has a broad rime with simple design. Later than mirrors with inscription "*Ri Guang*", the mirrors with inscription "*Zhao Ming*" first appeared in the reign of the Emperor Zhao and the Emperor Xuan of the Han Dynasty. The inscriptions on both mirrors were first carved in seal script and later in official script. The mirror is decorated with inscription "*Zhao Ming*" and "*Ri Guang*", which is transferred by Xiejiaji District Public Security Bureau in Huainan in September, 2010. It must be a practical commodity, with the casting technology under the standard level and a bigger shape.

The mirror with design of dragon and tiger facing each other in high relief is the origin of the mirror with portraits of deities and beasts. Five mirrors with design of dragon and tiger are listed in the book, most of which were unearthed in Shangyao Town and Xiejiaji District of Huainan. The mirror has a half-sphere-shaped knob and is decorated with the dragon and the tiger facing each other as the major motif. Two mirrors with single dragon design belong to the Three Kingdoms Period and Six Dynasties, with rough technology of casting.

There are four mirrors with portraits in the book, including a mirror with three-layer portraits, a mirror with four-layer portraits, a mirror with five-layer portraits and a mirror with portraits facing each other. The mirror with three-layer portraits is decorated with the Royal Lady of the West and the Royal Lord of the East on the top, immortals, Green Dragon and White Tiger on the middle and bottom and inscription on the rim. The mirror with five-layer portraits is decorated with beasts and birds at each layer, inscription "*Yi Guan*" at the forth layer and a band of inscription on the rim, which is similar with the mirror listed in the *A catalogue of Chinese Bronze Mirrors* and was cast at the same time.

The mirror with portraits of deities, as a new shape of bronze mirrors, prevailed between the middle and late Eastern Han Dynasty and the Three Kingdoms Period and Six Dynasties. As a treasure of Chinese art, it is decorated with deities in high relief such as the Royal Lord of the East, The Royal Lady of the West, Green Dragon and White Tiger, showing a strong and vivid aesthetic effect like a painting. These mirrors were mainly cast in Kuaiji and Echeng of the Wu region. Kuaiji (the present-day Shaoxing) became the center of the bronze mirror casting in the late Eastern Han Dynasty and Echeng (the present-day Ezhou City) later. These mirrors were widely used along both banks of the Yangtze River and rarely in the north of the Huai River. With frequent communication with the Wu State, the bronze culture of the Wu and Yue had permeated into the Huainan area since the late Spring and Autumn Period. Numerous porcelains and bronzes with the style of the Wu and Yue were unearthed here, including the bronze mirror of the Wu.

The Tang Dynasty was the peak of the feudal society. During this period, the casting technology and decorative art of the bronze mirror had been improved at a quick speed and made an epoch-making change, under the background of stable society, peaceful life and prosperous economy and culture. The bronze mirrors of the Tang Dynasty reached a peak, with heavy body, new shape, rich decorative themes and exquisite style.

The economy and culture of the Huainan region prospered in the Sui and Tang Dynasties. The Shouzhou Kiln produced yellow-glazed porcelains in the Tang Dynasty and flourished over four hundred years, which first appeared in the Southern and Northern Dynasties. The porcelains of the Shouzhou Kiln were transported into all over the country through convenient rivers, and goods from all over the country were transported back to Huainan. A number of the Tang tombs have been unearthed in Huainan since the founding of New China, with the bronze mirrors and yellow-glazed porcelains of Shouzhou Kiln, which reflect a glory of the Tang Dynasty.

Nine bronzes, three silver wares and a porcelain ewer of Shouzhou Kiln were unearthed from a brick-chambered tomb at Heinixiang (the present-day Ancheng Town), Tianjiaan District, Huainan City in 1957. The mirror with interlocking flowers unearthed from the tomb, as a bronze mirror of the Tang Dynasty, is decorated with three interlocking flowers spaced with three flying birds around the knob and the big interlocking flowers as the major motif, with 21.8cm diameter and 0.4cm thick of the rim, reflecting the prosperous scene of the Tang Dynasty. The yellow-glazed ewer of Shouzhou Kiln has spreading mouth with everted rim, swelling body and four loops, with 39.4cm high and 27.5cm diameter of the body. The remains unearthed reveal that the yellow-glazed porcelains of Shouzhou Kiln and the bronze mirror with interlocking flowers were very popular and buried with dead.

20 mirrors of the Tang Dynasty, with design of beasts, birds, phoenix, grapes, grapes, flowers and rosette, are listed in the book, covering round shape, water chestnut shape and mallow shape.

The mirrors of the Tang Dynasty, mostly the mirrors with flower design and the mirrors with auspicious beasts, were unearthed in Huainan. The flower design was one of the major decorative themes in the Tang Dynasty, expressing the people's love for life and peace at that time. The rosette design, with a strong Buddhist color, first appeared in the Sui Dynasty and reached a peak in the Tang Dynasty. The flower design found in Huainan includes design of interlocking flowers and birds, design of four interlocking flowers, design of six interlocking flowers and rosette design. There are seven mirrors with flower design listed in the book.

The design of auspicious beasts includes lion, unicorn, dragon, phoenix, peacock, crane, mandarin duck and parrot, among which some are the traditional patterns, such as dragon design; some innovative patterns from abroad, such as lion and grape designs. There are fourteen mirrors with auspicious beasts listed in the book, including mirrors with design of double phoenixes and auspicious beasts, mirrors with design of double phoenixes and double birds, mirrors with design of double phoenixes, double flying birds and clouds, mirrors with auspicious beasts and mirrors with design of auspicious beasts and grapes. The shapes of the mirror include round shape, water chestnut shape and mallow shape.

The mirror with double phoenixes and double auspicious beasts, as a treasure of the peak period of the bronze mirror casting between the Emperor Gaozong and the Emepror Dezong of the Tang, is decorated with two beasts running towards the right and two birds spreading wings and facing each other, which was unearthed at Tangshan Commune, Huainan City in 1960. As the representative of this kind of mirrors, the water-chestnut-shaped mirror is decorated with alternate arrangement of *Ruyi*-shaped flowers and bees and double phoenixes and double auspicious beasts spaced with interlocking flowers as the major motif, which was transferred by Xiejiaji District Public Security in Huainan City in September, 2010.

The mirror with design of auspicious beasts and grapes was closely related with Manichaeism in the Sassanian Dynasty of Persia. Auspicious beasts and grapes were regarded as the symbol of the power in Manichaeism. Grapes were brought by Zhang Qian to China in the reign of the Emperor Wu of the Han and were symbolized with plenty of offspring. The auspicious beasts represented warriors. The design of auspicious beasts and grapes had been widely used and become one of the most representative themes of decorative art since the introduction of Buddhism. The mirror of the Tang Dynasty is a peak of the history of the bronze mirrors in china. The design of auspicious beasts and grapes has a decorative effect of exquisite and mysterious, luxuriant and elegant. The mirror unearthed in Huainan shows the artistic features of this kind of bronze mirrors.

The mirror with coiling dragon design is also named the mirror with single dragon design. The design had been used in the Warring States Period and the Han Dynasty. The design was formed with double lines in the Han Dynasty. The design was carved in low relief in the Wei and Jin Dynasties. It became a vivid dragon flying in the Tang Dynasty. As recorded in the poem written by Li Bai, the mirror is called the mirror with coiling dragon design. The mirror was also named the Emperor's mirror. The mirror unearthed in Huainan is in shape of mallow and is decorated with a C-shaped dragon flying and looking back, reflecting the advanced technology of the bronze mirror casting of the Tang Dynasty.

After the downfall of the Tang Dynasty, China entered a chaotic period of the Five Dynasties and Ten Kingdoms Period. There was a political upheaval in the Song Period, with the Northern Song, Liao and Western Xia coexisting during the Northern Song Dynasty and the Southern Song and Jin confronting each other during the Southern Song Dynasty. With frequent wars and lack of raw materials, the bronze mirror making collapsed. According the records in the historical documents, the bronze mirror cast by the private must be tested by the government and sold by *liang* on the market. The inscriptions of Huzhou mirrors also reveal that the copper was very expensive. The industry of bronze mirror casting was seriously restricted, with thinner and thinner body. Until the Ming and Qing Dynasties, the bronze mirror was served widely as a practical commodity with simple design.

There are eighteen bronze mirrors of the Song and Jin Dynasties listed in the book, with story design, chrysanthemum design, geometric pattern and inscription.

This book includes three Huzhou mirrors in the shape of shield and mallow. The Huzhou mirror appeared in the late Northern Song Dynasty prevailed between the early and the middle Southern Song Dynasty. In the late Northern Song Dynasty, with the northern people migrating to the south and the economic center moving to the south, the handcraft industries developed promptly in the south and Huzhou, Raozhou, Lin'an and Ping'an became the center of the bronze mirror casting. The Huzhou mirrors were decorated with simple design and cast with inscription of the name of the maker and the price. The mirrors were cast by the government and private. The Huzhou mirrors in the book may be cast by the private, with rough technology.

In the Southern Song Dynasty, the Song and Jin were confronting each other by the Huai River. Some bronze mirrors of the Jin Dynasty were unearthed in Huainan. The Jin Dynasty was founded by the Jurchens. The bronze mirrors of the Jin represented plural cultures, with its unique rough and heavy style, which is distinguished from the Huzhou mirrors. The six bronze mirrors of the Jin in the book are decorated with traditional stories and flower design, with rough lines and simple layout. The mirror with pattern of legendary incident of Xu You and Chao Fu is similar with the mirror unearthed in Baoding, Hebei which also has a blank rectangular without inscriptions inside at the top. The mirror with the same design recorded in the *A Catalogue of Chinese Bronze Mirrors* is carved with inscription "*Xu You Xi Er, Chao Fu Yin Niu*", which marked that it was tested by the government in the early time. The Prohibition of Copper was carried out in the Jin Dynasty, and the copper casting by the private could be punished. Therefore it is assumed that the mirrors in Huainan and Baoding were cast privately as the imitation of the mirrors by the government. The mirror with pattern of boys riding is similar with the mirror unearthed in Wa County, Hebei in May, 1958, which has a bow-shaped knob on a flower-shaped base, the major motif of eight boys riding and circling in the same direction and a rectangular with inscription "*Jing Zi Ju Guan*" at one side. But the mirror in Huainan was badly corroded.

The industry of the bronze mirror casting changed in the Ming and Qing Dynasties, compared with the Song Period. Numerous imitations of the Han mirrors were cast, with heavy body. But with few raw materials and lower technology, the mirrors showed rough surface and unclear decorations. After the introduction of the grass mirror, the bronze mirror was only served as an ornament warding off evils.

There are twenty mirrors of the Ming and Qing Dynasty in the book, among which five mirrors with design of figures and treasures, a mirror with fish design, a mirror with Eight Diagrams design, three imitations of the Han mirror, and two mirrors with handles and flower design.

The mirror with design of figures and treasures is the representative of the Ming mirrors. Compared with the Song and Yuan Dynasties, the industry of the bronze mirror casting developed. With massive production, the bronze mirrors were decorated with new designs, in a better quality. The bronze mirror of the Ming Dynasty was a peak during the declined stage. The mirrors were decorated with pattern of Buddhism, such as the Eight Emblems with meaning of luck, safeness and long life. Among five mirrors with treasure design unearthed in Huainan, there is a treasure, with 40cm diameter and 1.4cm thick. The mirror is decorated with a band of inscription as the major motif and treasures design such as animals and clouds, composing a pleasant picture. The mirror may be cast by the government, with fine copper, clear decoration, and standard mold. The other four bronze mirrors are the common mirrors of the Ming Dynasty whose technology and design are inferior to the former.

In the Qing Dynasty, the bronze mirrors declined, with raw materials in a low quality, simple design and rough technology. The two mirrors with handle are the treasures of the bronze mirrors at the same time. The mirror with handle and rhomboid pattern is round in shape and is adorned with rhomboid pattern as the major motif and the brocade pattern as the ground motif. The mirror with regular layout and clear decoration may be cast by the government. The mirror with handle and inscription "*Li*" is decorated with inscription and interlocking flowers. The mirror with regular layout and bad raw material and rough technology may be cast by the private.

The bronze mirror is regarded as a symbol of Chinese traditional culture. The design of the bronze mirror, with concentrated connotation, reflects the rise and falls of the Chinese history, becomes the image of the real life and has a strong artistic appeal.

Taking a view of the developing history of the bronze mirror, we can feel its distinct characteristics of the time, appreciate its artistic connotation and know the creative power and imagination of the ancient people. With the changes of the times and dynasties, the bronze mirrors had been changed on shapes, designs and technology. The bronze mirror, as a valuable cultural heritage of the Chinese nation like other historical relics, is honored in the memories of the people.

Director of Huainan Museum
Shen Hanqing
January 8, 2011

图 版

Plates

单线连弧纹镜 战国

直径14厘米，边厚0.3厘米，重195克

1972年4月淮南市谢家集区红卫轮窑厂M4出土

　　圆形，三弦钮，圆钮座。钮外及缘内饰二周宽弦纹带，绕钮座的宽弦纹带呈凹弧面。主区纹饰是在素地上以镜钮为中心，环绕单线隆起的十一个内向连弧纹。连弧纹线条纤细，弧的曲度平缓。窄缘，边缘上卷。镜面有铁状锈蚀物，应是镜的附着物所致，在镜缘未锈蚀处可见光亮的镜体。

　　素地单线连弧纹铜镜发现较少。长沙楚墓发现两面，其M838出土的一面与此镜尺寸、布局基本相同，其时代定在战国楚国晚期早段，即公元前300年至公元前278年，在吴起拔郢之前。淮南这面铜镜镜体轻薄，有明显的早期特征，是本地区所见最早的楚式镜，该镜出土地点是淮南地区出土铜镜数量最多也最集中的区域，由此也证明，该地区在楚国迁都寿春城之前，这里已经是楚国人活动的区域。（沈汗青）

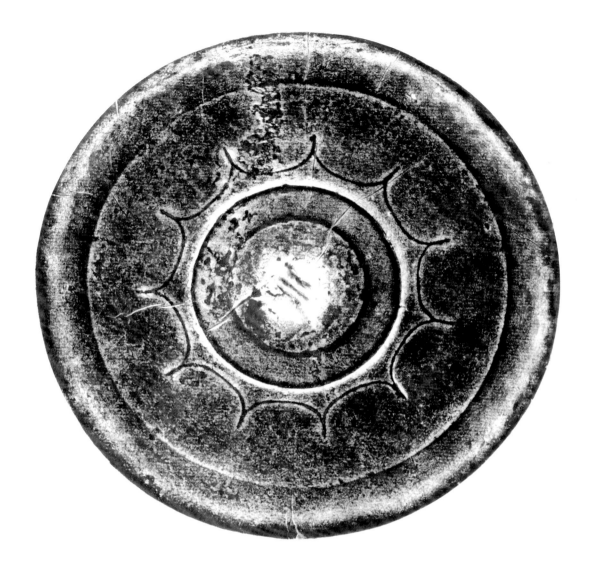

Mirror with design of linked arcs formed by single line   Warring States Period

Diameter: 14cm, Thickness of rim: 0.3cm, Weight: 195gram

Unearthed from the Tomb 4 of Hongwei Annular Kiln Works in Xiejiaji District, Huainan City in April, 1972

The mirror is round in shape. It has a knob with three-string design on a round base. A broad string band with concave surface adorns outside the base. The major motif is eleven linked arcs inward formed by single line around the base. Inner rim is decorated with a broad string band. The mirror has a narrow rim rolling upward. Rust can be seen on the surface.

The mirrors with linked arcs formed by single line are rarely found. The two mirrors with the same design unearthed from the Chu tomb in Changsha City, one of which, unearthed from Tomb 838, is similar with this mirror in size and design and is inferred as the mirror of the late Chu State in the Warring States Period (300AD — 278AD). The mirror with thin body holds the distinct features of the Chu mirror in early period and is the earliest mirror of the Chu mirror found in Huainan. The area from which the mirror was unearthed, have found bronze mirrors in a great number. All evidence proves that the Chu State had conducted activity at this area before moving the capital to Shouchun City. (Shen Hanqing)

云雷纹镜　战国

直径9.5厘米，边厚0.3厘米，重60克

1987年10月淮南市谢家集区唐山乡双古堆东侧砂场工地出土

　　圆形，三弦钮，圆钮座。钮座外和镜缘边各饰二周弦纹，弦纹之间满铺云雷纹。云雷纹为圆涡纹及两个底边相对的双线三角纹相间排列，呈四方连续式排列。在斜穿镜钮方向，有模制范线。卷缘。

　　战国时期云雷纹多作地纹，常出现于龙纹镜中，纯地纹镜比较少见。楚镜中的地纹除云雷纹外，还有羽状纹和云雷纹，是由同一印模连续压印而成。该镜体轻薄，较《中国铜镜图典》收录的直径15.5厘米云雷地纹镜和湖南长沙年佳湖出土的直径11厘米的同类镜直径都小，钮座所占镜背比例也小，其时代要稍早一些，时间应在楚国迁都寿春之前。（沈汗青）

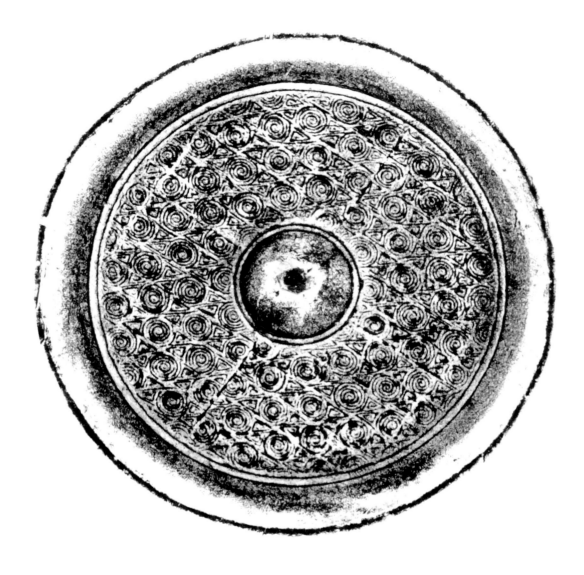

Mirror with design of cloud and thunder　Warring States Period

Diameter: 9.5cm, Thickness of rim: 0.3cm, Weight: 60gram

Unearthed from a Sand Workshop, east from Shuanggudui in Xiejiaji District, Huainan City in October, 1987

The mirror is round in shape. It has a knob with three-string design on a round base. Outside the base and inner rim are two band of string design. The ground is filled with design of cloud and thunder. The clouds and thunders, in the shapes of alternate arrangement of whorl pattern and two triangles formed by double lines, are arranged repeatedly toward four directions. The bottom sides of two triangles are opposing each other. A mark line of mold is slanting the knob. The mirror has a rim rolling.

In the Warring States Period (475 BC – 221 BC), the design of cloud and thunder used to be decorated as the ground motif and mostly on mirrors with dragon design. The mirrors with the design of cloud and thunder are rarely seen. The design of cloud with thunder and feather-like pattern were often used as the ground motif of the Chu mirror and were pressed continuously by the model. The mirror with thin body is shorter than the mirrors with the same design respectively recorded in the *A Catalogue of Chinese Bronze Mirror* with diameter 15.5cm and unearthed at Nianjia Lake, Changsha City, Hunan Province with diameter 11cm. The knob holds a tiny fraction compared with the ground. It is inferred that the mirror's age is the Chu State before moving the capital to Shouchun City.　(Shen Hanqing)

单线连弧纹镜　战国

直径14.4厘米，边厚0.3厘米，重230克

本馆旧藏

　　圆形，三弦钮，圆钮座。钮座和镜缘饰两周宽弦纹带，绕钮座的宽弦纹呈凹弧面，镜缘处的弦纹带较宽。主区饰十一个单线隆起的内向连弧纹。镜残有修，直径较本馆藏另一面同类镜直径稍大，两镜时代大致相同。（沈汗青）

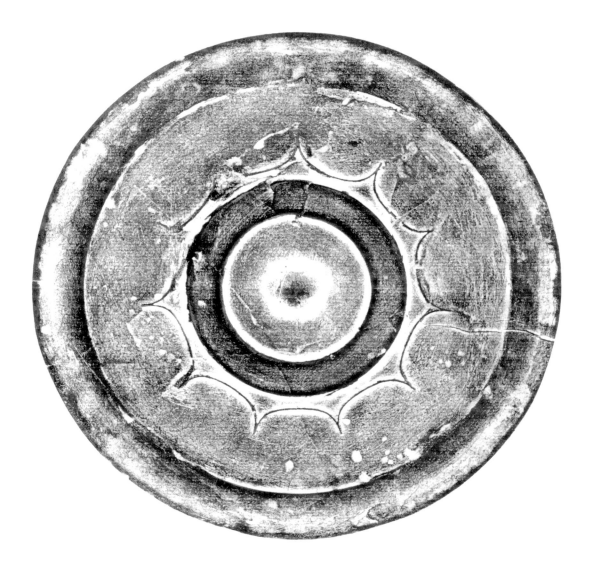

Mirror with design of linked arcs formed by single line Warring States Period

Diameter: 14.4cm, Thickness of rim: 0.3cm, Weight: 230gram

Collection of Huainan Museum

TThe mirror is round in shape. It has a knob with three-string design on a round base. A broad string band with concave surface adorns outside the base. The major motif is eleven linked arcs inward formed by single line. The mirror was once broken and repaired. The mirror is bigger in diameter than the mirror with the same design collected in Huainan museum and has the same time with it.   (Shen Hanqing)

羽状纹地四叶镜　战国

直径11.6厘米，边厚0.4厘米，重115克

1986年12月于淮南市谢家集区施家湖乡打击盗墓收缴

　　圆形，三弦钮，圆钮座。座外饰凸弦纹一周，且与主题纹饰四叶纹相连。四叶周围满铺羽状纹，每个羽状纹呈长方形，上下左右反复排列成四方连续式。钮座外十字形方向伸出四叶，叶有粗柄，叶面分叉呈山字形状，中间叶下饰有弧线。羽状地近缘处以凸弦纹为栏。宽素缘，卷边。

　　羽状纹地叶纹镜有四叶和八叶之分，四叶纹镜发现得较多，叶形的变化也最丰富。叶纹镜在战国中期出现。此镜属细涡粒状羽状纹上饰四叶纹，较变形粗羽状纹要早，时间在战国晚期楚国迁都寿春之前。

　　　　　　　　　　　　　　　　　　　　（沈汗青）

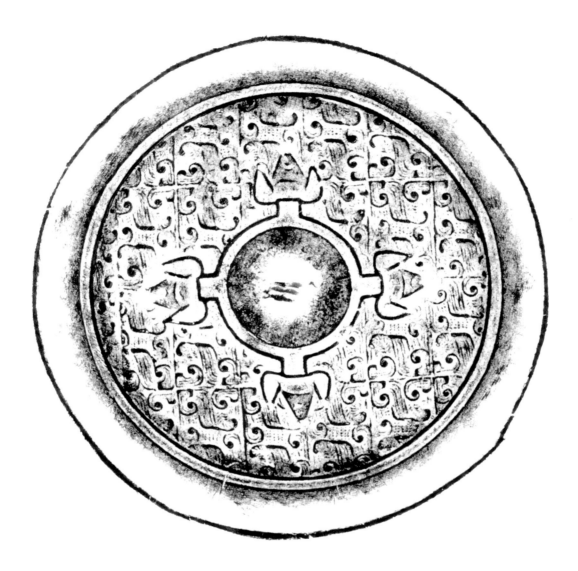

Mirror with feather-like pattern as ground motif and four-leaf design   Warring States Period

Diameter: 11.6cm, Thickness of rim: 0.4cm, Weight: 115gram

Got from an operation against tomb robbers in Shijiahu Town, Xiejiaji District, Huainan City in December, 1986

The mirror is round in shape. It has a knob with three-string design on a round base. Outside the base is a band of raised string pattern, joining to the subject designs of four-leaf pattern. Around four-leaf designs are feather-like patterns with rectangle shape toward four directions. The four-leaf design is stretching out of each direction of cross outside the base, which has sturdy petiole and is in the shape of "*Shan*" character. And the middle leaf is decorated with arc pattern. A band of raised string pattern is spaced between the ground motif and the rim. The mirror has a broad rim without design rolling upward.

Bronze mirrors with feather-like pattern as the ground motif and leaf design can be divided into two categories: four-leaf design and eight-leaf design. The mirrors with four-leaf design are commonly seen and have varied shape of leaf. The mirrors with leaf design appeared in the middle Warring States Period. The feather-like pattern on this mirror is in shape of granulated fine whorl and earlier than stylized heavy feather-like pattern, so the mirror is inferred as a bronze mirror of the Chu State before moving the capital to Shouchun City in the late Warring States Period.   (Shen Hanqing)

羽状纹地花叶纹镜　战国

直径13.6厘米，厚0.5厘米，重148克

1958年淮南市谢家集区唐山公社九里大队出土

　　圆形，三弦钮，方钮座，镜背满饰羽状纹。此镜采用四方连续图案方法，羽状纹两两相对应，横置排列成十行，羽翅的对应间有十分密集细小的乳突，共三行六列，与羽状纹、主纹构成三层纹饰。主纹是从方形钮座四角向外伸出的对称长杆花叶，形如"J"形，每支杆上有两个心形花瓣，共八花四长叶。宽缘卷沿。

　　羽状纹，也有学者称之为变形羽状兽纹、羽翅纹等，是截取蟠螭纹躯体的一部分为一个长方形，有规律连续排列形成的四方连续图案。这种图案在装饰镜背的时候常常布满镜背，密集而整齐，有较强的装饰效果。此镜纹饰精细繁缛，但不失雅致，是文化特征较明显的楚式镜。（沈汗青）

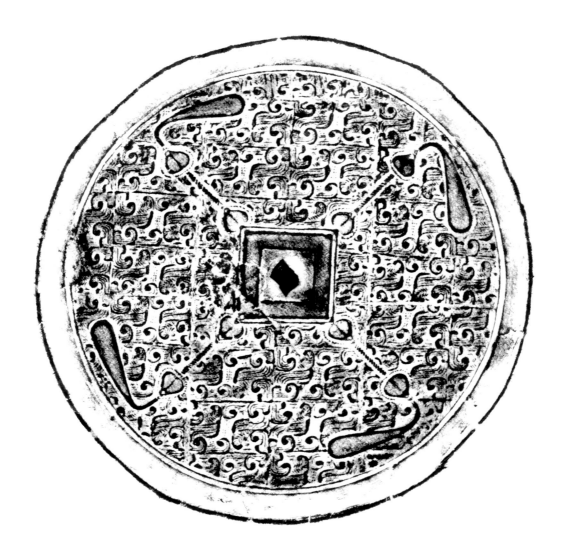

Mirror with feather-like pattern as ground motif and design of flower and leaf Warring states Period

Diameter: 13.6cm, Thickness: 0.5cm, Weight: 148gram

Unearthed at Jiuli Brigade, Tangshan Commune, Xiejiaji District, Huainan City in 1958

The mirror is round in shape. It has a knob with three-string design on a square base. It is decorated with feather-like pattern repeatedly arranged toward four directions as the motif ground. The three-layer design of the mirror composes of feather-like pattern corresponding in twos and arranging in ten lines, nipple pattern spacing with corresponding area of feather-like pattern and arranging in three lines and ten rows and motif design. Outside each corner of the square is a long J-shaped leaf pattern stretching

out and each leaf has a heart-shaped petal. The mirror has a broad rim rolling upward.

The feather-like pattern, also called "stylized animal with feather pattern" or "wing with feather pattern", is composed of the organized, linked arrangement of a rectangle part of interlaced-hydras pattern. It often regularly fills up in the ground and has a strong decorative effect. The mirror with exquisite design is a typical mirror of the Chu State.   (Shen Hanqing)

四山镜 战国

直径13.7厘米，厚0.4厘米，重165克

1957年淮南市唐山公社邱家岗出土

圆形，三弦钮，三重方钮座。钮座四角饰四片花瓣，主纹为四山字纹，山字底边与方钮座四边平行排列，间饰四花，以羽纹为地，构成三层重叠式图案，布局细致，主次分明。窄斜素缘。

山字纹镜在战国时十分流行，多以羽状纹、草叶纹作地纹。上饰三山、四山、五山或六山纹，尤以四山纹为多。镜中的山字，其寓意有不同解释，一般认为是从青铜器上的勾连云雷纹演化而来。在圆形镜背上以三个或数个山字纹作纹饰，是比较难以排列布局

的，但是我们现在见到的每一面山字纹镜均十分匀称美观，古代工匠技艺之精巧可见一斑。此镜四个山字均朝左向倾斜，避免了构图的呆板，产生了律动；虽然单个山字缺少平衡，但整体有一种旋转的韵律。方形钮座四角伸出四叶纹，四山之间饰四瓣花纹，下层再以细密的羽状纹铺地，使观者感受到镜背纹饰繁缛精细，有强烈的美感。该镜胎体轻薄，能够保存如此完好十分难得。（沈汗青）

Mirror with inscription of four "*Shan*" characters Warring States Period

Diameter: 13.7cm, Thickness: 0.4cm, Weight: 165 gram

Unearthed at Qiujiagang, Tangshan Commune, Huainan City in 1957

The mirror is round in shape. It has a knob with three-string design on a three-layer square base. A petal casts outside each corner of the square. The mirror is decorated with a three-layer overlapping pattern consisting of the inscription of four "*Shan*" characters symmetrically arranged, four flowers with which four "*Shan*" are spaced and feather-like pattern as ground motif. The bottom strokes of the characters are in parallel with the four sides of the square. The decoration of the mirror has an exquisite layout and shows a distinction between the primary design and the lesser one. It has an inclined narrow rim without design.

During the Warring States Period (475 BC – 221 BC), the mirrors with inscription of "*Shan*" character prevailed among the populace, most of which are adorned with feather-like pattern or leaf pattern as the ground motif. The mirrors were usually decorated with inscription of three, four, five or six "*Shan*" characters, especially four "*Shan*" characters design more. The "*Shan*" character is given different meaning. It is generally thought that "*Shan*" is derived from thunder pattern on the bronzes. It is hard to arrange three or several "*Shan*" characters on a round surface. The ancient craftsmen were great talents with considerable creative spirit, so every mirror with inscription of "*Shan*" characters found shows us aesthetic and symmetrical design. The four "*Shan*" characters inclining to left form circulating composition as a whole. The mirror with intricate and elegant decorations brings a strong aesthetic feeling. It is rare that the mirror with thin body is kept in good condition.   (Shen Hanqing)

羽状纹地四山四鹿纹镜　战国

直径15.7厘米，边厚 0.5厘米，重230克

1987年12月淮南市谢家集区红卫轮窑厂出土

　　圆形，三弦钮，以双层方形宽带为钮座。镜背通体以精美的羽状纹为地，呈四方连续排列，四山纹粗壮有力，以鹿形瑞兽间隔。鹿作回首状，小短尾，三足落地，右前腿抬起弯曲，身饰鳞状纹，造型生动。山字向左倾斜，中间一笔向左伸向镜缘，两侧的竖划上端向内折成尖角。宽缘，边缘上卷。

　　该镜制作十分规整，模范精细，为战国晚期楚国铜镜。此镜1987年在淮南市谢家集区红卫轮窑厂发现时已残破，后经修复完整。山字纹镜中饰瑞兽类纹饰的比较罕见，尤显此镜珍贵。（沈汗青）

Mirror with inscription of four "*Shan*" characters,

design of four deer and feather-like pattern as ground motif   Warring States Period

Diameter: 15.7cm, Thickness of rim: 0.5cm, Weight: 230gram

Unearthed from the Hongwei Annular Kiln Works in Xiejiaji District, Huainan City in December, 1987

The mirror is round in shape. It has a knob with three-string design on a two-layer square base, and is decorated with feather-like pattern arranged toward four directions as ground motif. Four strong and powerful "*Shan*" characters are spaced with vivid deer which are looking back and filled scale pattern in the body. The "*Shan*" character is inclined to the left and the middle stroke goes toward the rim. The tops of the strokes on both sides stretch inward in a closed angle shape. The mirror has a broad rim rolling upward.

This mirror with perfect structure and exquisite layout is inferred as a bronze mirror of the Chu State in the late Warring States Period. It is a pity that the mirror was once broken when it was unearthed from the Hongwei Annular Kiln in Huainan City in 1987. The mirror swith inscription of "*Shan*" characters and mythical creature design are rarely found, so this mirror is particularly valuable.   (Shen Hanqing)

羽状纹地变形兽纹镜 战国
直径12.9厘米，边厚0.3厘米，重130克
本馆旧藏

　　圆形，三弦钮，圆钮座。座外饰一周凹弧面宽带纹和一周弦纹。主区以羽状纹为地，上饰五个变形兽纹。兽纹呈几何图案状，尾部呈如意云头，身部呈"C"形弯曲。缘处以弦纹为栏，宽素缘，缘上卷。

　　此类变形兽纹镜发现较少，湖南常德德山楚墓出土一面，比此镜略大。这种变形兽纹十分夸张，几乎看不到兽纹的特征，已经变成几何纹和花草纹，十分耐人寻味。（沈汗青）

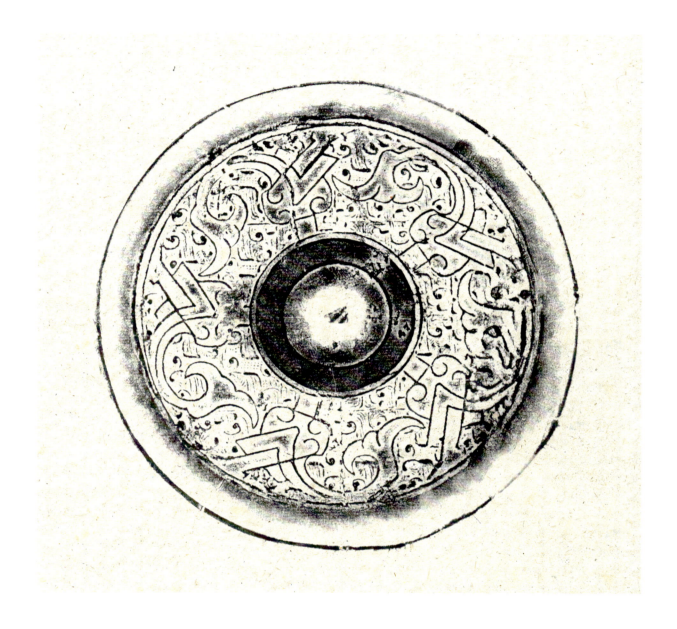

Mirror with feather-like pattern as ground motif and stylized animal pattern   Warring States Period

Diameter: 12.9cm, Thickness of rim: 0.3cm, Weight: 130gram

Collection of Huainan Museum

The mirror is round in shape. It has a knob with three-string design on a round base. Outside the base are a broad band with concave surface and a band of string pattern. The ground is decorated with feather-like pattern as ground motif and five stylized animal patterns. The animal pattern has a geometry-shaped head, an end with S-shaped cloud design and a C-shaped body. The edge of feather-like pattern is adorned with a band of string design. The mirror has a broad rim without design rolling upward.

It is rare to find the mirrors with feather-like pattern as ground motif and stylized animal pattern. The mirror with the same design, but a little bigger, was once unearthed from the Chu tomb in De Hill, Changde City, Hunan Province. The exaggerated pattern of stylized animal holds no features of animal pattern and is in the shape of geometric pattern and the flower and leaf design, which is very interesting.   (Shen Hanqing)

羽状纹地四叶镜 战国

直径11.3厘米，边厚0.3厘米，重68克

1972年淮南市谢家集区红卫轮窑厂出土

　　圆形，三弦钮，圆钮座。钮座饰有一周凸弦纹，四周等距伸出四桃形叶，双层，外层叶由放射形短线构成，形似茸毛，叶无柄，紧贴钮座。四周满铺羽状地纹，羽状地细密，有模印羽状地纹痕迹和范线。此镜造型规范，模范细腻。属细涡粒状羽状纹，时代较早，应不晚于战国晚期楚国迁都寿春之前。（沈汗青）

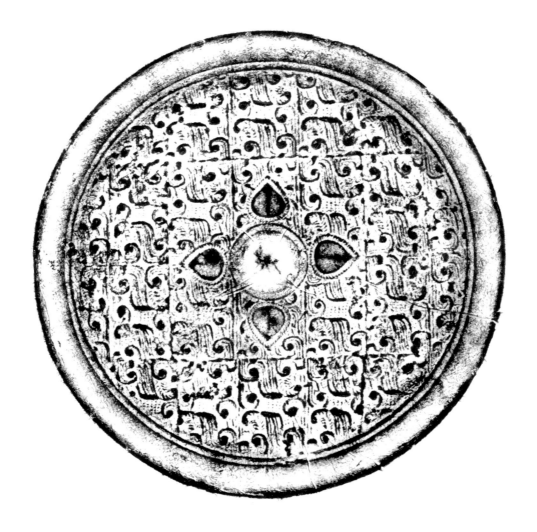

Mirror with feather-like pattern as ground motif and four-leaf design Warring States Period

Diameter: 11.3cm, Thickness of rim: 0.3cm, Weight: 68gram

Unearthed at Hongwei Annular Kiln Works, Xiejiaji District, Huainan City in 1972

The mirror is round in shape. It has a knob with three-string design on a round base. Outside the base is a band of raised string pattern. Four peach-shaped leaves are stretching out around the band in the same distance, which has two layouts and no petiole. Outer layout of peach-shaped leaf comprises short radiative lines which look like fuzz. The feather-like pattern is decorated as ground motif, on which mold mark can be found. This mirror with perfect structure, exquisite layout and feather-like pattern in the shape of granulated fine whorl, is inferred as a bronze mirror not later than the Chu State moving the capital to Shouchur City in the late Warring States Period. (Shen Hanqing)

羽状纹地四叶镜 战国
直径12.8厘米，边厚0.6厘米，重270克
1958年淮南市唐山公社九里大队出土

　　圆形，三弦钮，方形双层钮座。钮座四边中间各伸出一单片桃形叶纹，叶片中饰对称斜线纹表现叶之脉络，向镜钮方向整齐排列，并以两个相连的短弧线横穿叶片，四叶下满铺羽状地纹。卷缘。（沈汗青）

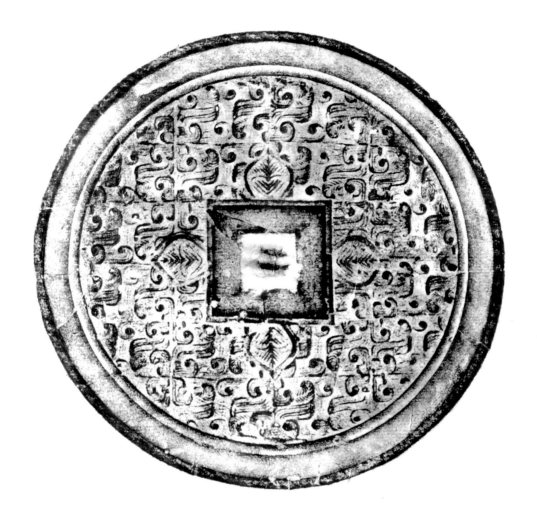

Mirror with feather-like pattern as ground motif and four-leaf design   Warring States Period

Diameter: 12.8cm, Thickness of rim: 0.6cm, Weight: 270gram

Unearthed at Jiuli Brigade, Tangshan Commune, Huainan City in 1958

The mirror is round in shape. It has a knob with three-string design on a two-layer square base. A peach-shaped leaf is stretching out of each middle side of the square, which is decorated with slanted-line pattern as leaf vein and two short arc lines crossing the leaf. The feather-like pattern is adorned as ground motif. The rim is rolling upward.   (Shen Hanqing)

龙纹镜 战国

直径11.6厘米，边厚0.25厘米，重97克

1982年8月淮南市赖山公社莲花大队出土

　　圆形，三弦钮，圆钮座。座外环两周凸弦纹，内饰栉齿纹。主区纹饰以云锦纹铺地，上均匀分布四龙纹。龙首靠近缘部，腹部呈"S"形弯曲，作张牙舞爪状，缠绕环转，动感十足。主区与镜缘处饰绞索纹。凹弧面宽素缘，卷沿。此镜地纹与主纹层次分明，四龙造型简洁，为战国楚国晚期典型的龙纹镜。

（沈汗青）

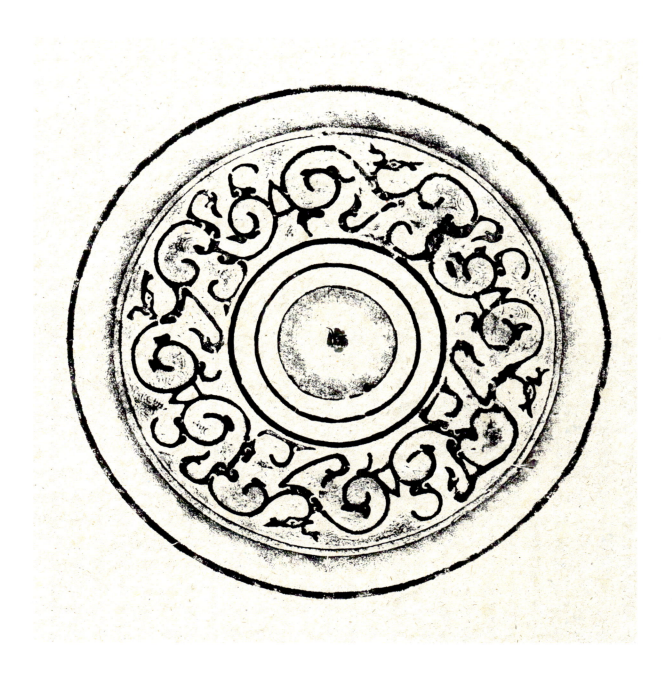

Mirror with dragon design Warring States Period

Diameter: 11.6cm, Thickness of rim: 0.25cm, Weight: 97gram

Unearthed at Lianhua Brigade, Laishan Commune, Huainan City in August, 1982

The mirror is round in shape. It has a knob with three-string design on a round base. Outside the base are two bands of raised string design with fine-toothed pattern inside. The ground is decorated with design of Yun brocade as the ground motif and four dragons. The dragon has an S-shaped body and is making threatening gesture. Inside the rim is the twisted pattern. The mirror has a broad rim with concave surface which has no design and is rolling. The mirror, with a distinction between ground motif and major motif and simple dragon pattern, is inferred as a typical mirror of the late Chu State in the Warring States Period. (Shen Hanqing)

龙纹镜　战国

直径12.7厘米，边厚0.4厘米，重150克

20世纪80年代后期征集

　　圆形，桥钮，圆钮座。座外环绕一周凹弧面宽带
纹。主区纹饰两侧以弦纹和栉齿为栏，主纹在云雷纹
地上饰四龙。龙首大张口，作吞钮座状，肢爪伸张，

身躯弯卷，勾连交错，变化复杂。宽凹弧面缘，缘边
卷起。（沈汗青）

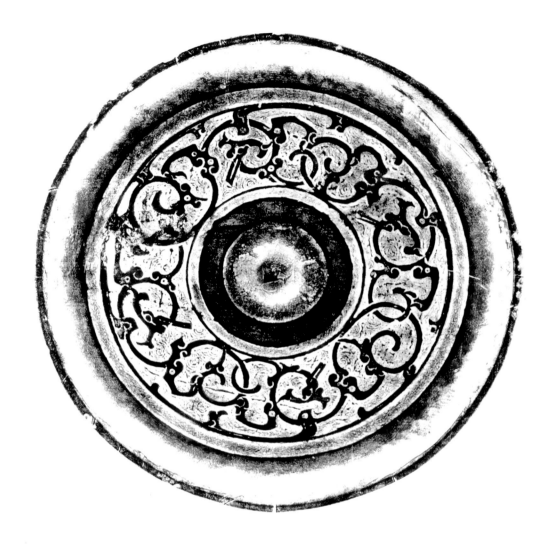

Mirror with dragon design   Warring States Period

Diameter: 12.7cm, Thickness of rim: 0.4cm, Weight: 150gram

Collected in late 1980s

The mirror is round in shape. It has a bridge-shaped knob on a round base. Outside the base is a broad band with concave surface. Inside the rim are the string design and fine-toothed design. The ground is filled with design of cloud and thunder and is decorated with four dragons on the ground motif. The dragon is swallowing the knob, stretching its paws and curving its body. The mirror has a broad rim with concave surface which is rolling upward.   (Shen Hanqing)

蟠螭连弧纹镜 战国

直径16.3厘米，边厚0.5厘米，重326克

本馆旧藏

　　圆形，弦钮，圆钮座。钮有修。座外围一周凹面弦纹宽带，主区由地纹和主纹组合而成。地纹为云雷纹；地纹之上饰八个内向连弧纹宽带，将镜背分成内外两区，两区各饰四蟠螭：内区蟠螭向右运动，外区蟠螭向左运动。内外蟠螭上下勾连。蟠螭大张口，小圆目，前足伸，后足踏镜缘或连弧纹，尾部翻卷。此镜以三层纹饰构成了一幅细密繁缛的浅浮雕图案，是晚期楚镜之佳品。（王莉）

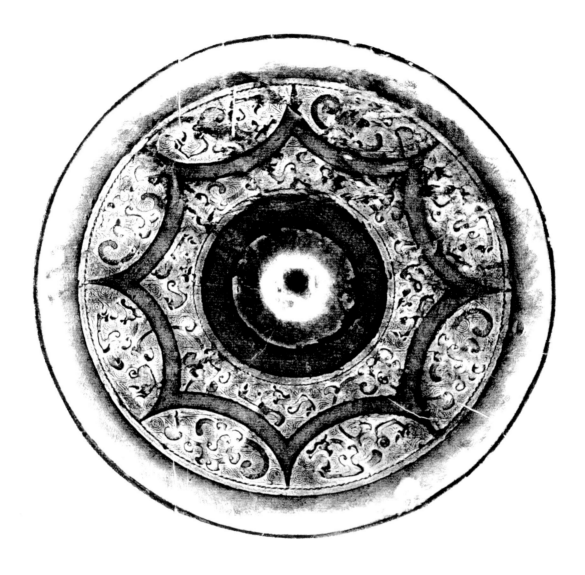

Mirror with design of interlaced hydras and linked arcs   Warring States Period

Diameter: 16.3cm, Thickness of rim: 0.5cm, Weight: 326gram
Collection of Huainan Museum

The mirror is round in shape. It has a repaired knob with string design on a round base. Outside the base is a broad band of string design with concave surface. The ground is decorated with design of cloud and thunder as ground motif. The major motif of each part spaced with a broad band of eight linked arcs inwards, is adorned with four interlaced-hydras patterns moving towards

the right on inner part and the left on outer part. The interlaced hydras with mouth opening, small round eyes and rolling tail, is stretching its front paws out and keeping the back paws at the rim or arc pattern. The mirror with exquisite decoration of a three-layer bas relief is a treasure of the Chu bronze mirror in the late period. (Wang Li)

龙纹镜 战国

直径23.8厘米，边厚0.5厘米，重818克

2010年9月淮南市谢家集公安分局移交

　　圆形，宽弦钮，圆形钮座。七个浅凹弧面连弧纹绕钮座一周，镜背以细密的云雷纹铺地，外饰一圈凹弧面宽带纹。主区在云雷纹地上饰八龙纹。龙大口，小圆目，长舌卷起，角部后翻，身躯平起，足踏镜缘，身形变化复杂，缠绕交错，勾连奇曲。外以一周细弦纹和栉齿纹为栏。宽素缘，缘边卷起，窄平。此镜形制硕大，纹饰繁缛华丽，是战国晚期楚镜的代表作品。（沈汗青）

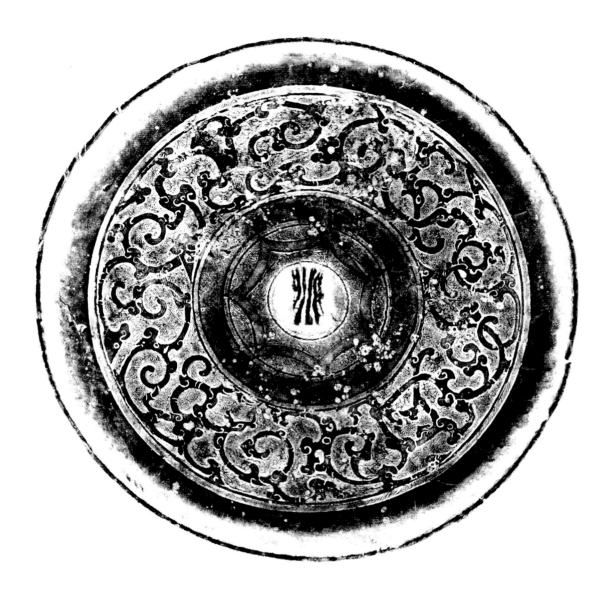

Mirror with dragon design   Warring States Period

Diameter: 23.8cm, Thickness of rim: 0.5cm, Weight: 818gram

Transferred by Xiejiaji District Pubic Security Bureau in Huainan City in September, 2010

The mirror is round in shape. It has a knob with broad string design on a round base. Around the base are seven linked arcs with concave surface and a broad band with concave surface. The ground is decorated with the design of cloud and thunder as ground motif. Eight dragons, as major motif, are in shape of big mouth, small round eyes, rolling tongue and twisted body. A band of thin-string design and fine-toothed patter adorn inside the rim. The mirror has a broad rim without design and rolling. The mirror with exquisite decoration and in large size is a typical mirror of the Chu State in the late Warring States Period.   (Shen Hanqing)

羽状纹地四叶镜 战国

直径13厘米，边厚0.6厘米，重278克

2010年8月淮南市谢家集区李郢孜镇塌陷区改造工程谢家集小区21号楼工地出土

　　圆形，三弦钮，小圆钮座。钮座双层，仅比镜钮稍大，此种钮座十分少见。座外等距伸出四桃形叶，叶形饱满，中间隆脊，短粗无柄，长度不及钮座直径。镜背满铺羽状地纹，羽状地纹较大，但十分清晰、规整，每一羽尾卷而凸起，极细密，是羽状地纹中比较少见的精细作品。羽状地纹边缘以弦纹为栏。镜缘弧起，缘宽。

　　羽状地纹镜早期采用模印制范，一面直径不足10厘米的镜上，有时有多达30个羽状纹模印痕迹，模印之间的连接处多见不规则接缝。脱范时，为保护镜体，多将泥范揭破，故很少有完全相同的铜镜，是一镜一范所致。而此镜羽状地纹和四叶纹观察不到任何模印的接范痕，陈佩芬先生在观察有些铜镜花纹上具有明显的缩蜡痕迹后认定"山字纹镜从羽翅纹的地纹看，它是用失腊法铸造的。"此镜纹饰清晰，铸造精良，镜体厚重，已无楚镜之轻薄特征，是楚国末期用失腊法铸造的，弥足珍贵。（沈汗青）

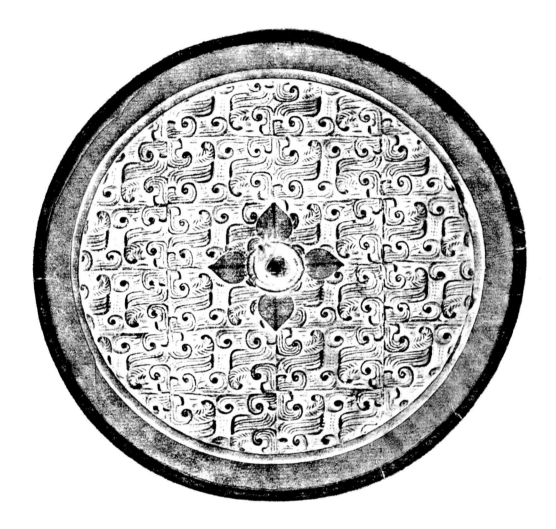

Mirror with feather-like pattern as ground motif and four-leaf design Warring States Period

Diameter: 13cm, Thickness of rim: 0.6cm, Weight: 278gram

Unearthed at a construction site of No.21 Building, Xiejiaji Area under a project of rebuilding subsidence area, in Liyingzi Town, Xiejiaji District, Huainan City in August, 2010

The mirror is round in shape. It has a knob with three-string design on a two-layer round base which is a little bigger than the knob and not commonly seen. Four peach-shaped leaves with plump shape and raised ridge are stretching out of the base in the same distance. The feather-like pattern with neat, clear and big shape is adorned as ground motif. It is rare to see such exquisite feather-like pattern with back part rolling and raised. The edge of feather-like pattern is adorned with a band of string design. The mirror has a broad rim raised in arc shape.

In the early period, casting of the mirror with feather-like pattern as motif ground used the technology of molding. Even over 30 mold marks with irregular joint could be found in a mirror less than diameter 10cm. In order to protect the mirror, the clay model was often broken when casting. So each mirror owns its only mold and it is rare to find the same mirrors. But in this mirror, any mold mark can not be found. Mr. Chen Peifen observed clear wax marks on ground motif of feather-like pattern and inferred that the mirror with inscription of "Shan" character was cast by lost-wax method. The mirror with clear design, exquisite cast and thick body, was cast by lost-wax method in the late Chu State and of high value, which hadn't owned the light and thin features of bronze mirror of the Chu State.　(Shen Hanqing)

龙纹镜　战国

直径16.3厘米，边厚0.7厘米，重305克

2010年9月淮南市谢家集区公安分局移交

　　圆形，三弦钮，云雷纹圆钮座。外饰绞索纹和凹弧面宽带弦纹各一周，主区纹饰以云雷纹铺地，三只龙环绕钮座均匀分布，龙头部靠近镜缘，张口吐舌作回首反顾状，身躯右旋，两足前后伸张，踏于镜缘，后足勾缠于菱形纹中。龙首大眼，长舌下勾，头顶后部伸出长弯角，身躯动感极强，与菱形纹勾连交错。主纹两侧以高凸弦纹和栉齿纹为廓。镜缘略凹弧，卷缘。（沈汗青）

Mirror with dragon design   Warring States period

Diameter: 16.3cm, Thickness of rim: 0.7cm, Weight: 305gram

Transferred by Xiejiaji District Public Security Bureau in Huainan City in September, 2010

The mirror is round in shape. It has a knob with three-string design on a round base with design of cloud and thunder. Outside the base are a band of twisted rope pattern and a broad string band with concave surface. The ground is decorated with design of cloud and thunder as ground motif and three dragons around the base. The dragon is looking back and is standing at the rim. The dragon design with mouth opening and tongue showing is interlocked with lozenge pattern. Inside the rim are the raised string design and fine-toothed pattern. The rim has a concave surface and is rolling.   (Shen Hanqing)

龙纹镜 战国

直径23.2厘米，边厚1.1厘米，重984克

1987年6月淮南市谢家集区唐山乡双古堆墓葬出土

　　圆形，三弦钮，云雷纹圆钮座。钮座环绞索圈、栉齿纹、凹弧面宽带纹、弦纹各一周。主区以云雷纹为地，饰三龙和三菱形纹。三龙等距均匀布置，龙角近钮座，首部呈四分之三侧目，双面，张大口露齿，口吐长舌向上卷起，引颈昂首，身体作腾飞状，勾曲伸展，羽状翅布满身躯。其中二龙头部左顾，一龙右顾，三龙身体向右运动，龙身近缘处环绕绞索纹和栉齿纹各一周。凹弦面宽缘，高卷。

　　此镜体形硕大，较少见。山东临沂银雀山第四号西汉早期墓所出铜镜和《中国铜镜图典》收录的一面铜镜与此镜相似。镜背的龙纹造型写实，头部双目，在同类镜中罕见。镜背龙纹盘曲交错，气韵生动，虽出土于汉初墓葬中，但其整体风格为楚镜造型，可谓是楚镜最后的辉煌了。（沈汗青）

Mirror with dragon design   Warring States Period

Diameter: 23.2cm, Thickness of rim: 1.1cm, Weight: 984

Unearthed from the Shuanggudui tomb, Tangshan Town, Xiejiaji District, Huainan City in June, 1987

The mirror is round in shape. It has a knob with three-string design on a round base with design of cloud and thunder. Around the base are four bands of twisted rope pattern, fine-toothed pattern, broad concave surface and string design. The ground is decorated with design of cloud and thunder as ground motif and three dragons and lozenges designs as major motif in the same distance. The dragon with mouth opening and tongue rolling upward is trying to fly. Two dragons are looking to the left, and one is looking to the right. The dragons with feather-like pattern in body are moving towards the right. Inside the rim are bands of twisted rope pattern and fine-toothed pattern. The mirror has a broad rim with concave surface which is rolling.

The mirror is in a large size and is rare. It is similar with two mirrors respectively unearthed from Tomb 4 of the early Western Han Dynasty at Yinque Hill, Linyi City, Shangdong Province and recorded in *A Catalogue of Chinese Bronze Mirror*. The dragon design with realistic shape and two eyes is uncommon. Although the mirror was unearthed from early Han tomb, it holds the shape of the Chu bronze mirror and is regarded as the final treasure of the Chu bronze mirror.   (Shen Hanqing)

蟠螭菱纹镜　西汉
直径7.1厘米，边厚0.2厘米，重29克
1990年3月淮南市唐山乡打击盗墓收缴

　　圆形，三弦钮，圆钮座。座外环一周宽带弦纹，主纹区以卷云纹铺地，上饰三条变形蟠螭龙纹，蟠螭间分别有一连体菱形纹，镜体薄。镜缘内卷，宽凹。

蟠螭纹镜流行于战国晚期，是这一时期较常见的一种铜镜，西汉早期的铜镜仍保留其遗风。（文立中）

Mirror with design of interlaced hydras and lozenge   Western Han Dynasty

Diameter: 7.1cm, Thickness of rim: 0.2cm, Weight: 29gram

Gotten on operation of fighting tomb robbers at Tangshan Town, Huainan City in March, 1990

The mirror is round in shape. It has a knob with three-string design on a round base. Outside the base is a broad band of string design. The ground is decorated with cirrus cloud design as ground motif and three stylized interlaced-hydras designs as major motif. Each interlaced hydras spaced with lozenge interlocked with it. The mirror has a thin body and a broad rim holding concave surface and rolling inwards. The mirror with interlaced-hydras design was popular in the late Warring States Period and kept in the early Western Han Dynasty.   (Wen Lizhong)

圈带叠压蟠螭镜　西汉
直径10.5厘米，边厚0.25厘米，重85克
2010年9月淮南市谢家集公安分局移交

　　圆形，三弦钮，圆钮座。座外环一周凹面宽带纹，其外由主纹和地纹构成，地纹为云雷纹，其上饰相互勾连的蟠螭纹，蟠螭勾首、曲身、卷尾，呈"C"形，蟠螭身上叠压一周凹面宽带纹，上饰四乳钉。宽卷缘。

　　此镜为西汉早期镜，延续了战国时期铜镜的形制特点和纹饰风格。铜镜的地纹到西汉中期后就逐渐消失，此镜地纹已趋于简单，属于过渡时期风格。（汪茂东）

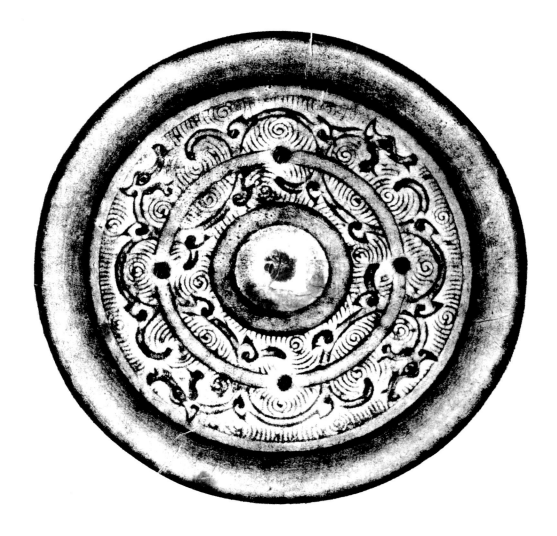

Mirror with overlaid band and coiled serpent design　Western Han Dynasty

Diameter: 10.5cm, Thickness of rim: 0.25cm, Weight: 85gram

Transferred by Xiejiaji District Public Security Bureau, in Huainan City in September, 2010

The mirror is round in shape. It has a knob with three-string design on a round base. Outside the base is a broad band with concave surface. The ground is decorated with design of cloud and thunder as ground motif and coiled serpent design interlaced. A broad band with concave surface and nipple pattern is overlaid on the C-shaped design of coiled serpent. The mirror has a broad rim rolling.

The mirror, as a mirror of the early Western Han Dynasty, holds the features of shape and decoration of the bronze mirror in the Warring States Period. The ground motif had been disappearing since the middle Western Han Dynasty. The mirror with simple ground motif shows a decoration style in transitional period.　(Wang Maodong)

相思铭蟠螭镜　西汉

直径11.1厘米，边厚0.5厘米，重155克

1957年淮南市谢家集区赖山公社出土

　　圆形，三弦钮，双螭龙纹钮座。座外饰两周弦纹、两周绳纹，弦纹内有十三字，篆文，铭："愁思以悲，愿君毋说，相思愿毋绝"。主区纹饰为以三股凸起的细线条勾勒的蟠螭纹，纹饰勾曲缠绕。镜缘外沿上卷。此式铭文镜，于西汉墓中经常出土，尚保留着战国晚期铜镜的特征，流行于西汉早期。（沈汗青）

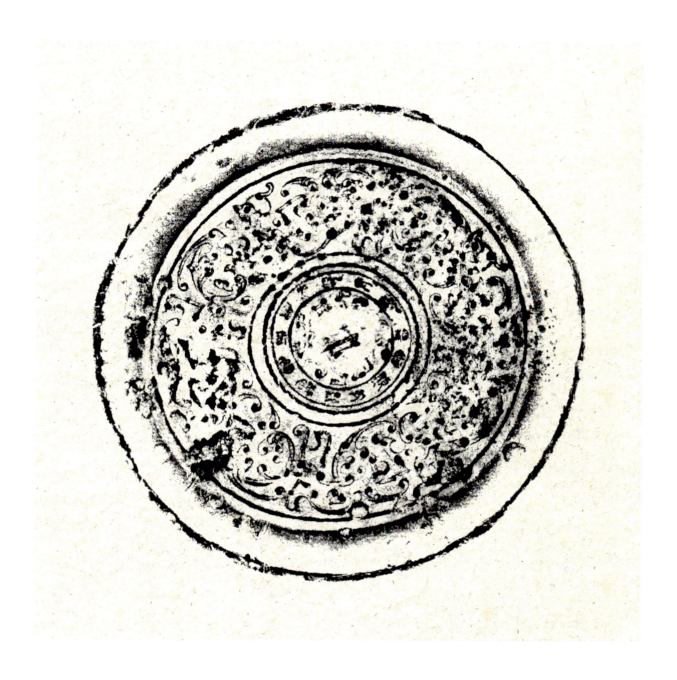

Mirror with inscription of "*Xiang Si*" and interlaced hydras design   Western Han Dynasty

Diameter: 11.1cm, Thickness of rim: 0.5cm, Weight: 155gram

Unearthed at Laishan Commune, Xiejiaji District, Huainan City in 1957

The mirror is round in shape. It has a knob with three-string design on a hydras-dragon-shaped base. Outside the base are two bands of string pattern, two bands of rope pattern. Inside the string pattern has thirteen characters in seal script, "*Chou Si Yi Bei, Yuan Jun Wu Shuo, Xiang Si Yuan Wu Jue*". The major motif is interlaced hydras design formed by three raised lines. The mirror has a rim rolling upward. The mirror with a band of inscription is the earliest mirror with inscription in history of Chinese bronze mirror. The mirrors with inscription were often found from the Western Han tomb. It keeps the features of the bronze mirror in the late Warring States Period and was popular in the early Western Han Dynasty.   (Shen Hanqing)

蟠螭菱纹镜　西汉
直径11.8厘米，边厚0.5厘米，重141克
1957年淮南市赖山公社出土

圆形，三弦钮，云雷纹钮座。座外饰一周凹弧面宽带弦纹。主区以钮座边缘和镜缘内的两周栉齿纹为廓，在云雷纹地上饰三蟠螭纹和三菱形纹。镜背有修，纹饰较模糊，可辨识蟠螭纹与菱形纹以双线勾勒，勾连缠绕，腹部为菱形叠压。凹弧面宽缘，镜缘高卷。（沈汗青）

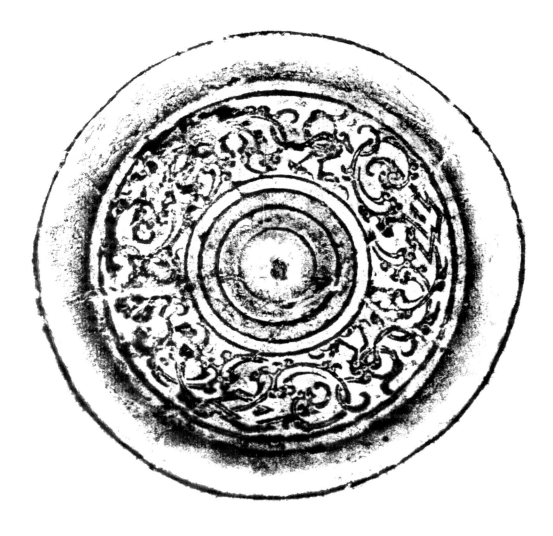

Mirror with design of interlaced hydras and lozenge   Western Han Dynasty

Diameter: 11.8cm, Thickness of rim: 0.5cm, Weight: 141gram

Unearthed at Laishan Commune, Huainan City in 1957

The mirror is round in shape. It has a knob with three-string design on a base with design of cloud and thunder. Outside the base is a broad band of string design with concave surface. The bands of fine-toothed pattern adorn respectively outside the string band and inside the rim. The ground is decorated with design of cloud and thunder as ground motif and three designs of interlaced hydras and lozenge as major motif. The mirror was once broken and the decoration is not clear. The design of interlaced hydras and lozenge is formed by double lines and is interlocked each other. The mirror has a broad rim holding concave surface and rolling upward.   (Shen Hanqing)

大乐贵富铭四叶蟠螭镜　西汉

直径18.5厘米，厚0.8厘米，重518克

1997年底淮南市唐山镇第三砖厂出土

　　圆形，三弦钮，弦纹钮座，背部由两个双绳纹圆圈分成两区。中心区域饰双螭纹，外区为铭文带，铭文为篆体"大乐贵富，千秋万岁，宜酒食"，间隔一个鱼纹。双绳纹圆圈带伸出四株火焰状叶纹，将外区分成四等份，每区饰一组蟠螭纹。蟠螭张口，小圆眼，眼上置一长角，两爪向左右舒张，身体盘旋弯曲。

　　该镜为西汉早期铜镜，形制较大。纹饰用并行三条凸起的细线构成，线条流转圆畅，细腻而繁缛。蟠螭纹下有不均匀的斜线纹和羽状纹作地，保留战国羽状地的特点。四组叶纹和四组蟠螭两两相对，十分匀称。主纹外饰一周突起的绳纹。镜缘窄而高卷。（沈汗青）

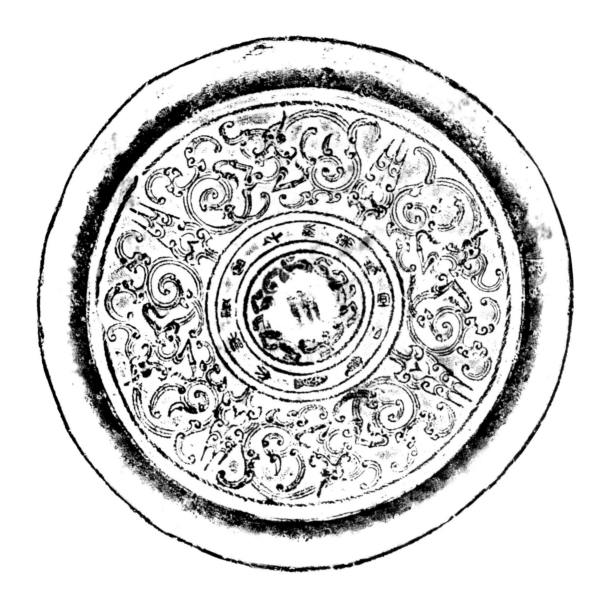

Mirror with inscription of "*Da Le Gui Fu*" and design of four-leaf and interlaced hydras   Western Han Dynasty

Diameter: 18.5cm, Thickness: 0.8cm, Weight: 518gram

Unearthed from the Third Brickyard, Tangshan Town, Huainan City in the end of 1997

The mirror is round in shape. It has a knob with three-string design on a base with string design. The ground is divided into two parts by two bands of rope pattern formed by double lines. The inner part is adorned with interlaced-hydras design and a band of inscription in seal script "*Da Le Gui Fu, Qian Qiu Wan Sui, Yi Jiu Shi*". Each character is spaced with fish design. Four designs of flame-shaped leaf are stretching out of the band of rope design and divide the outer part into four equal areas. Each area is decorated with interlaced-hydras design in the shape of mouth opening, small round eyes, long horn, paws stretching out and curved body.

As a mirror of the early Western Han Dynasty, the mirror is in a big size and the exquisite design is formed by three raised lines. The ground is adorned with pattern of slanted-line and feather-like with the shape in the Warring States Period as ground motif. Each design is opposite each other. The mirror has a narrow rim rolling upward.   (Shen Hanqing)

大乐贵富铭四叶蟠螭镜　西汉

直径16.8厘米，边厚0.6厘米，重392克

2010年9月淮南市谢家集公安分局移交

　　圆形，三弦钮，双龙钮座。绕钮座有四周绳纹，环铭居中，篆书"大乐贵富，千秋万岁，宜酒食"，以一个写实的鱼纹间隔。主区有四个火焰状叶纹，自钮座伸出，将镜背分成四区，四叶纹中间饰四蟠螭纹。蟠螭张口，圆目，曲角，身躯勾连盘曲，细腻繁缛。四叶纹和蟠螭纹均以三单线平行勾勒，局部用双线或四层线处理，镜背华美繁丽，是西汉早期的典型器。（沈汗青）

Mirror with inscription of "*Da Le Gui Fu*" and design of four-leaf and interlaced hydras   Western Han Dynasty

Diameter: 16.8cm, Thickness of rim: 0.6cm, Weight: 392gram

Transferred by Xiejiaji District Public Security Bureau, Huainan City in September, 2010

The mirror is round in shape. It has a knob with three-string design on a base with dragon design. Outside the base are four bands of rope design and a band of inscription in seal script "*Da Le Gui Fu, Qian Qiu Wan Sui, Yi Jiu Shi*". Each character is spaced with fish design. Four designs of flame-shaped leaf are stretching out of the base and space the design of interlaced hydras in shape of mouth opening, round eyes, rolling horn and curved body into four parts. The design is formed by three lines and its part is carved by double or four lines. The mirror is inferred as a mirror of the early Western Han Dynasty.   (Shen Hanqing)

大乐贵富铭四叶蟠螭镜　西汉

直径 12.9厘米，边厚0.4厘米，重228克

2010年淮南市谢家集公安分局移交

圆形，三弦钮，双蟠龙钮座。座外饰四周弦纹，弦纹中间有十一字篆书铭："大乐贵富、千秋万岁、宜酒食"，以鱼纹结句。外侧弦纹伸出四火焰状叶纹，将镜背分成四区，每区置一蟠螭纹，蟠螭首部二二相对，蟠首双目，大张口，顶部有角向后弯下，口吐长舌，向上翻卷，身躯勾连缠绕，尾部卷起，后足踏镜缘。四叶纹和蟠螭纹以双线勾勒，近缘处以细弦纹为栏。纹饰繁缛华丽，宽素缘上卷。此镜纹饰细腻繁丽，流行于西汉早期。（沈汗青）

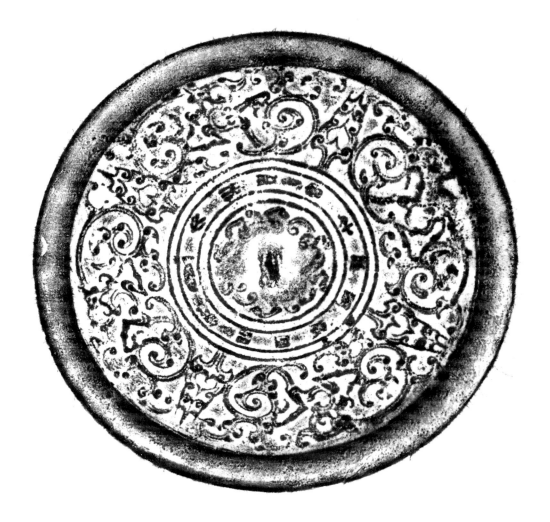

Mirror with inscription of "*Da Le Gui Fu*" and design of four-leaf and interlaced hydras Western Han Dynasty

Diameter: 12.9cm, Thickness of rim: 0.4cm, Weight: 228gram

Transferred by Xiejiaji District Public Security Bureau in Huainan City in 2010

The mirror is round in shape. It has a knob with three-string design on a base with coiled dragon design. Outside the base are four bands of string design and a band of inscription in seal script "*Da Le Gui Fu, Qian Qiu Wan Sui, Yi Jiu Shi*". Each character is spaced with fish design. Four designs of flame-shaped leaf are stretching out of the base and space the design of interlaced hydras

in shape of mouth opening, round eyes, rolling horn and curved body into four parts. The design is formed by double lines. Inside the rim is decorated with a band of string design. The mirror has a broad rim showing no design and rolling upward. The mirror is inferred as a mirror of the early Western Han Dynasty. (Shen Hanqing)

大乐贵富铭四叶蟠螭镜 西汉
直径13.2厘米，边厚0.5厘米，重172克
本馆旧藏

　　圆形，桥钮，双螭龙钮座。座外饰两周弦纹，弦纹内置一圈铭文带，篆体，漫漶不清，试识为"大乐贵富，千秋……宜酒食"，以一鱼纹结句。弦纹外伸出均匀对称的四株火焰状叶纹，将镜背分成四区，每区置一组蟠螭纹。叶纹、蟠螭纹均以三线勾勒，使镜背纹饰曲线流转、繁缛富丽。主纹外以一圈绳纹为栏。缘宽，高卷边。此类镜在西汉早期流行，其镜钮、纹饰特征还保留着战国晚期风格。（沈汗青）

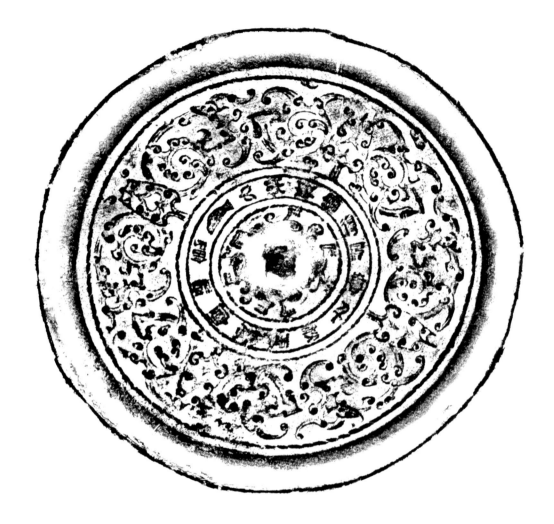

Mirror with inscription of "*Da Le Gui Fu*" and design of four-leaf and interlaced hydras   Western Han Dynasty

Diameter: 13.2cm, Thickness of rim: 0.5cm, Weight: 172gram

Collection of Huainan Museum

The mirror is round in shape. It has a bridge-shaped knob on a base with coiled dragon design. Outside the base are two bands of string design and a band of unclear inscription in seal script "*Da Le Gui Fu, Qian Qiu... Yi Jiu Shi*". Each character is spaced with fish design. Four designs of flame-shaped leaf are stretching out of the base and space the design of interlaced hydras into four parts.

The design is formed by three lines. Inside the rim is a band of rope design. The mirror has a broad rim rolling upward. The mirror is inferred as a mirror of the early Western Han Dynasty and keeps the features of knob and design of the bronze mirror in the late Warring States Period.   (Shen Hanqing)

大乐贵富铭蟠螭博局镜　西汉

直径10.1厘米，边厚0.5厘米，重116克
1972年淮南市唐山公社九里大队出土

　　圆形，三弦钮，双蟠龙钮座。座外饰双线方框，上为十五字篆文铭："大乐富贵，得所好，千秋万岁，延年益寿"，以一鱼纹结句。方框外四边中部伸出双线勾勒的"T"形博局纹，镜缘处伸出"L"形纹与之对应，四角与"V"形纹相对，"TLV"形纹内皆加饰二道细凸线，并将镜背分为四等八区，每区内饰一蟠螭纹。云雷纹铺地，蟠螭勾连变形，叠压于博局

纹之下。宽素卷缘。

　　此类镜是蟠螭纹博局镜的早期形式。在河北满城窦绾墓中出土一面，直径18.8厘米；安徽六安经济技术开发区发现一面，直径8.8厘米。淮南发现两面。另一面1987年5月出土于淮南市唐山镇双古堆汉墓。可知此类镜流行西汉中期。（沈汗青）

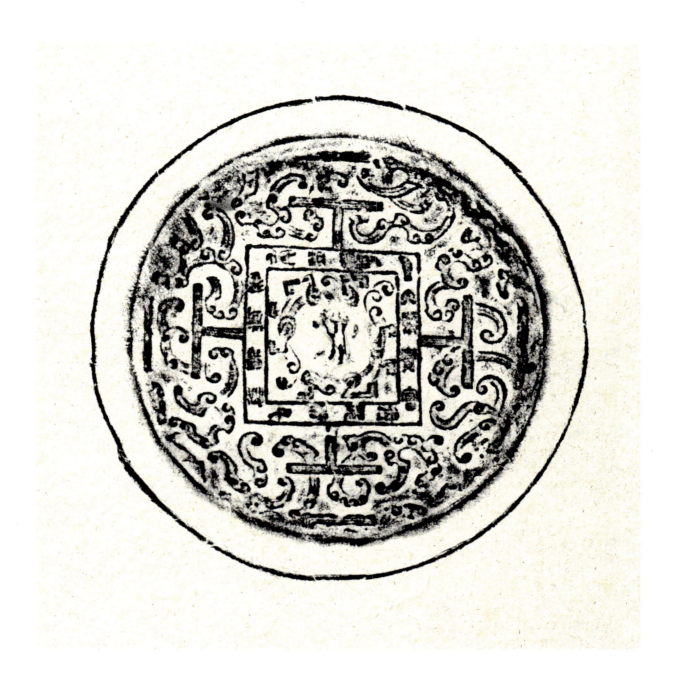

Mirror with inscription of "*Da Le Gui Fu*" and design of interlaced hydras and gambling   Western Han Dynasty

Diameter: 10.1cm, Thickness of rim: 0.5cm, Weight: 116gram

Unearthed at Jiuli Brigade, Tangshan Commune, Huainan City in 1972

The mirror is round in shape. It has a knob with three-string design on a base with coiled dragon design. Outside the base is a square framed with double lines and carved inscription in seal script "*Da Le Gui Fu, De Suo Hao, Qian Qiu Wan Sui, Yan Nian Yi Shou*" on it. Each character is spaced with fish design. T-shaped gambling design formed by double lines is stretching out of each middle side of the square, corresponding with L-shaped design stretching out of the rim. Each corner of the square corresponds with V-shaped design. The design with T-shaped, L-shaped and V-shaped is decorated with two raised lines and divides the ground into quarters and eight parts. Each part is adorned with interlaced-hydras design overlaid by gambling design. The ground is decorated with design of cloud and thunder as ground motif. The mirror has a broad rim showing no design and rolling.

The mirror is the early shape of mirror with gambling design. In the Tou Wan tomb in Mancheng, Heibei Province unearthed a mirror with diameter 18.8cm. At Liu'an Economic and Technical Development Zone discovered a mirror with diameter 8.8cm. Two mirrors were found in Huainan City, one of which was unearthed from the Han tomb at Shuanggudui, Tangshan Town, in Huainan City in May, 1987. The mirror with gambling design was popular in the middle Western Han Dynasty.   (Shen Hanqing)

草叶纹日光镜　西汉

直径13.7厘米，厚0.4厘米，重341克

本馆旧藏

　　圆形。半球钮，柿蒂纹方钮座。钮座外有凹弧面大方格，格内有铭文一周："见日之光，天下大明"，四角各有小方格，格内饰短斜线。外区在大方格的四角各伸出双叶一花苞纹，四乳钉居大方格中间位置，将外区四分，乳钉两侧各一对单层草叶纹。镜缘为凸起的十六组连弧纹，向内环绕。

　　日光镜流行于西汉中晚期到东汉中期，较星云纹和博局纹铜镜要早，反映了西汉时期社会稳定清静无为的审美趋向，与战国晚期繁缛神秘的蟠螭纹相比，更贴近自然和现实生活状态。汉代用花叶纹装饰铜镜，与唐代花鸟纹镜有异曲同工之妙，都是对生活领悟的写照。（沈汗青）

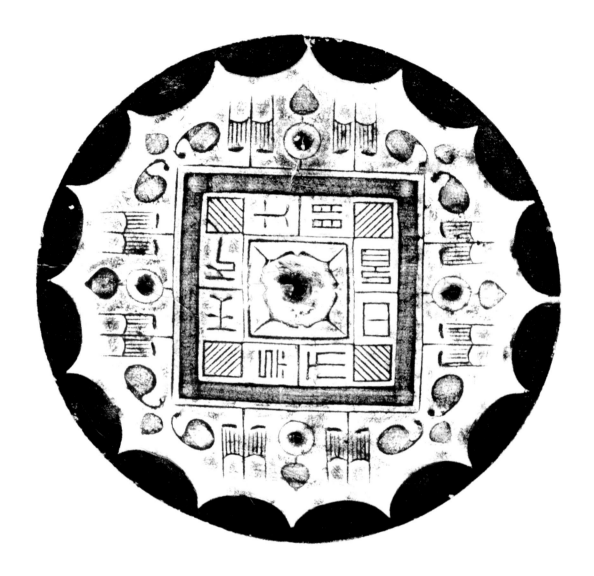

Mirror with inscription of "*Ri Guang*" and grass-leaf design   Western Han Dynasty

Diameter: 13.7cm, Thickness: 0.4cm, Weight: 341gram

Collection of Huainan Museum

The mirror is round in shape. It has a half-sphere-shaped knob on a base with kaki calyx design. Outside the base is a square with concave surface. The square surrounds a band of inscription "*Jian Ri Zhi Guang, Tian Xia Da Ming*". A little square with short slanted lines pattern is on each corner of the square. A design of bud with two leaves is stretching out of each corner of the square. Outside the middle sides of the square are four nipples. A couple of grass-leaf design is on both sides of each nipple. The rim is decorated with sixteen raised and linked arcs inside.

The mirror with inscription of "*Ri Guang*" was popular from middle and late Western Han Dynasty to early Eastern Han Dynasty and was earlier than mirror with nebular design and mirror with gambling design. Compared with overelaborated and mysterious design of interlaced-hydras of the late Warring States Period, the design on the mirror with inscription of "*Ri Guang*" expresses the aesthetic tendency of yearning for social stability and nature and reflects vividly a real life picture. The design of flower and leaf in the Han Dynasty, as the same as the meaning of the design of flower and bird in the Han Dynasty, represent the understanding for the life.   (Shen Hanqing)

草叶纹日光镜 西汉

直径11.5厘米，边厚0.3厘米，重170克

1988年12月安徽省寿县第二砖厂出土

圆形，圆钮，柿蒂纹方钮座。座外饰一周凹弧面方框，框内有八字铭文，顺时针方向旋读："见日之光，天下大明"，篆书。框内四角各有一叶纹，框外四角伸出对称带茎双叶纹，框四边中间置一乳钉，其上伸出一叶纹，两侧饰对称单层草叶纹。内向十六连弧纹缘。日光镜流行于西汉中期，是西汉时期代表性镜式之一。此镜纹饰构图疏密得当，严谨而不失活泼。（于怀珍）

Mirror with inscription of "*Ri Guang*" and grass-leaf design Western Han Dynasty

Diameter: 11.5cm, Thickness of rim: 0.3cm, Weight: 170gram

Unearthed from the Second Brickyard in Shou County, Anhui Province in December, 1988

The mirror is round in shape. It has a round knob on a base with kaki calyx design. Outside the base is a square with concave surface. Inside the square is the inscription with eight characters "*Jian Ri Zhi Guang, Tian Xia Da Ming*" in seal script. A grass-leaf is on each corner of the square. A design of two leaves with stems is stretching out of each corner of the square. Outside the middle sides of the square are four nipples out of each which a grass leaf is stretching. Both sides of the nipple are surrounded with grass-leaf design. The rim is decorated with sixteen linked arcs inside. The mirror with inscription of "*Ri Guang*" was popular in the middle Western Han Dynasty and was one of the representative bronze mirrors of the Western Han Dynasty. The mirror has a proper layout and vivid decoration. (Yu Huaizhen)

连峰钮星云纹镜　西汉
直径11厘米，厚0.4厘米，重217克
1958年淮南市谢家集区唐山公社出土

　　圆形，连锋式钮，又称之为博山炉式钮，由七乳构成。圆钮座为凹弧面卷曲形成的云纹，云纹外有一周略微凸起的弦纹。钮座外环绕向内弧的小连弧纹，以斜栉纹包围一周。中区主纹饰四分，四个较大的乳钉之间有五枚小乳钉，形成四组星云纹，每区以三弦曲线相连，五枚小乳钉以三弦小曲线从外侧包围。四

个星云区呈四组弧边。外区与中区间以斜栉纹环绕，镜缘以十六组向内弧的连弧纹装饰。

　　星云纹镜，又名百乳镜。一般认为，星云纹镜出现于汉武帝时期，流行于西汉的昭宣时期。西汉中期以后少见。制作工艺在汉镜中是比较精良的。因其纹饰状如星云，所以有星云纹之说。（沈汗青）

Mirror with a continuous peak-shaped knob and nebular design   Western Han Dynasty

Diameter: 11cm, Thickness: 0.4cm, Weight: 217gram

Unearthed at Tangshan Commune, Xiejiaji District, Huainan City in 1958

The mirror is round in shape. It has a continuous peak-shaped knob which is also called Boshan-incense-burner-shaped knob and includes seven nipples. The base is decorated with cloud design formed with concave surface coiling and surrounded with a band of raised string pattern. Outside the base is a band of linked arcs inside. The major motif is four groups of nebular design including four bigger nipples spaced with four nipples. Each of four groups is connected by a three-string band. Both sides of the major motif have two bands of fine-toothed pattern. The rim is decorated with a band of sixteen linked arcs inside.

The mirror with nebular design is also named mirror with one-hundred-nipples design. It was thought that this kind of mirror appeared in the Emperor Wu of Han and was popular in the period of the Emperor Xuan and the Emperor Zhao of Han. It had been less since the middle Western Han Dynasty. It has refined craftsmanship and the decoration pattern in the shape of nebula is called nebular design.   (Shen Hanqing)

日光镜　西汉
直径7.3厘米，边厚0.3厘米，重53克
1977年4月于淮南市赖山公社廿店大队沈塘村征集

　　圆形，半球钮，圆钮座。座外饰一周内向八连弧纹，连弧纹与钮座间各饰四个短弧线和四个凸起小三角形，两两相对。中区为两圈栉齿纹中夹一圈铭文带。铭文为阳文，篆书"见日之光，天下大明"八字，每字间以"☺"或"◈"形符号相隔。宽素平缘。

　　西汉武帝以后铜镜纹饰出现了较大变化，日光镜中的主题纹饰趋于简化，给人以明净快洁之感，铭文装饰逐渐成为铜镜纹饰的主要组成部分。此面日光镜可谓此类型的代表之作。（刘继武）

Mirror with inscription of "*Ri Guang*"   Western Han Dynasty

Diameter: 7.3cm, Thickness of rim: 0.3cm, Weight: 53gram

Collected at Shentang Village, Niandian Brigade, Laishan Commune in Huainan City in April, 1977

The mirror is round in shape. It has a half-sphere-shaped knob on a round base. Outside the base is a band of eight linked arcs inward. Between the arcs and the base are four short arcs and four raised triangles alternately arranged. Both sides of the major motif are adorned with two bands of fine-toothed pattern. The major motif is the band of inscription with eight characters "*Jian Ri Zhi Guang, Tian Xia Da Ming*" in seal script and relief, which were spaced with ☺-shaped or ✦-shaped pattern. The mirror has a broad and flat rim without design.

The mirror decoration had been a big change since the Emperor Wu of Western Han. The major motif on the mirror with inscription of "*Ri Guang*" trended to simplification and showed a bright and clean effect. The inscription had become a main part of the mirror design. This mirror is regarded as a representative mirror with inscription "*Ri Guang*".   (Liu Jiwu)

连弧纹日光镜　西汉

直径7.6厘米，边厚0.5厘米，重86克

本馆旧藏

　　圆形，乳钮，圆钮座。内区饰内向八连弧纹，钮座间饰以日月和三线纹；外区主纹为铭文圈带，铭"见日之光，天下大明"，铭带内外两侧以栉齿纹为廓。素缘。

　　日光镜为汉镜中出土数量较多、流行时间较长的镜种之一。此镜日纹上饰三线纹表达太阳光芒，并在铭文里采用"见日之光，天下大明"的诠释，反映了汉代人对日月的崇拜。（汪茂东）

Mirror with linked arcs design and inscription of "*Ri Guang*"   Western Han Dynasty

Diameter: 7.6cm, Thickness of rim: 0.5cm, Weight: 86gram

Collection of Huainan Museum

The mirror is round in shape. It has a nipple-shaped knob on a round base. Outside the base are the crescent design and three straight lines alternately arranged which are surrounded with a band of eight linked arcs inside. The major motif is a band of inscription "*Jian Ri Zhi Guang, Tian Xia Da Ming*". Both sides of the major motif are decorated with a band of fine-toothed pattern.

The mirror has a rim without design.

The mirror with inscription of "*Ri Guang*" is one of bronze mirrors which were unearthed in a great number and were popular for a long time. The three straight lines are regarded as the symbol of the sunlight. And the inscription expresses the people's worship for the sun in the Han Dynasty.   (Wang Maodong)

日光昭明重圈铭文镜 西汉

直径10.7厘米，边厚0.5厘米，重197克
2010年9月淮南市谢家集公安分局移交

　　圆形，半球钮，圆钮座。钮座外环饰一周十二个联珠纹，三个一组间以四条短线纹。其外饰两周凸宽带纹，内区有铭，为"见日之光，长毋相忘"；外区亦饰铭文，为"内清质以昭明，光辉象夫日月，心忽

而愿忠，然而不泄"。铭文内、外两侧各饰一周栉齿纹。缘厚，向内微坡，素面。

　　此镜铸工精美，铭文清晰，字体飘逸自然，品相上乘，是重圈铭文镜中的上品。（汪茂东）

Mirror with circles of inscriptions "*Ri Guang*" and "*Zhao Ming*"　　Western Han Dynasty

Diameter: 10.7cm, Thickness of rim: 0.5cm, Weight: 197gram

Transferred by Xiejiaji District Public Security Bureau in Huainan City in September, 2010

　　The mirror is round in shape. It has a half-sphere-shaped knob on a round base. Outside the base are twelve beads surrounded, which are spaced with four short lines in threes and has two raised bands. Between the bands has a band of inscription "*Jian Ri Zhi Guang, Chang Wu Xiang Wang*". The major motif is the inscription of "*Nei Qing Zhi Yi Zhao Ming, Guang Hui Xiang Fu Ri Yue, Xin Hu Er Yuan Zhong, Ran Er Bu Xie*". Both sides of the inscription are decorated with a band of fine-toothed pattern. The heavy rim without design is slanting inside.

　　The mirror with exquisite decoration and natural touch is the treasure of the mirror with inscription circles.　(Wang Maodong)

日光镜 *西汉*
直径6.7厘米，边厚0.1厘米，重38克
本馆旧藏

　　圆形，半球钮，圆钮座。纹饰分内外两区，内区为一圈内向八连弧纹，内以若干道短弧形和直线作简单装饰；外区主纹，为夹于两周栉齿纹间的铭文带，铭文为"见日之光，天下大明"，每字间隔以月牙纹和"◈"纹，字体较为特别，有的学者认为是篆隶式变体。宽素平缘。日光镜流行于西汉中晚期到东汉中期，纹饰简明清新，与战国时期楚镜的神秘风格明显不同，是汉镜中常见的一种样式。（文立中）

inscription of "*Ri Guang*"   Western Han Dynasty

Diameter: 6.7cm, Thickness of rim: 0.1cm, Weight: 38gram

Collection of Huainan Museum

The mirror is round in shape. It has a half-sphere-shaped knob on a round base. Outside the base is a band of eight linked arcs inward. Between the arcs and the base are four short arcs and four raised triangles arranged alternately. Both sides of the major motif are adorned with two bands of fine-toothed pattern. The major motif is the band of inscription with eight characters "*Jian Ri Zhi Guang, Tian Xia Da Ming*". The characters were carved in form changing between seal and official scripts and were spaced with crescent design and ❖-shaped pattern. The mirror has a broad and flat rim without design. The mirror with inscription of "*Ri Guang*" was popular from middle and the late Western Han Dynasty to the middle Eastern Han Dynasty. Differed from the mysterious style of the Chu mirror in the Warring States Period, this kind of mirror with simple decoration was a common bronze mirror of the Han Dynasty.   (Wen Lizhong)

连弧纹昭明镜　西汉
直径8.9厘米，边厚0.4厘米，重163克
2010年9月淮南市谢家集公安分局移交

　　圆形，半球钮，圆钮座。钮座外有一周内向八连
弧纹，连弧纹与钮座间有若干短直线条装饰。主区为
铭文圈带，铭文"内清以昭明，光日"，篆书，字体
方正，每字间以"而"形符号相隔，铭文带两侧以斜
向栉齿纹为廓。宽素缘。

　　昭明镜流行于西汉中后期，以西汉后期最为盛
行，是出土最多、流行范围最广的西汉铜镜之一。昭
明镜以文字为主要装饰，为研究古代文字提供了重要
的历史资料。（任胜利）

Mirror with linked arcs design and inscription of "*Zhao Ming*"   Western Han Dynasty

Diameter: 8.9cm, Thickness of rim: 0.4cm, Weight: 163gram

Transferred by Xiejiaji District Public Security Bureau in Huainan City in September, 2010

The mirror is round in shape. It has a half-sphere-shaped knob on a round base. Outside the base is a band of eight linked arcs inside. Between the arcs and the base are several short lines. The major motif is a band of inscription "*Nei Qing Yi Zhao Ming, Guang Rì*" in seal script which is spaced with *Er*-character-shaped pattern. Both sides of the major motif are decorated with a band of fine-toothed design. The mirror has a broad rim without design.

The mirror with inscription of "*Zhao Ming*" was popular from the middle to the late Western Han Dynasty and reached its peak in the late Western Han Dynasty. It was one of the Han mirrors which were unearthed in a great number and were popular widely. This kind of mirror mainly decorated with inscription provides important historical information for studying ancient characters.   (Ren Shengli)

连弧纹昭明镜 西汉

直径10.3厘米，边厚0.3厘米，重163克

1988年5月淮南市唐山乡双古堆东墓出土

　　圆形，半球钮，圆钮座。座外环以一周宽带弦纹和一周内向八连弧纹，其间填饰简单短直线装饰；主纹为一周铭文圈带，铭"内清以昭明，光日月"，篆书，字体方正，每字间以"而"形符号相隔，两侧以栉齿纹为廓。宽镜缘，平素。（陶冶强）

Mirror with linked arcs design and inscription of "*Zhao Ming*" Western Han Dynasty

Diameter: 10.3cm, Thickness of rim: 0.3cm, Weight: 163gram

Unearthed at Shuanggudui tomb, Tangshan Town in Huainan City in May, 1988

The mirror is round in shape. It has a half-sphere-shaped knob on a round base. Outside the base are a band of string pattern and a band of eight linked arcs which is filled with short lines in blank. The major motif is a band of inscription "*Nei Qing Yi Zhao Ming, Guang Ri Yue*" in seal script which is space with *Er*-character-shaped pattern. Both sides of the major motif are decorated with a band of fine-toothed pattern. The mirror has a broad and flat rim without design. (Tao Zhiqiang)

连弧纹昭明镜　西汉

直径11.4厘米，边厚0.6厘米，重239克

2010年9月淮南市谢家集公安分局移交

　　圆形，圆钮，圆钮座。座外饰一周凸弦纹圈带，内以短弧线纹连接钮座，其外饰一周内向八连弧纹。中区有一周铭文圈带，顺时针方向旋读，铭文"内清以昭明，光象日月"，篆隶之间书体，字间有"而"形符号，铭文两侧环以栉齿纹为廓。宽素平缘。

　　汉代铜镜的铭文字体可以分为两种：一种是篆书隶化的书体，是从篆书向隶书蜕变的一种反映；另一种字体方整，与汉代印文字体如出一辙。文字书体的演化也成为判断汉代铜镜时代的依据之一。（单超）

Mirror with linked arcs design and inscription of "*Zhao Ming*"   Western Han Dynasty

Diameter: 11.4cm

Transferred by Xiejiaji District Public Security Bureau in Huainan City in September, 2010

The mirror is round in shape. It has a round knob on a round base. Outside the base is adorned with a band of raised string pattern connected with the base through short arcs and a band of eight linked arcs inside. The major motif is a band of inscription "*Nei Qing Yi Zhao Ming, Guang Xiang Ri Yue*" in form changing between seal and official scripts which is spaced with *Er*-character-shaped pattern. Both sides of the inscription are decorated with fine-toothed pattern. The mirror has a broad and flat rim without design.

The inscription on the Han mirrors have two writing styles, including form changing between seal and official scripts and seal script. The time of the Han mirrors can be referred on the basis of the styles of inscription.   (Shan Chao)

连弧纹日光镜 西汉

直径6.4厘米，边厚0.15厘米，重34克

本馆旧藏

　　圆形，半球钮，圆钮座。纹饰分内外两区，内区为连弧纹，连弧与钮座之间有短弧线和凸起的三角装饰，外区为铭文带一周，铭文为"见日之光，天下大明"，每字间分别有"◈"纹与短弧线交错相隔，铭文带两侧以栉齿纹为栏。素镜缘较宽。（文立中）

Mirror with linked arcs design and inscription of "*Ri Guang*"   Western Han Dynasty

Diameter: 6.4cm, Thickness of rim: 0.15cm, Weight: 34gram

Collection of Huainan Museum

The mirror is round in shape. It has a half-sphere-shaped knob on a round base. Outside the base are the arcs and triangles in relief which are surrounded with linked arcs. The major motif is the inscription of "*Jian Ri Zhi Guang, Tian Xia Da Ming*" which are spaced ❖ with -shaped patterns and short arcs alternately arranged. Both sides of the major motif are decorated with a band of fine-toothed pattern. The broad rim without design is slanting inside.   (Wen Lizhong)

连弧纹昭明镜 西汉

直径9.7厘米，边厚0.5厘米，重215克

1977年8月淮南市物资回收公司拣选

　　圆形，半球钮，圆钮座。座外饰内向十二连弧
纹，连弧纹内饰四组短线、弧线装饰。主纹区为铭
文圈带，两侧有栉齿纹为栏，内铭"内清以昭明，光夫
日月"，篆书，字体方正，间以"而"字。素宽缘。

　　镜上有铭始于战国晚期，汉武帝以后铭文逐渐
成为铜镜纹饰的重要组成部分，而此镜完全以铭文为
主题内容，镜缘宽大，主要流行于西汉晚期至东汉早
期。（闫晓娟）

Mirror with linked arcs design and inscription of "*Zhao Ming*"   Western Han Dynasty

Diameter: 9.7cm, Thickness of rim: 0.5cm, Weight: 215gram

Got from a material recycling company in Huainan City in August, 1977

The mirror is round in shaped. It has a half-sphere-shaped knob on a round base. Outside the base is a band of twelve linked arcs inside. Between the base and the arcs are four groups of short lines and arcs. The major motif is a band of inscription "*Nei Qing Yi Zhao Ming, Guang Fu Ri Yue*" in seal script which is spaced with *Er*-character-shaped pattern. Both sides of the major motif are decorated with a band of fine-toothed pattern. The mirror has a broad rim without design.

The mirror with inscription appeared in the late Warring States Period. The inscription had become the main decoration on the mirror since the Emperor Wu of Han. This mirror with inscription as the major motif and broad rim was popular from the late Western Han Dynasty to the early Eastern Han Dynasty.   (Yan Xiaojuan)

连弧纹昭明镜　西汉

直径8.8厘米，边厚0.4厘米，重137克
2010年9月淮南市谢家集公安分局移交

　　圆形，半球钮，圆钮座。座外围饰内向十二连弧纹，在座外和连弧纹间的空白处填以短直线、弧线装饰。主纹区为一周铭文带："内清质以昭明，象日月"，每一字间加一"而"形符号，篆书，字体方正。主纹两侧以栉齿纹为廓。宽素平缘。

　　昭明连弧纹镜在我国各地皆有出土，是西汉铜镜中分布范围最广的镜式，它始于西汉宣昭时期，以西汉后期到东汉早期最为盛行。该镜铭与常见完整的昭明镜铭文相比，有减字现象，可见当时对镜铭的完整性并无严格要求。此外，该镜的连弧纹其弧度甚曲，大小略有差异，与常见的规整连弧不同，应为工匠制模时雕刻而成。这种随意性体现了铜镜发展到汉代，已经不再是贵族的专用品，成为广大普通百姓皆可使用的日常用品了。（吴琳）

Mirror with linked arcs design and inscription of "*Zhao Ming*"   Western Han Dynasty

Diameter: 8.8cm, Thickness of rim: 0.4cm, Weight: 137

Transferred by Xiejiaji District Public Security Bureau in Huainan City in September, 2010

The mirror is round in shape. It has a half-sphere-shaped knob on a round base. Outside the base is a band of twelve linked arcs inside. Between the base and the arcs are short straight lines and arcs. The major motif is a band of inscription "*Nei Qing Zhi Yi Zhao Ming, Xiang Ri Yue*" in seal script which is spaced with Er-character-shaped pattern. Both sides of the major motif are decorated with a band of fine-toothed pattern. The mirror has a broad rim without design.

The mirror with linked arcs design and inscription of "*Zhao Ming*" was unearthed at all parts of the country and was used widely in the Western Han Dynasty. It appeared in the reign of the Emperor Xuan and Emperor Zhao of Western Han and was popular from the late Western Han Dynasty to the early Eastern Han Dynasty. Compared with the mirror with inscription of "*Zhao Ming*", it has inscription with characters reduced, which shows that the number of characters was not required strictly. Known from the arc patterns standardized, the arc patterns on this mirror has different and arbitrary radians, which reflects that the bronze mirror was not only used as an exclusive article for noblemen and had become an article for daily use since the Han Dynasty. (Wu Lin)

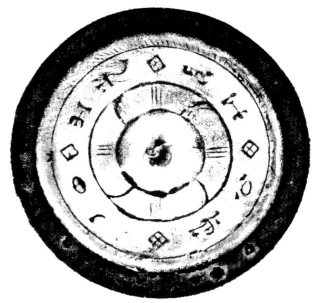

日光镜 西汉

直径6厘米，边厚0.2厘米，重37克

2010年9月淮南市谢家集公安分局移交

圆形，半球钮，圆钮座，座外有数道短弧线、直线装饰。主纹区为一周铭文带："见日之光，长不相忘"，其中"见"和"相"字在铸造时脱范不佳，缺失部分；字体介于篆隶之间，富于变化，每两字间加一"◈"形符号。主纹外环一周栉齿带为界。宽素平缘。

日光镜是汉镜中出土数量多、流行范围广的镜类之一，在我国的许多地区都有发现，是典型的汉式镜之一。但此镜铭文在日光镜中较为少见，"长不相忘"表达了铜镜除了照面的实用价值以外，还被赋予了表达相思的社会功能。（吴琳）

Mirror with inscription of "*Ri Guang*" Western Han Dynasty

Diameter: 6cm, Thickness of rim: 0.2cm, Weight: 37gram

Transferred by Xiejiaji District Public Security Bureau in Huainan City in September, 2010

The mirror is round in shape. It has a half-sphere-shaped knob on a round base. Outside the base are several arcs and short straight lines. The major motif is a band of inscription "*Jian Ri Zhi Guang, Chang Bu Xiang Wang*", among which characters of "*Jian*" and "*Xiang*" lost parts. The characters were carved in form changing between seal and official scripts and were spaced with ◈-shaped pattern. The major motif ends with a band of fine-toothed pattern. The mirror has a broad and flat rim without design.

The mirror with inscription of "*Ri Guang*" is one of bronze mirrors which were unearthed in a great number and were popular in Han Dynasty. It was found in most provinces of China and is one of mirrors with features of the Han Dynasty. The inscription on this mirror is rare to be found on the mirror with inscription of "*Ri Guang*". The inscription of "*Chang Bu Xiang Wang*" expresses not the practical value of the bronze mirror reflecting the images but also the social function implying yearning between lovers. (Wu Lin)

连弧纹昭明镜　西汉

直径6厘米，边厚0.3厘米，重35克
2010年9月淮南市谢家集公安分局移交

圆形，半球钮，圆钮座。座外饰内向八连弧纹，连弧纹内饰四短弧线纹，各连弧之间饰折线纹。主纹为一周铭文圈带，顺时针方向旋读，铭"内清以昭明，光象日月"，篆隶体，其中"清"字省略了偏旁"氵"，字间不规律夹以"而"形符号。铭文外环以栉齿纹为廓。素缘。

昭明镜流行时间较长，从西汉中期一直延续到东汉早期，是汉镜中出土数量较多、流行时间较长的镜类之一。（单超）

Mirror with linked arcs design and inscription of "*Zhao Ming*"　Western Han Dynasty

Diameter: 6cm, Thickness of rim: 0.3cm, Weight: 35gram
Transferred by Xiejiaji District Public Security Bureau in Huainan City in September, 2010

The mirror is round in shape. It has a half-sphere-shaped knob on a round base. Outside the base is a band of eight linked arcs inside. Between the base and the arcs are four short arcs. Between two arcs is adorned with a broken line. The major motif is a band of inscription "*Nei Qiing Yi Zhao Ming, Guang Xiang Ri Yue*" in form of changing between seal and official scripts. The "*Qing*" character lost 氵-shaped side and the characters are spaced with *Er*-character-shaped pattern. The major motif is surrounded with a band of fine-toothed pattern. The mirror has a rim without design.

The mirror with inscription of "*Zhao Ming*" was popular from the middle Western Han Dynasty to the early Eastern Han Dynasty. It is one of the Han mirrors which were unearthed in a great number and were popular for a long time.　(Shan Chao)

日光镜 西汉

直径8.1厘米，边厚0.4厘米，重114克

2010年9月淮南市谢家集公安分局移交

　　圆形，半球钮，圆钮座。座外饰一周内向八连弧纹，连弧内置若干短弧线、直线装饰，连弧外饰铭文圈带一周，铭文"见日之光，天下大明"，每字间以"𠃌"或"◈"字相间，两侧饰栉齿纹为廓。宽素缘。

　　日光镜流行于西汉中晚期，这是我国铜镜发展的重要时期，在考古发掘中，日光镜出土的数量较多，反映出当时铜镜的使用相当普遍。（任胜利）

Mirror with inscription of "*Ri Guang*"   Western Han Dynasty

Diameter: 8.1cm, Thickness of rim: 0.4cm, Weight: 114gram

Transferred by Xiejiaji District Public Security Bureau in Huainan City in September, 2010

The mirror is round in shape. It has a half-sphere-shaped knob on a round base. Outside the base are a band of eight linked arcs inward and the design of several arcs and short straight lines. The major motif is a band of inscription with characters "*Jian Ri Zhi Guang, Tian Xia Da Ming*" which are spaced with ꙩ-shaped or ❖-shaped pattern. The bands of fine-toothed pattern adorn both sides of the major motif. The mirror has a broad and flat rim without design.

The mirror with inscription of "*Ri Guang*" was popular in the middle and late Western Han Dynasty which is the important period for developing the bronze mirror. The fact that the mirrors with inscription of "*Ri Guang*" were unearthed in a great number shows that it was in common use at that time.   (Ren Shengli)

连弧纹昭明镜　西汉

直径8.3厘米，边厚0.35厘米，重109克
本馆藏品

　　圆形，半球钮，圆钮座。座外饰一周内向十二连弧纹，主区为两圈栉齿纹中夹一圈带铭文，铭文"内清以昭明，光象日月"。每两字之间置一"而"形符号，使铭文整体布局规整、美观，字体方正工整，篆书但有所隶化。宽素平缘。

　　铜镜上铸铭最早出现于战国末期，西汉初年镜铭也仅是纹饰上的点缀。武帝以后铭文逐渐成为铜镜纹饰的重要组成部分，有的铜镜则完全以铭文为主要装饰。这种以铭文为主纹或铭文与其他纹饰共同组成主纹的现象在中国铜镜铸造史上延续相当长时期，直至唐代有所改变。（刘继武）

Mirror with linked arcs design and inscription of "*Zhao Ming*" Western Han Dynasty

Diameter: 8.3cm, Thickness of rim: 0.35cm, Weight: 109gram

Collection of Huainan Museum

The mirror is round in shape. It has a half-sphere-shaped knob on a round base. Outside the base is a band of twelve linked arcs inside. The major motif is a band of inscription "*Nei Qing Yi Zhao Ming, Guang Xiang Ri Yue*" which is spaced with *Er*-character-shaped pattern. The characters are arranged in a symmetrical and beautiful layout and in square and upright form changing between the seal and official scripts. Both sides of the major motif are decorated with a band of fine-toothed pattern. The mirror has a broad and flat rim without design.

The mirror with inscription appeared in the late Warring States Period. The inscription had become the main decoration on the mirror since the Emperor Wu of Han. Some mirrors are decorated completely with inscription. The major motif composing of inscription or inscription with other design had been used for a long time till the Tang Dynasty. (Liu Jiwu)

四乳四虺镜　西汉

直径13.8厘米，边厚0.6厘米，重489克

2009年11月淮南市谢家集区唐山镇夏郢孜西路出土

　　圆形，半球钮，双层柿蒂纹钮座。座外环一周素面宽带纹，两侧以栉齿纹为栏。外区四个带座乳钉将主区分成四部分，每区饰一双线勾勒的虺纹，虺呈钩形，头右尾左，昂颈回首，抬尾下卷。虺身两侧各填饰一只禽鸟纹。主纹外侧环以斜向栉齿纹为廓。宽素

平缘。整镜体厚质实。

　　此镜以乳钉分区，形成汉式镜中以钮座为中心严谨对称的纹饰格局，而四虺均作头右尾左的装饰又使铜镜纹饰在严谨中透出律动之感。（刘继武）

Mirror with design of four nipples and four serpents   Western Han Dynasty

Diameter: 13.8cm, Thickness of rim: 0.6cm, Weight: 489gram

Unearthed at west road, Xiayingzi, Tangshan Town, Xiejiaji District in Huainan City in November, 2009

The mirror is round in shape. It has a half-sphere-shaped knob on a base with a two-layer design of kaki calyx. Outside the base is a broad band without design, each side of which has a band of fine-toothed pattern. The major motif is divided into four parts by four nipples with the bases. Each part is decorated with a serpent design formed by double lines. The serpent in shape of hook has a head turning round in the right, a raising neck and a tail rolling downward in the left. Each side of the serpent has a bird. The major motif ends with a band of fine-toothed design. The rim without design is broad and has a flat surface. The mirror has a heavy body.

The mirror has a symmetrical layout with knob as the center and nipple as dividing line. The serpent design with head in right and tail in left bring a rhythmic beauty to the mirror.   (Liu Jiwu)

四乳四虺镜　西汉
直径8.3厘米，边厚0.4厘米，重128克
1988年2月魏家菜地出土，1989年4月于淮南市潘集区贺疃乡魏桥村魏永严处征集

圆形，半球钮，圆钮座。座外饰四组短线和凸弦纹装饰，主纹以两周栉齿纹为廓，内为相间环绕的四乳四虺，四乳有圆座，四虺呈钩形躯体，同形，虺身两侧点缀禽鸟纹。素宽平缘。此镜模铸精良，造型饱满，动感极强。（陶佳）

Mirror with design of four nipples and four serpents　Western Han Dynasty
Diameter: 8.3cm, Thickness of rim: 0.4cm, Weight: 128gram
Unearthed at Wei's vegetable plot; Collected from Wei Yongyan at Weiqiao Village, Hetong Town, Panji District in Huainan City in April, 1989

The mirror is round in shape. It has a half-sphere-shaped knob on a round base. Outside the base are four groups of short lines and a band of raised string design. Each side of the major motif has a band of fine-toothed pattern. The major motif is design of four nipples with bases and four hook-shaped serpents with bird design on both sides. The rim without design is broad and has a flat surface. The mirror with delicate mold and luxuriant decoration has a strongly kinetic effect.　(Tao Jia)

四乳四虺镜　西汉

直径9.9厘米，边厚0.4厘米，重174克
本馆旧藏

　　圆形，半球钮，圆钮座。座外环一周凸起的宽弦纹带，两者之间的空白处填以若干斜线纹作简单装饰。主纹为四乳四虺，乳钉较平，下有圆形座，虺呈"S"形，是简化变形了的虺纹，腹下点缀有禽鸟纹饰。主纹内外两侧以栉齿纹为廓。宽素平缘。

　　四乳四虺镜在许多地区都有出土，从汉武帝时期一直延续到东汉前期都很流行。该镜纹饰布局严谨，以四乳将镜背分成四区，每区一虺，首尾相连，并以钮为中心呈中心对称布局。其制作精良，表面泛银光，为此类镜中的代表器。（吴琳）

Mirror with design of four nipples and four serpents　Western Han Dynasty

Diameter: 9.9cm, Thickness of rim: 0.4cm, Weight: 174gram
Collection of Huainan Museum

　　The mirror is round. It has a half-sphere-shaped knob on a round base. Outside the base is a band of raised string pattern. The base and the sting pattern are spaced with slanted lines. The major motif is design of four nipples with round bases and four S-shaped simplified serpents with bird design below the body. The band of fine-toothed pattern adorns each side of the major motif. The rim without design is broad and has a flat surface.

　　The mirror with design of four nipples and four serpents has been found in many places and was popular from the Emperor Wu of Han to the early Eastern Han Dynasty. This mirror has a symmetrical layout with the knob as the center, four parts divided by four nipples and a serpent on each part. It shows refined craftsmanship and is a rare treasure.　(Wu Lin)

四乳四虺镜 西汉

直径17.9厘米，边厚0.5厘米，重711克

1988年5月淮南市唐山乡双古堆东出土

圆形，乳钮，柿蒂钮座。镜背以一周宽带弦纹分内外两区：内区在柿蒂四叶间作简单装饰，外环一周栉齿纹；外区饰四乳四虺，四乳有座，四虺呈钩形，头部上扬，卷尾，其身躯上下两侧各饰一只神鸟，其上神鸟展翅腾飞，其下神鸟倒立，两侧以栉齿纹为廓。宽素缘。（汪茂东）

Mirror with design of four nipples and four serpents   Western Han Dynasty

Diameter: 17.9, Thickness of rim: 0.5cm, Weight: 711gram

Unearthed from east of Shuanggudui at Tangshan Town in Huainan City in May, 1988

The mirror is round in shape. It has a nipple-shaped knob on a base with kaki calyx design. The ground is divided into two parts by a broad band with string pattern. Around the kaki calyx design is decorated with simple design and is surrounded with a band of fine-toothed pattern. Outer part is adorned with design of four nipples with bases and four hook-shaped serpents with raising head, rolling tail and a bird on each side. Each side of outer part has a band of fine-toothed pattern. The mirror has a broad rim without design.   (Wang Maodong)

上大山见仙人铭博局镜　　新莽

直径14.3厘米，厚0.5厘米，重459克

2006年6月淮南市谢家集区赖山窑厂砖墓出土

　　圆形，乳钮，方形钮座。自内向外共有七层纹饰：座外方格内有十二小乳钉呈方形排列。小乳钉间有十二辰铭，其中"午"字铭漏，疑为模范不清所致；直线方框，呈"V"形槽；中区主纹饰由博局、八乳划分为四方八区，依次是青龙配禽鸟、朱雀配神鹿、白虎配独角兽、玄武配羽人，羽人为侧身嬉戏状；一周环铭："上大山兮，见仙人，食玉英，饮澧泉，驾交龙兮，乘浮云，宜官秩，保子孙"；中区与外区间隔以栉纹和锯齿纹；宽缘略高，缘上饰以流云纹。

　　博局镜，又名规矩镜，流行于西汉中晚期至东汉早期。博局镜的定名源于国家博物馆所藏铜镜拓本"刻娄博局去不祥"。淮南市博物馆所藏此镜与前所述铜镜时代相当，大致在王莽到东汉早期。博局镜在各地出土较多，南北方均有。汉代盛行博戏，有六黑六白棋子，二人对博。此镜是博局镜中的佳品，虽出土于小型砖室墓中，但纹饰精美，品相甚佳，由于地下保存条件较好，镜背纹饰如同刚刚脱模，十分夺目，实属难得。（沈汗青）

Mirror with inscription of "*Shang Da Shan Jian Xian Ren*" and gambling design   Xin Dynasty

Diameter: 14.3cm, Thickness: 0.5cm, Weight: 459gram

Unearthed at a brick tomb of Laishan Kiln Workshop in Xiejiaji District, Huainan City in June, 2006

The mirror is round in shape. It has a nipple-shaped knob on a square base and a seven-layer decoration. Twelve nipples arranged in a square adorn outside the square and is spaced with twelve Earthly Branches, among which "*Wu*" character was lost. Each corner of the square corresponds with a V-shaped design. The major motif is decorated with Green Dragon with bird, Scarlet Bird with deer, White Tiger with unicorn and Somber Warrior with winged figure and is spaced with design of gambling and eight nipples. Outside the major motif is a band of inscription "*Shang Da Shan Xi, Jian Xian Ren, Shi Yu Ying, Yin Li Quan, Jia Jiao Long Xi, Cheng Fu Yun, Yi Guan Zhi, Bao Zi Sun*". Inside the rim are a band of fine-toothed pattern and a band of saw pattern. The raised rim is decorated with drifting cloud.

The mirror with gambling design, also called the mirror with standard design, was popular from middle and the late Western Han Dynasty to the early Eastern Han Dynasty. Its name is originated from rubbings "*Ke Lou Bo Ju Qu Bu Xiang*" of bronze mirror collected at the National Museum. The mirror has the similar time with the mirror of the National Museum, which is from the Xin Dynasty to the early Eastern Han Dynasty. The mirrors with gambling design were unearthed in a great number in the North and the South. Gambling is derived from the board game Liubo, a prevailing game in the Han Dynasty. The game was played between two players with each player having six men. The mirror was found at a brick tomb in a small scale but was kept in good condition. It is a rare treasure with clear and exquisite decoration. (Shen Hanqing)

八乳四神博局镜　新莽

直径 14厘米，边厚0.5厘米，重374克

2010年8月淮南市谢家集区李郢孜镇谢家集新村出土

　　圆形，半球钮，圆形钮座。环钮座饰八个带座小乳钉，小乳钉间饰弯钩形弧线组成的小弧线。外钮饰凹面大方框，方框内角处各置一短弧线构成的小草纹。环方框外每边有两较大带座乳钉，方框中部的乳钉间各伸出一"T"形博局纹，对置处饰"L"形博局纹，方框对角处饰"V"形博局纹。"TLV"间环置四神，分别饰白虎配羽人、朱雀、玄武、青龙均配禽鸟。镜背空隙处填饰弯钩状的短弧线纹，状如草叶，近缘处以栉齿纹为栏。宽缘，缘上饰锯齿纹一周，凸弦纹两周，弦纹内饰变形的四神纹。

　　此镜十分精美，博局纹见棱见角，神兽禽鸟纹线条纤细，但非常清晰，整个镜背繁而有序，层次分明，极富华美之感。最有特色的是镜缘部分，将四神拉长变形饰于缘面。镜的主题纹和镜缘各饰一组四神图案，比较少见。（沈汗青）

Mirror with design of eight nipples, four deities and gambling Xin Dynasty

Diameter: 14cm, Thickness of rim: 0.5cm, Weight: 374gram

Unearthed at Xiejiaji new village, Liyingzi Town, Xiejiaji District in Huainan City in August, 2010

The mirror is round in shape. It has a half-sphere-shaped knob on a round base. Around the base is a band of eight nipples which are spaced with hook-shaped arcs. Outside the band is a square with concave surface. Inside each corner of the square is a leaf design formed by arcs. Each side of the square has two bigger nipple designs with the bases. A T-shaped design is stretching out of the middle side of the square and is put in the middle of two nipple designs, corresponding with L-shaped design stretching out of the rim. Each corner of the square corresponds with V-shaped design. Around the design of T-shaped, L-shaped and V-shaped are four deities which are White Tiger with winged figure, Scarlet Bird with animal and bird, Somber Warrior with animal and bird and Green Bird with animal and bird. The ground is decorated with leaf pattern formed by hook-shaped arcs. Inside the rim is the fine-toothed design. On the Broad rim are a band of saw design and two bands of raised string design with stylized four-deity pattern.

The mirror with exquisite designs and clear lines shows a well-arranged decoration and has a strong effect of elegance. The most unique feature of the mirror is the rim with stylize four-deity design. It is rare to find the mirror with four-deity design as major design and on the rim. (Shen Hanqing)

新有善铜铭八乳瑞兽博局镜　新莽

直径13.9厘米，边厚0.5厘米，重465克

本馆旧藏

　　圆形，半球钮，圆钮座。座外环一周双线方框纹，框内饰一周弦纹，框外置"TLV"组合成的博局纹，在"T"纹两侧各饰一带座乳钉，共八个，每一乳钉下阳线勾画一瑞兽，分别为青龙、白虎、朱雀、玄武四神等。其外环一周铭文圈带，铭文"新有善铜出丹阳，和以银锡清且明，左龙右虎尚四彭"，篆书。宽缘，上饰一周变形蟠虺纹。该镜纹饰精细，模铸规范，从其铭文和宽缘上的纹饰推断，新为新莽，应是王莽时期产品。（陶治强）

Mirror with inscription of "*Xin You Shan Tong*" and design of eight nipples, animals and gambling Xin Dynasty

Diameter: 13.9cm, Thickness of rim: 0.5cm, Weight: 465gram

Collection of Huainan Museum

The mirror is round in shape. It has a half-sphere-shaped knob on a round base. Outside the base are a string band and a square formed by double lines. Outside the square is the TLV-shaped gambling design. Each side of T-shaped design has a nipple design with bases. Below each nipple is an animal, such as Green Dragon, White Tiger, Scarlet Bird or Somber Warrior. Outside the major motif has a band of inscription in seal script "*Xin You Shan Tong Chu Dan Yang, He Yi Yin Xi Qing Qie Ming, Zuo Long You Hu Shang Si Peng*". The broad rim is adorned with a band of stylized coiled serpent design. The mirror has an exquisite decoration and a delicate mold. Base on the inscription and the design, it was inferred as a mirror of the reign of Wang Mang.   (Tao Zhiqiang)

四乳神兽镜　东汉

直径9.6厘米，边厚0.4厘米，重185克

本馆旧藏

　　圆形，半球钮，柿蒂纹钮座。主纹为四乳神兽，四乳将镜背纹饰分为四区，四乳有座，外环一周弦纹，内填短线条。四区内饰神兽，形态各异。宽缘，缘上内外两侧饰宽带纹，中间夹饰一周双线波折纹。

（陶治强）

Mirror with design of four nipples and mythical creatures　Eastern Han Dynasty

Diameter: 9.6cm, Thickness of rim: 0.4cm, Weight: 185gram

Collection of Huainan Museum

The mirror is round in shape. It has a half-sphere-shaped knob on a base with kaki calyx design. The major motif is design of four nipples with bases and mythical creatures. The mythical creatures are spaced with four nipples. The major motif is surrounded with a band of string pattern. The broad rim is adorned with two broad bands and a band of wave pattern formed by double lines between the broad bands.　(Tao Zhiqiang)

四乳八鸟镜 东汉

直径8.2厘米，边厚0.4厘米，重130克
2010年9月淮南市谢家集公安分局移交

　　圆形，圆钮，圆钮座。座外以短线和栉齿纹装饰。主纹为四乳八鸟，四乳有座。八鸟两两相对，分置于四乳间。禽鸟纹样简洁，二歧冠、覆羽翼、翘尾，纹饰两侧以斜向栉齿纹为廓。宽缘，素面。

　　四乳八鸟镜流行于西汉晚期到东汉早期，纹饰布局采用了当时流行的以四乳钉为基点组织主题纹饰的四分法，八鸟虽有图案化倾向，但形象自然，使人感觉生动活泼。（任胜利）

Mirror with design of four nipples and eight birds　Eastern Han Dynasty

Diameter: 8.2cm, Thickness of rim: 0.4cm, Weight: 130gram
Transferred by Xiejiaji District Public Security Bureau in Huainan City in September, 2010

　　The mirror is round in shape. It has a round knob on a round base. Outside the base are short lines and a band of fine-toothed pattern. The major design is the design of four nipples with bases and eight birds. Four nipples are spaced with two birds facing each other. The bird is in a simple shape and has two pileums, feathered wing and raising tail. The band of fine-toothed pattern adorns each side of the major motif. The mirror has a broad rim without design.

　　The mirror with design of four nipples and four birds was popular from the late Western Han Dynasty to the early Eastern Han Dynasty. Base on the nipples as the centers, its major motif is arranged. The bird was patterned but has a natural shape, which bring a vivid effect.　(Ren Shengli)

四乳龙凤镜 东汉

直径11.4厘米，边厚0.4厘米，重297克

1977年8月淮南市物资回收公司拣选

　　圆形，乳钮，圆钮座。座外环一周宽带弦纹，内饰短直线、月牙状弧线纹等与钮座相连；主区纹饰由四乳钉将其分为四区，乳钉有座，间饰龙纹、凤纹，空白处填以云朵纹。龙，作腾飞状；凤，昂首、卷尾，两侧以斜栉齿纹为廓。宽缘，上饰锯齿波折纹一周。龙凤纹是汉代铜镜中常见的纹饰，寓意龙凤呈祥，反映出汉人对美好生活的向往。（汪茂东）

Mirror with design of four nipples, dragon and phoenix   Eastern Han Dynasty

Diameter: 11.4cm, Thickness of rim: 0.4cm, Weight: 297gram

Got from a material recycling company in Huainan City in August, 1977

The mirror is round in shape. It has a nipple-shaped knob on a round base. Outside the base is a broad band of string design. Between the base and the band are designs of short lines and crescent-shaped arcs linked with the base. The major motif is divided into four parts by four nipples with bases. Each part is arranged alternately dragon or phoenix and filled with cloud design in blank. The bands of fine-toothed design adorn the major motif. The broad rim is decorated with a band of wave design. The Han mirror was often decorated with the design of dragon and phoenix which means prosperity brought by dragon and phoenix and represents good wish of people of the Han Dynasty for beautiful life.   (Wang Maodong)

四乳四凤镜　东汉

直径10.9厘米，边厚0.3厘米，重159克
1982年12月淮南市宫集公社林巷一队出土

　　圆形，乳钮，圆钮座。座外环一周宽带弦纹，内饰六道三斜线纹与钮座相连。主纹为四乳四凤，四乳有座，四凤形态相似，皆昂首、长卷尾、展翅，两侧饰栉齿纹为廓。宽缘，上饰三角锯齿纹一周，锯齿纹间饰短斜线纹，其外环一周双线波折纹。

　　《说文解字》释："凤，神鸟也。"在古代的传说中，凤为群鸟之首，羽翼最美，飞时百鸟随之，在古人心中是吉祥之鸟。由于凤鸟能给人们带来祥瑞和吉庆，铜镜常用凤鸟图案，表达了人们的美好愿望。
（汪茂东）

Mirror with design of four nipples and four phoenixes　Eastern Han Dynasty

Diameter: 10.9cm, Thickness of rim: 0.3cm, Weight: 159gram
Unearthed at Linxiang First Brigade, Gongji Commune in Huainan City in December, 1982

　　The mirror is round in shape. It has a knob with nipple design on a round base. Outside the base is a broad band of string design. Inside the band are six groups of three short lines linked with the base. The major motif is the design of four nipples on bases and four phoenixes with head raising, tail roiling and wings spreading. The bands of fine-toothed design adorn both sides of the major motif. The broad rim is decorated with a band of saw pattern filling short lines in blank and a band of wave pattern formed by double lines.

　　It is recorded in *Shuo Wen Jie Zi* that phoenix is a mythical bird. In ancient legend, phoenix with the most beautiful wings is head of birds. When it flies, it is followed by birds. It is regarded as the symbol of luck. For this reason, the bronze with phoenix design represent good wish of people.(Wang Maodong)

四乳八鸟镜　东汉
直径9厘米，边厚0.5厘米，重168克
1976年3月淮南市物资回收公司拣选

圆形，半球钮，圆钮座。座外环一周凸弦纹，内饰二组短线相间纹饰与钮座相连。主题纹饰以四个带座乳钉分为四区，每区饰两只禽鸟，两两相对，两鸟之下靠钮座一侧饰"日"纹或"月"纹，间隔排列，两侧环以栉齿纹为廓。宽厚缘，缘向内微坡，素面。
（汪茂东）

Mirror with design of four nipples and eight birds　Eastern Han Dynasty
Diameter: 9cm, Thickness of rim: 0.5cm, Weight: 168gram
Got from a material recycling company in Huainan City in March, 1976

The mirror is round in shape. It has a half-sphere-shaped knob on a round base. Outside the base are two short lines linked with the base at intervals and a band of raised string pattern. The major motif is divided into four parts by four nipples with bases. Each part has two birds facing each other. Between two birds and above the base is adorned alternately with the crescent design or design in shape of "*Ri*" character. The bands of fine-toothed pattern adorn both sides of the major motif. The broad and thick rim without design is slanting inside.　(Wang Maodong)

四乳八鸟镜　东汉

直径9.9厘米，边厚0.6厘米，重239克

2010年9月淮南市谢家集公安分局移交

　　圆形，半球钮，圆钮座。座外饰四组短线和逆向旋纹，外环素面宽弦纹带，主区纹饰以两周斜向栉齿纹为界，内饰四乳八鸟：四乳带圆座，八鸟两两相对，有冠羽，身体饰简单纹样。宽素平缘。此镜规矩厚重，镜的材质含锡量高，纹饰清晰，黑漆古亮丽，镜背至今尚可照人。（孙梅）

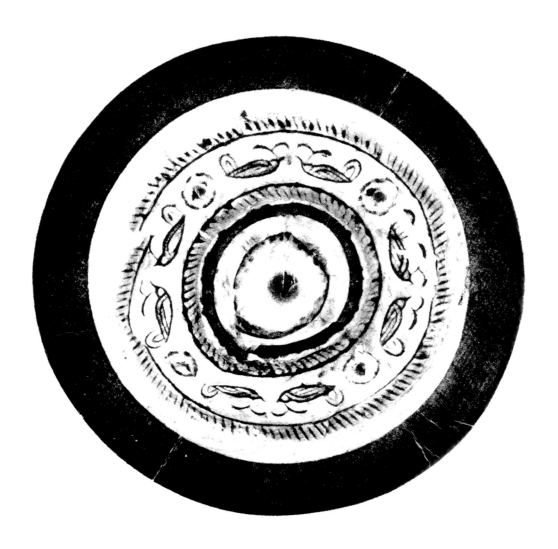

Mirror with design of four nipples and eight birds Eastern Han Dynasty

Diameter: 9.9cm, Thickness of rim: 0.6cm, Weight: 239gram

Transferred by Xiejiaji District Public Security Bureau in Huainan City in September, 2010

The mirror is round in shape. It has a half-sphere-shaped knob on a round base. Outside the base are four groups of short lines, a band of string pattern and a broad band of string pattern. The major motif is surrounded with two bands of fine-toothed pattern. The major motif is the design of four nipples on round bases and eight birds. Four nipples are spaced with two birds facing each other. The bird with pileum and feather is decorated with simple design. The rim without design is broad and has a flat surface. The thick and heavy mirror with a high content of tin has a pleasing cover of black patina. The shiny side of the mirror can reflect the image up to now.　(Sun Mei)

四乳四神镜　东汉
直径9.9厘米，边厚0.3厘米，重179克
本馆旧藏

圆形，半球形钮，圆钮座。座外饰一周凸弦纹，内以四组短线和四组弧线纹装饰。主纹以两周栉齿纹带为廓，四枚带座乳钉将主纹分为四区，单线勾勒的青龙、白虎、朱雀、玄武四神环绕排列其间。宽缘，缘上饰双线波折纹。

汉代铜镜装饰多以单线或双钩阳线的表现技法出现于镜背，并且围绕镜钮组成同心圆的多层连续图案，又喜用四分法把纹样四等分，构成既对称又连续的装饰图案。此镜的四神造型生动，有写实风格，栩栩如生，极富动感。（王莉）

Mirror with design of four nipples and four deities   Eastern Han Dynasty

Diameter: 9.9cm, Thickness of rim: 0.3cm, Weight: 179gram
Collection of Huainan Museum

The mirror is round in shape. It has a half-sphere-shaped knob on a round base. Outside the base is a band of raised sting pattern. Inside the band are two short lines and arc-shaped lines arranged alternately. The bands of fine-toothed design adorn the major motif. The major motif is the design of Green Dragon, White Tiger, Scarlet Bird and Sober Warrior spaced with nipples with bases. The broad rim is decorated with wave pattern formed by double lines.

The patterns of the Han bronze mirrors formed mostly with hook-shaped single line or double lines are arranged in multi-layer continuous concentric circles and appear in a balanced and continuous layout by quartering. The design of four deities with vivid shape and natural style has a strong dynamic effect.   (Wang Li)

四乳禽鸟镜 东汉

直径7.7厘米，边厚0.4厘米，重105克

本馆旧藏

　　圆形，半球钮，圆钮座。座外饰一圈凸弦纹和短线装饰纹。主纹饰为四乳四鸟相间环列，四乳有座，四禽鸟昂首展翅，同向，呈飞翔状。外区饰两周栉齿纹。斜缘。

　　此镜以四乳钉为基点，将镜背均匀分为四个区域，主题纹饰列置其间。这种布局在西汉晚期后大量流行。禽鸟采用了浅线和浮雕式手法，造型简约，纹饰由线条式的平面变化为半立体式。这种装饰方法流行于东汉中期，后逐渐演化成高浮雕装饰。（闫晓娟）

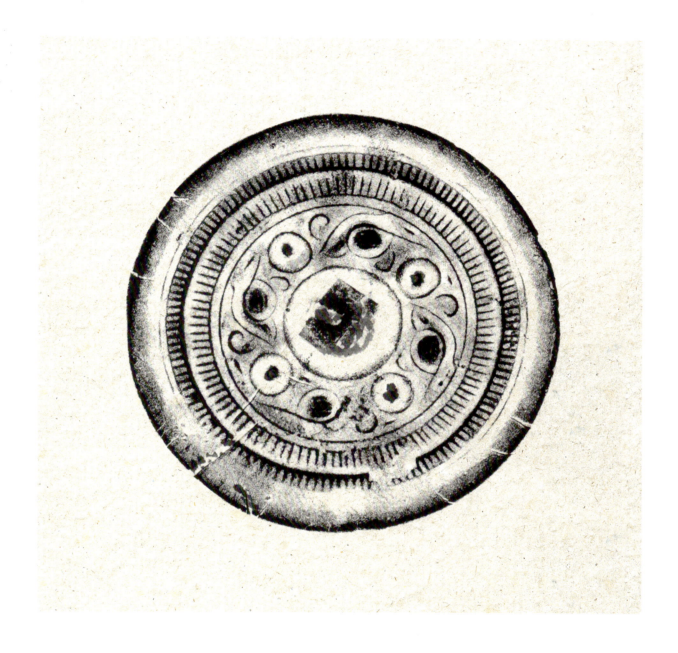

Mirror with design of four nipples and birds Eastern Han Dynasty

Diameter: 7.7cm, Thickness of rim: 0.4cm, Weight: 105gram

Collection of Huainan Museum

The mirror is round in shape. It has a half-sphere-shaped knob on a round base. Outside the base are short lines and a band of raised string pattern. The major motif is the design of four nipples with bases and four flying birds alternately arranged. Two bands of fine-toothed pattern adorns outside the base. The mirror has a slanting rim.

The mirror is decorated with four nipples with which the major motif is spaced. The layout had been more popular since the late Western Han Dynasty. The bird with simple shape is formed with low lines and carved in relief. The decoration in low relief was used in the middle Eastern Han Dynasty and gradually became the decoration in high relief. (Yan Xiaojuan)

四乳八鸟镜 东汉

直径8.2厘米，边厚0.5厘米，重135克
1984年6月淮南市物资回收公司拣选

圆形，半球钮，圆钮座。钮座外饰二组短线纹，外环宽带弦纹一周。主纹由四带座乳钉分为四区，每区各饰一对禽鸟，两两相对，两侧栉齿纹为廓。宽缘，素面无纹。此镜鸟纹线条洗练、形态生动自然。

（汪茂东）

Mirror with design of four nipples and eight birds Eastern Han Dynasty

Diameter: 8.2cm, Thickness of rim: 0.5cm, Weight: 135gram
Got from a material recycling company in Huainan City in June, 1984

The mirror is round in shape. It has a half-sphere-shaped knob on a round base. Outside the base is adorned with designs of two short lines linked with the base at intervals and a broad band of string pattern. The major motif is divided into four parts by four nipples with bases. Each part has two birds facing each other. The bands of fine-toothed pattern adorn both sides of the major motif. The mirror has a broad rim without design. The bird design in the mirror is cast with simple lines and has a vivid and natural shape.

(Wang Maodong)

四乳龙虎镜　东汉

直径10厘米，边厚0.4厘米，重198克
本馆旧藏

　　圆形，半球钮，圆钮座。主纹以钮为中心呈对称布局，四个带座乳钉将纹饰分为四区，每区饰一神兽，为双龙双虎，间隔排列，两侧以栉齿纹为廓。宽缘，上饰双线波折纹。

　　汉代铜镜纹饰多以双钩阳线绘画的表现技法出现于镜背，再用四分法把主纹分成四等份，且纹饰围绕镜钮组成多层同心圆，构成既对称又连续的圆形装饰图案。此镜做工考究，纹饰清晰精美，为汉镜之佳品。（刘继武）

Mirror with design of four nipples, dragons and tigers　Eastern Han Dynasty

Diameter: 10cm. Thickness of rim: 0.4cm, Weight: 198gram
Collection of Huainan Museum

The mirror is round in shape. It has a half-sphere-shaped knob on a round base. The major motif is the design of two dragons and two tigers alternately arranged and spaced with four nipples with bases. The bands of fine-toothed pattern adorn the major motif. The broad rim is decorated with wave pattern formed with double lines.

The patterns of the Han bronze mirrors formed mostly with hook-shaped double lines are arranged in multi-layer continuous concentric circles and appear in a balanced and continuous layout by quartering. The mirror with delicate craftsmanship and exquisite design is the treasure of the Han bronze mirrors. (Liu Jiwu)

四乳龙虎镜 东汉
直径9.8厘米，边厚0.35厘米，重183克
本馆旧藏

　　圆形，半球钮，圆钮座。纹饰以两周栉齿纹分区。内区座外饰短线，短线之间饰一弧形短线条，外环一宽带弦纹。中区以四带座乳钉分成四区，每区内饰一瑞兽，为双龙双虎，相间环绕。虎身体粗壮，圆目突出，身饰斑线纹；龙首前伸，尾部上翘，作奔走状。宽缘，上饰一周双线波折纹，且每一波折间填以一点珠纹。（陶治强）

Mirror with design of four nipples, dragons and tigers　Eastern Han Dynasty
Diameter: 9.8cm, Thickness of rim; 0.35cm, Weight: 183gram
Collection of Huainan Museum

　　The mirror is round in shape. It has a half-sphere-shaped knob on a round base. The major motif is adorned with two bands of fine-toothed pattern. Outside the base is adorned with design of short lines spaced with arc-shaped lines and surrounded with a band of string pattern. The major motif is the design of two running dragons and two tigers with streak pattern alternately arranged and spaced with four nipples with bases. The broad rim is adorned with a band of wave pattern formed with double lines and filled with beads in blank. (Tao Zhiqiang)

四神博局镜　东汉

直径10厘米，边厚0.3厘米，重151克
1999年安徽省寿县埝口魏岗孜窑厂出土，2001年6月征集

　　圆形，半球形钮，柿蒂钮座。座外围一周双线方格纹，方格外饰青龙、白虎、朱雀、玄武四神，四神按东、南、西、北方位排列，每个神兽的上下前后分别置TLV形博局纹以间隔，外以一周栉齿纹带为廓。宽缘，缘内侧饰双线三角纹。

　　此镜纹饰简洁规整，但简洁而不失饱满，规整中尤见灵动。（王莉）

Mirror with design of four deities and gambling　Eastern Han Dynasty

Diameter: 10cm, Thickness of rim: 0.3cm, Weight: 151gram
Unearthed at Weigangzi Kiln Workshop in Niankou, Shou County, Huainan City in 1999; Collected in June, 2001

The mirror is round in shape. It has a half-sphere-shaped knob on a base with kaki calyx design. Outside the base is adorned with a square formed by double lines. Outside the square is decorated with four deities of Green Dragon, White Dragon, Scarlet Bird and Somber Warrior arranged in order of east, south, west and north, which are spaced with TLV-shaped design. Outside the major motif is adorned with a band of fine-toothed pattern. The mirror has a broad rim. Inner the rim has a band of triangle pattern formed by double lines.

The decoration of the mirror has a simple layout but a strongly vivid effect. (Wang Li)

八乳禽兽博局镜 东汉

直径18厘米，边厚0.5厘米，重832克

本馆旧藏

　　圆形，半球钮，圆钮座。纹饰分内外两区：内区是九个带座小乳钉纹环绕镜钮，钮外环一周双弦纹和双线方框纹；外区为"TLV"形式的博局纹，在双线方框的四边等距置八个带座乳钉纹，乳钉和博局纹之间的空白处填以八只禽兽纹，计有青龙、白虎、玄武、禽兽等。镜缘内侧有一周栉齿纹为界。镜缘较宽，缘面上饰有两组纹饰，内为一周三角锯齿纹，外为流云纹。博局镜流行于西汉中晚期至东汉早期，此镜有王莽到东汉早期特征。（程东雯）

Mirror with design of eight nipples, animals and gambling   Eastern Han Dynasty

Diameter: 18cm, Thickness of rim: 0.5cm, Weight: 832gram

Collection of Huainan Museum

The mirror is round in shape. It has a half-sphere-shaped knob on a round base. The ground has two parts. Inner part has a band of nine nipples with bases around the base, a band of string design and a square formed by double lines. Outer part is adorned with design of T-shaped, L-shaped and V-shaped. Each side of the square has two nipples in the same distance. The nipple design and the pattern of T-shaped, L-shaped and V-shaped are spaced with animals design, including Green Dragon, White Tiger, Somber

Warrior and animals and so on. Inside the rim has a band of fine-toothed pattern. A broader rim is adorned with a band of saw pattern and a band of design of drifting clouds. The mirror with gambling design was popular from the middle and late Western Han Dynasty to early Eastern Han Dynasty. The mirror shows the features of the mirror with gambling design from Xin Dynasty to early Eastern Han Dynasty.   (Chen Dongwen)

尚方作镜铭八乳禽兽纹博局镜　　东汉

直径15.5厘米，边厚0.5厘米，重373克

2006年6月淮南市谢家集区赖山窑厂砖墓出土

圆形，半球钮，柿蒂纹钮座。座外环一双线方框，框外饰"TLV"纹组合成的博局纹，在"T"纹两侧各饰一乳钉，计八个，每乳钉下对应有一只禽鸟。

其外环一周铭文圈带，铭"尚方作镜真大巧，上有山人不□□□玉泉"。尖缘，上饰三角锯齿纹两周，其间夹一层波折纹。（陶治强）

Royal-made Mirror with inscription and design of eight nipples, animals and gambling   Eastern Han Dynasty

Diameter: 15.5cm, Thickness of rim: 0.5cm, Weight: 373gram

Unearthed at Laishanyao Kiln Workshop in Xiejiaji District, Huainan City in June, 2006

The mirror is round in shape. It has a half-sphere-shaped knob on a base with kaki calyx design. Outside the base is adorned with a square formed by double lines. Outside the square is adorned with TLV-shaped gambling design. Each side of T-shaped design has a nipple. Below each nipple has an animal. Outside the major motif has a band of inscription "*Shang Fang Zuo Jing Zhen Da Qiao, Shang You Shan Ren Bu*□□□*Yu Quan*". The sharp rim is decorated with two bands of saw pattern and a band of wave pattern among them.   (Tao Zhiqiang)

新有善铜铭禽兽纹简化博局镜　东汉

直径11.9厘米，边厚0.4厘米，重293克
1977年8月淮南市物资回收公司拣选

　　圆形，乳钮，圆钮座。座外饰一双线方框，框内饰对角线穿越钮座，框外四边各置一双线"T"形纹，为简化博局纹，框外四角各饰一带座乳钉，将主纹四等分，其内饰双凤双虎，两两相对。凤，昂首，长尾上卷，展翅飞翔；虎，昂首，卷竖尾，前肢下蹲，后肢后撑，作奔跑状。外饰铭文圈带一周，铭"亲（新）有善同（铜）出丹阳，和以锡银清且明"，外以一周栉齿纹为廓。宽缘，缘上饰三角锯齿纹一周、卷云纹一周。此镜虽铭"新有善铜"，但从其简化博局纹及其工艺特征看，时代要晚一些。（汪茂东）

Mirror with inscription of "*Xin You Shan Tong*" and design of animals and simple gambling   Eastern Han Dynasty

Diameter: 11.9cm, Thickness of rim: 0.4cm, Weight: 293gram

Got from a material recycling company in Huainan City in August, 1977

The mirror is round in shape. It has a nipple-shaped knob on a round base. Outside the base is adorned with a square formed by double lines. Inside the square have diagonal lines across the base. A T-shaped simple gambling design is stretching out of each side of the square. A nipple with a base adorns each corner of the square and divides the major motif into four parts. The major motif is the design of flying phoenix and running tiger facing each other.

Outside the major motif have a band of inscription "*Xin You Shan Tong Chu Dan Yang, He Yi Xi Yin Qing Qie Ming*" and a band of fine-toothed pattern. The broad rim is decorated with a band of saw pattern, a band of cirrus cloud design. Although it is recorded in the inscription that its time is Xin Dynasty, the simple gambling design and its craftsmanship appeared in later time.   (Wang Maodong)

新有善铜铭禽兽简化博局镜　东汉

直径11.7厘米，边厚0.45厘米，重301克
2005年4月淮南市谢家集区李一矿河西村安居工程工地汉墓出土

　　圆形，半球钮，圆钮座。座外围一周双线方框，框内四角各饰一组月牙纹，框外四角各置一带座乳钉，中间饰一双线"T"形符号的简化博局纹，并填以七只形态各异的禽兽纹。外环以一圈铭文："新有善

铜出丹阳，和以银锡"，字体瘦长，外饰一周栉齿纹为廓。宽缘，上饰三角锯齿纹和双线波折纹各一周。此镜镜体浑厚，纹饰规整，模铸精良。（陶治强）

Mirror with inscription of "*Xin You Shan Tong*" and design of animals and simple gambling   Eastern Han Dynasty

Diameter: 11.7cm, Thickness of rim: 0.45cm, Weight: 301gram

Unearthed from the Han Tomb at a construction site west of Liyikuanghe Village under a Comfortable Housing Project in Xiejiaji District, Huainan City in April, 2005

The mirror is round in shape. It has a half-sphere-shaped knob on a round base. Outside the base is adorned with a square formed by double lines. Each corner inside the square has a crescent-shaped design. Each corner of the square has a nipple design with a base. A T-shaped simple gambling design is stretching out of the middle of each side of the square. The major motif is seven different animals. Inside the rim is adorned with a band of inscription "*Xin You Shan Tong Chu Dan Yang, He Yi Yin Xi*" and a band of fine-toothed pattern. The broad is decorated with a band of saw pattern and a band of wave pattern formed by double lines. The mirror with a heavy body has a delicate decoration and exquisite mold.   (Tao Zhiqiang)

八乳博局镜 *东汉*

直径12.6厘米，边厚0.4厘米，重294克

2005年4月淮南市谢家集区李一矿河西村安居工程工地出土

　　圆形，半球钮，圆钮座。座外围以双线方格纹，方格内饰两条对角线与钮座相连，空白处填以草叶纹装饰。主题纹饰为"TLV"格式的博局纹，其间等距排列八个乳钉纹，乳钉有座，座外环一周弦纹，内以四组三道短线装饰，弦纹环带外出六条右向旋转的涡纹，犹如日之火焰。主题纹饰外以一周栉齿纹为栏。宽缘，缘上饰一周锯齿纹和一周双线波折纹。（文立中）

Mirror with design of eight nipples and gambling   Eastern Han Dynasty

Diameter: 12.6cm, Thickness of rim: 0.4cm, Weight: 294gram

Unearthed at a construction site west of Liyikuanghe Village under a Comfortable Housing Project in Xiejiaji District, Huainan City in April, 2005

The mirror is round in shape. It has a half-sphere-shaped knob on a round base. Outside the base is adorned with a square formed by double lines. Inside the square have two diagonal lines across the base and grass blades design in the blank. The major motif is gambling design with TLV-shaped and a band of eight nipples design with bases in the same distance. The base of

nipple design is decorated with a band of string design with three short lines in four groups. Six arcs rolling towards the right are stretching out of the band and are in shape of flame-shaped whorl inside the rim has a band of fine-toothed design. The broad rim is decorated with a band of saw pattern and a band of wave pattern formed by double lines.   (Wen Lizhong)

八连弧云雷纹镜　东汉

直径15.4厘米，边厚0.5厘米，重371克
1972年11月淮南市物资回收公司拣选

　　圆形，半球钮，圆钮座。座外有一周形似双瓣幼芽的装饰，间以四字铭。其外环饰宽弦纹带一周，主区饰内向八连弧纹一周，外区由八个涡纹及并行弧线组成的云雷纹带一周，以栉齿纹为廓。斜缘，素面无纹。

　　连弧云雷纹镜是东汉前期具有新风格的镜类之一，布局上可看做西汉连弧纹昭明镜的简化形式，其内区仍为一圈连弧纹，但昭明镜的铭文带却被纤细变形的云雷纹所代替。（刘继武）

Mirror with design of eight linked arcs and cloud and thunder   Eastern Han dynasty

Diameter: 15.4cm, Thickness of rim: 0.5cm, Weight: 371gram

Got from a material recycling company in Huainan City in November, 1972

The mirror is round in shape. It has a half-sphere-shaped knob on a round base. Outside the base is adorned with design of buds with two leaves spaced with four characters and surrounded with a broad string band. The major motif has a band of eight linked arcs inside and a band of cloud and thunder design formed with arcs spaced with whorl pattern. The major motif ends a band of fine-toothed pattern.

The mirror has a slanting rim without design.

The mirror with design of linked arcs and cloud and thunder appeared in early Eastern Han Dynasty. The motif was evolved from the mirror with linked arcs design and inscription of "*Zhao Ming*", which remained inner band of linked arcs and replaced the inscription with stylized design of cloud and thunder.(Liu Jiwu)

湅治铅华铭连弧镜 东汉

直径14.6厘米，边厚0.7厘米，重553克

本馆旧藏

　　圆形，半球钮，联珠纹钮座。在两周栉齿纹之间饰有一周宽带弦纹和一周内向八连弧纹，空白处填以短直线、弧线组成的复合纹样。其外环一周铭文圈带，铭文："湅治铅华清而明，以之为镜宜文章，延年益寿辟不祥，（与）天无极而日月光，千秋万"，篆书，字体方正。外以栉齿纹为廓。素宽平缘。

　　此镜纹饰布局层次清晰，模范规整，是同类镜中的典型器。（于怀珍）

Mirror with inscription of "*Lian Zhi Qian Hua*" and design of linked arcs   Eastern Han Dynasty

Diameter: 14.6cm, Thickness of rim: 0.7cm, Weight: 553gram

Collection of Huainan Museum

The mirror is round in shape. It has a half-sphere-shaped knob on a base with continuous beads. Between fine-toothed bands have a broad string band and a band of eight linked arcs and is decorated with short lines and arcs in blank. The outer band of inscription of "*Lian Zhi Qian Hua Qing Er Ming, Yi Zhi Wei Jing Yi Wen Zhang, Yan Nian Yi Shou Bi Bu Xiang, Tian Wu Ji Er Ri Yue*

Guang, Qian Qiu Wan" in seal script, is surrounded with a band of fine-toothed pattern. The mirror has a broad and flat rim without design.

The mirror with symmetrical and clear layout is the treasure of this kind of mirrors.   (Yu Huaizhen)

长宜子孙铭连弧云雷纹镜　东汉

直径20.7厘米，边厚0.6厘米，重864克
本馆旧藏

　　圆形，半球钮，柿蒂纹钮座，四柿叶间各一字铭，合为"长宜子孙"，篆书。其外为一周短直线纹和一周凸弦纹带，中区饰内向八连弧纹，连弧间有短线纹和小乳钉，隐喻日、月、山川。外区饰八组云雷纹，云雷纹由圆圈涡纹与对置的双重三角纹组成，两侧以两周短直线纹装饰。宽素平缘。

　　连弧纹镜始于战国晚期，流行于西汉至东汉中期。这面连弧纹镜与河南洛阳东汉中期墓出土镜纹饰相同，应在东汉早期。此镜造型规整、纹饰清晰、镜体敦厚，是汉镜中的佳品。（文立中）

Mirror with design of linked arcs and cloud and thunder and inscription of "*Chang Yi Zi Sun*"   Eastern Han Dynasty

Diameter: 20.7cm, Thickness of rim: 0.6cm, Weight: 864gram

Collection of Huainan Museum

The mirror is round in shape. It has a half-sphere-shaped knob on a base with kaki calyx design, four leaves of which are spaced with inscription of "*Chang Yi Zi Sun*" in seal script. Outside the base have a band of fine-toothed pattern and a band of raised string pattern. The major motif is a band of eight linked arcs inside and eight groups of cloud and thunder design. Inside the arcs are adorned with short lines and nipples representing sun, moon and mountains. The design of cloud and thunder is formed with whorl pattern and opposite overlapping triangles pattern and

is surrounded with two short lines at both sides. The mirror has a broad and flat rim without design.

The mirror with linked arcs design appeared in late Warring States Period and was popular from the Western Han Dynasty to the middle Eastern Han Dynasty. Similar with the decoration of the mirror of Eastern Han Dynasty unearthed in Luoyang, Henan, it is referred as a mirror of early Eastern Han Dynasty. The mirror with symmetrical layout, clear decoration and heavy body is the treasure of Han mirrors.   (Wen Lizhong)

四乳四兽镜 东汉
直径9.6厘米，边厚0.5厘米，重181克
本馆旧藏

　　圆形，半球钮，圆钮座。座外环一周弦纹。主纹为四乳四兽，四乳有座，间饰相同的四兽，形似蛙状，皆一足前伸，后足粗壮，长须飘扬。外侧以一周栉齿纹为栏。斜缘，缘上饰两组纹饰，内为三角锯齿纹，外为双线水波纹。该镜纹饰简练自然，兽纹形态生动，别具一格。（程东雯）

Mirror with design of four nipples and four animals Eastern Han Dynasty

Diameter: 9.6cm, Thickness of rim: 0.5cm, Weight: 181gram

Collection of Huainan Museum

The mirror is round in shape. It has a half-sphere-shaped knob on a round base. Outside the base is surrounded a band of string pattern. The major motif is the design of four nipples with bases and four frog-shaped animals spaced with nipples. Outside the major motif is adorned with a band of fine-toothed pattern. The slanted rim is decorated with a band of saw pattern and a band of wave pattern formed by double lines. The mirror with refined decoration and vivid animal design has an unique style.   (Chen Dongwen)

龙虎纹博局镜 东汉

直径11.7厘米，边厚0.4厘米，重286克

本馆旧藏

圆形，半球钮，柿蒂纹钮座。座外环一弦纹宽带框，框内置星月纹，框外饰博局纹，博局纹之间饰龙虎纹，两两相对，作奔走状，外侧以斜向栉齿纹为廓。宽缘，缘中饰双线波折纹。（汪茂东）

Mirror with design of dragon, tiger and gambling Eastern Han Dynasty

Diameter: 11.7cm, Thickness of rim: 0.4cm, Weight: 286gram

Collection of Huainan Museum

The mirror is round in shape. It has a half-sphere-shaped knob on a base with kaki calyx design. Outside the base has a square formed by string design. Inside the square is adorned with crescent design. The gambling design adorns outside the square, which is spaced with design of dragon and tiger running and facing each other. The motif ends with a band of fine-toothed pattern. The broad rim is decorated with wave pattern formed by double lines. (Wang Maodong)

四神简化博局镜　东汉

直径11厘米，边厚0.5厘米，重234克
淮南市废品收购站拣选

圆形，半球钮，圆钮座。座外双阳线勾勒方框，方框内四角各有一"小"字形花叶纹，框外四边中点各向外伸出一个双线"T"形纹，而四角与外圈向内伸出的四个双线"V"形纹相对，并将内区等分为四份，内饰四神，按东西南北四方分别为青龙、白虎、朱雀、玄武，外以一圈栉齿纹为廓。宽平缘，上饰一周双线三角纹。此镜中无一般规矩镜中常见的双线"L"形纹，为早期简化博局镜。

四神博局镜出现于西汉中晚期，以王莽时最为流行和精美。简化博局镜流行于东汉中晚期。（刘继武）

Mirror with design of four deities and simple gambling　Eastern Han Dynasty

Diameter: 11cm, Thickness of rim: 0.5cm, Weight: 234gram
Collected at a recycling center in Huainan City

The mirror is round in shape. It has a half-sphere-shaped knob on a round base. Outside the base is adorned with a square formed by double lines. Each corner inside the square has a grass blade design in shape of "*Xiao*" character. A T-shaped design formed by double lines is stretching out of the middle of each side of the square. The V-shaped design formed by double lines and stretching out of the rim corresponds with each corner of the square and divides the ground into quarters. Each quarter is adorned with a deity, Green Dragon in east, White Tiger in west, Scarlet Bird in south and Somber Warrior in north. The major motif ends with a band of fine-toothed pattern. The broad rim is adorned with design of triangle formed by double lines. The mirror has not L-shaped design and is an early mirror with simple gambling design.

The mirror with design of four deities and gambling appeared in middle and late Western Han Dynasty and was popular in Xin Dynasty. The mirror with simple gambling design was popular in middle and late Eastern Han Dynasty. (Liu Jiwu)

简化博局镜 东汉
直径10.1厘米，边厚0.5厘米，重245克
本馆旧藏

　　圆形，半球钮，圆钮座。座外有一双线方框纹，方框内四角有二条对角线与钮座相连。方框外是简化博局纹。其间点缀八个卷云纹，镜缘内侧与主区纹饰间有一周栉齿纹、两周弦纹。镜缘较宽，缘面上饰有两组纹饰，内为三角锯齿纹，外为波折纹。博局镜流行于西汉中晚期至东汉早期，到东汉中后期博局纹及其相间的纹饰逐步简化。（程东雯）

Mirror with simple gambling design　Eastern Han Dynasty
Diameter: 10.1cm, Thickness of rim: 0.5cm, Weight: 245gram
Collection of Huainan Museum

　　The mirror is round in shape. It has a half-sphere-shaped knob on a round base. Outside the base has a square formed by double lines. Inside the square have two diagonal lines across the base. The simple gambling design adorns outside the square and is spaced with cirrus clouds design. There are a band of fine-toothed pattern and two bands of string pattern between the rim and the major motif. The broad rim is decorated with a band of saw pattern and a band of wave pattern. The mirror with gambling design was popular from middle and late Western Han Dynasty to early Eastern Han Dynasty. Its decoration was simplified in middle and late Eastern Han Dynasty.　(Chen Dongwen)

禽鸟简化博局镜　东汉
直径9.5厘米，边厚0.3厘米，重128克
本馆旧藏

　　圆形，半球钮，圆钮座。座外为一双线方格，方格外四角各饰一对禽鸟纹，隔角相对而望，其下有两片叶纹。方格四边中间各出一"T"形双线纹，外围有一周栉齿纹为廓。缘面较宽，上有一组锯齿纹，外侧为斜面。

　　此镜纹饰简练，纹饰生动自然。（陶佳）

Mirror with design of birds and simple gambling　Eastern Han Dynasty
Diameter: 9.5cm, Thickness of rim: 0.3cm, Weight: 128gram
Collection of Huainan Museum

　　The mirror is round in shape. It has a half-sphere-shaped knob on a round base. Outside the base is adorned with a square formed by double lines. Each corner of the square has a couple of birds facing each other and a grass blade design. A T-shaped design formed by double lines is stretching out of the middle of each side of the square. The major motif ends with a band of fine-toothed design. The broad rim is decorated with a band of saw pattern and has a slanted surface.

　　The mirror with gambling design was popular from middle Western Han Dynasty to early Eastern Han Dynasty. The mirror has a vivid and natural decoration.　(Tao Jia)

简化博局镜 东汉

直径9.8厘米，边厚0.4厘米，重205克
2010年9月淮南市谢家集公安分局移交

　　圆形，圆钮，圆钮座。座外饰双线方框纹，内有两条对角线穿过钮座，方框外四边中间各饰一双线"T"纹，外环两道细弦纹，空白处以三道短弧线作简单装饰。外区纹饰为双线三角纹，每一三角间皆饰一珠点，外区饰一周细弦纹和一周栉齿纹为栏。宽缘，缘上饰双线三角纹。

　　博局镜流行于西汉中晚期至东汉早期，但此镜仅有四个"T"形纹，而且整个纹饰布局和内容也简化到仅有一周双线三角纹，为典型的简化博局镜，流行于东汉中晚期。此镜含锡量较高，纹饰清晰，模铸规范，是同类镜中的精品。（孙梅）

Mirror with simple gambling design   Eastern Han Dynasty

Diameter: 9.8cm, Thickness of rim: 0.4cm, Weight: 205gram

Transferred by Xiejiaji District Public Security Bureau in Huainan City in September, 2010

The mirror is round in shape. It has a round knob on a round base. Outside the base has a square formed by double lines. Inside the square have two diagonal lines across the base. A T-shaped design is stretching out of each side of the square and is embraced with two short arcs. Outside T-shaped designs is surrounded with two bands of string pattern and a band of triangle pattern formed by double lines and is spaced with a small boss. Inside the rim have a band of string pattern and a band of fine-toothed design. The broad rim is decorated with triangle design formed by double lines.

The mirror with gambling design was popular from middle and late Western Han Dynasty to early Eastern Han Dynasty. This mirror has T-shaped simple gambling design and a band of triangle pattern formed double lines as major motif and is a typical mirror with simple gambling design which was popular in middle and late Eastern Han Dynasty. The mirror with high content of tin, clear decoration and delicate mold is a rare treasure.   (Sun Mei)

四神简化博局镜　东汉

直径10.2厘米，边厚0.4厘米，重189克
本馆旧藏

圆形，半球钮，圆钮座。座外弦纹内饰短直线纹，主纹以四乳分区，四乳靠近钮座，与"V"形符号的简化博局纹相对，四区内填饰青龙、白虎、朱雀、玄武四神图案，两侧以栉齿纹为廓；宽缘，上饰一周双线波折纹。四神，又称四灵、四象等，在汉代铜镜纹饰中常用，取其吉祥辟邪之意。（陶治强）

Mirror with four deities and simple gambling   Eastern Han Dynasty

Diameter: 10.2cm, Thickness of rim: 0.4cm, Weight: 189gram

Collection of Huainan Museum

The mirror is round in shape. It has a half-sphere-shaped knob on a round base. Outside the base is adorned with a string band with short lines. The ground is divided by four nipples around the base into four parts. Each nipple design corresponds with a simple V-shaped gambling design. Each part fills respectively with Green Dragon, White Tiger, Scarlet Bird and Somber Warrior.

The major motif ends with a band of fine-toothed pattern. The broad rim is decorated with a band of wave pattern formed by double lines. Four Deities, also called Four Intelligent Creatures or Animals of Four Quarters, were often seen in Han mirrors and has the meaning of bring luck and counteracting evil.   (Tao Zhiqiang)

五乳神兽镜 东汉

直径13.9厘米，边厚0.5厘米，重485克

本馆旧藏

　　圆形，半球钮，圆钮座。座外环两周弦纹，内作简单装饰。主题纹饰为五乳神兽，五乳有座，外环一周弦纹，内以四组三道弦纹装饰，主区五乳间饰以神兽，分别为羽人、青龙、白虎、朱雀、玄武，线条细腻，形象生动，主纹内外两侧以栉齿纹带为栏。镜缘较宽，缘上饰锯齿纹一周，双线三角纹一周，双线三角纹间每一折内饰一点珠纹。

　　五乳神兽镜流行于西汉晚期到东汉中期，四灵和羽人纹饰透出了汉代黄老思想。此镜纹饰繁丽，制作精细。（文立中）

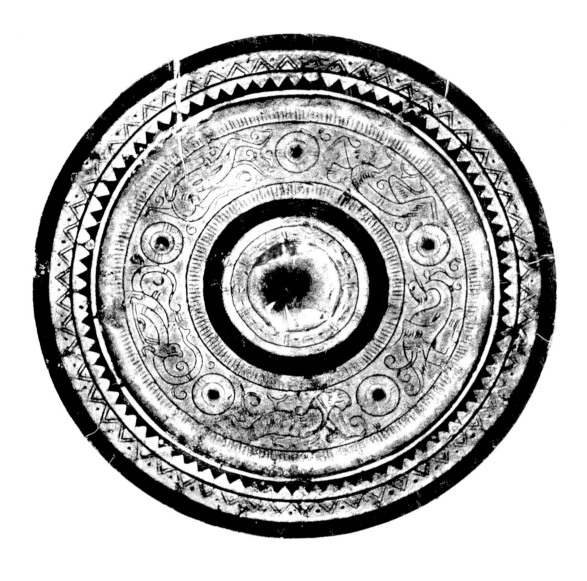

Mirror with design of five nipples and mythical animals   Eastern Han Dynasty

Diameter: 13.9cm, Thickness of rim: 0.5cm, Weight: 485gam

Collection of Huainan Museum

The mirror is round in shape. It has a half-sphere-shaped knob on a round base. Outside the base have two bands of string pattern inside which is adorned with simple design. The major motif is the design of five nipples with bases and mythical animals. It is surrounded with a band of string pattern spaced with four groups of three arcs. The mythical animals with delicate lines and vivid shapes are winged figure, Green Dragon, White Tiger, Scarlet Bird and Sober Warrior, which are apace with nipples. Two bands of fine-toothed pattern adorn both sides of the major motif. On the broad rim has a band of saw pattern and a band of triangle pattern formed with double lines and filled beads in blank.

The mirror with design of five nipples and mythical animals was popular from the late Western Han Dynasty to the middle Eastern Han Dynasty. Four Intelligent Creatures reflects the ideas of Huang-Lao School. This mirror shows exquisite decoration and refined craftsmanship.   (Wen Lizhong)

六乳神兽镜 东汉

直径13.4厘米，边厚0.5厘米，重411克

1982年12月淮南市官集公社林巷一队出土

圆形，乳钮，柿蒂纹钮座。座外饰一周细弦纹和宽带弦纹，内作若干简单装饰；主纹为六乳神兽，六乳有座，外环以细弦纹，且内作短线纹装饰，神兽分别为青龙、白虎、朱雀、玄武、独角兽、羽人，为细线条勾勒，形态生动，两侧皆以栉齿纹为廓。宽缘，上饰三角锯齿纹和双线波折纹两周，其间饰一周弦纹。此镜制范精细，纹饰布局均匀，四神造型饱满，是此类镜中的佳品。（汪茂东）

Mirror with design of six nipples and mythical animals   Eastern Han Dynasty

Diameter: 13.4cm, Thickness of rim: 0.5cm, Weight: 411gram

Unearthed at Linxiang First Brigade, Gongji Commune in Huainan City in December, 1982

The mirror is round in shape. It has a nipple-shaped knob on a base with kaki calyx design. Outside the base have a band of string pattern and a broad band of string pattern, between which is adorned with simple design. The major design is the design of six nipples with bases and mythical animals, which is adorned with short lines and surrounded with string pattern. The mythical animals are formed with fine lines and in vivid shapes of Green Dragon, White Tiger, Scarlet Bird, Somber Warrior, unicorn and winged figure. The bands of fine-toothed pattern adorn both sides of the major motif. On the broad rim has saw pattern and wave pattern formed with double lines, which are spaced with string pattern. The mirror with delicate mold, symmetrical layout and vivid design, is the treasure of the bronze mirror.   (Wang Maodong)

七乳神兽镜　东汉

直径16.4厘米，边厚0.5厘米，重717克

1958年淮南市唐山公社出土

　　圆形，乳钮，圆钮座。座外环九个带座乳钉，外环一周细弦纹，弦纹两侧空白处填以简单装饰。镜背以一周宽带弦纹隔开，外区饰七乳七神兽，七乳有座，神兽分别为羽人、青龙、凤鸟、朱雀、白虎、神鹿等，皆为细线条勾画，刻画细腻，形态生动；两侧以斜向栉齿纹为廓。宽缘，上饰三角锯齿纹和双线波

折纹各一周。

　　汉代铜镜背面装饰的乳钉纹有单有双，七乳间配七神兽，古人称为"七子镜"。此镜模范规整清晰，纹饰层次分明，线条简约流畅，属此类汉镜中的佳品。（汪茂东）

Mirror with design of seven nipples and mythical animals Eastern Han Dynasty

Diameter: 16.4cm, Thickness of rim: 0.5cm, Weight: 717gram

Unearthed at Tangshan Commune in Huainan City in 1958

The mirror is round in shape. It has a nipple-shaped knob on a round base. Outside the base is surrounded with nine nipples with bases. The nipples are also surrounded with a band of string pattern and a broad band of string pattern, between which is adorned with simple design. The major motif is the design of seven nipples with bases and seven mythical animals including winged figure, Green Dragon, phoenix, Scarlet Bird, White Tiger and deer. The animals are formed with fine lines and have vivid shapes. The bands of fine-toothed pattern adorn both sides of the major motif. On the broad rim has a band of saw pattern and a band of wave pattern formed with double lines.

In Han Dynasty, the nipples adorn the back of the mirror in odd number or even number. The mirror with design of seven nipples and seven mythical animals was called Qi Zi Mirror in ancient time. The mirror with exquisite and clear decoration is the treasure of the bronze mirrors.   (Wang Maodong)

七乳四神禽兽镜 东汉
直径11.6厘米，边厚0.5厘米，重262克
1984年6月淮南市物资回收公司拣选

　　圆形，圆钮，圆钮座。座外饰四组短直线和一周凸弦纹。主纹以两周栉齿纹为廓，内饰七乳七兽，七乳有座，外围六内向连弧纹；七瑞兽分别为青龙、白虎、朱雀、玄武、神鹿、吉羊、羽人。宽缘，上饰一周锯齿纹和一周双线波折纹。

　　此镜在七乳钉外饰连弧纹，比较少见，使用时间也短，仅在王莽时期及稍后的时间内偶见。镜背纹饰线条流畅，禽兽动感十足，栩栩如生。（闫晓娟）

Mirror with design of seven nipples, four deities and animals   Eastern Han Dynasty

Diameter: 11.6cm, Thickness of rim: 0.5cm, Weight: 262gram

Got from a material recycling company in Huainan City

The mirror is round in shape. It has a round knob on a round base. Outside the base have four groups of short straight lines and a band of raised string pattern. Both sides of the major motif are surrounded with two bands of fine-toothed pattern. The major motif is the design of seven nipples with bases, outside which is adorned with six linked arcs inward, and seven mythical animals including Green Dragon, White Tiger, Scarlet Bird, Somber Warrior, deer,

ram and winged figure. The broad rim has a band of saw pattern and a band of wave pattern formed with double lines.

The design of seven nipples adorned with linked arcs is rare to be found on the mirror decoration. It was used in a small account during Xin Dynasty and later time. This mirror has vivid decoration with flowing lines.   (Yan Xiaojuan)

龙虎对峙镜 东汉
直径19.55厘米，厚0.5厘米，重762.5克
1958年淮南市唐山公社出土

　　此镜形制较大，纹饰繁缛精美，是东汉时期铜镜中的珍品。

　　圆形，乳钮，圆钮座。中区有一高浮雕硕大盘龙，环绕乳钉与虎对峙，龙虎皆饰突起的羽状纹。龙纹形态较虎纹要大，二兽均大张口、怒目、侧身，龙爪弯曲，龙后羽展开，卷曲至虎首下。此镜高浮雕、细线与面结合，遒劲有力，十分生动。中区与外区间以双细线弦纹。外区六个四叶柿蒂座小乳钉分成六个

环绕区。一、二区各饰一匹飞马，前马张口回首，后马张口低首，马首后鬃毛直立，两飞马鬃前有反文铭，应是马的自铭："赤诵马"和"王桥马"。三区饰螭龙，侧身，头部有后飘长角，作飞奔状。四区饰鸟瞰状螭龙，龙首伏于腹上，双目怒视。独角后甩。五区饰长颈回首状龙，张口圆目。六区饰正面螭龙，口部夸张有巨齿。中区与外区饰双弦纹，间以环绕的栉纹。镜缘饰变形勾连螭纹。（沈汗青）

Mirror with design of dragon and tiger facing each other   Eastern Han Dynasty

Diameter: 19.55cm, Thickness: 0.5cm, Weight: 762.5gram

Unearthed at Tangshan Commune in Huainan City in 1958

The mirror with shape in a large scale and exquisite decoration is a treasure of the bronze mirrors in Eastern Han Dynasty.

The mirror is round in shape. It has a nipple-shaped knob on a round base. Around the base is the design of bigger dragon and tiger facing each other and adorned with raised feather-like pattern, both which have opening mouth, glaring eyes. The inner and outer parts are divided with string pattern formed with double lines. The outer part is adorned with design of flying horse with inscription of "*Chi Song Ma*", flying horse with inscription of "*Wang Qiao Ma*", hornless dragon, bird looking at dragon, dragon looking back and the front of dragon, which are spaced with nipples design with bases decorated with kaki calyx. The rim is decorated with stylized design of hornless dragon.   (Shen Hanqing)

张氏铭龙虎镜 东汉

直径14.8厘米，边厚1.1厘米，重812克
本馆旧藏

　　圆形，乳钮，圆钮座。钮座两侧饰一龙一虎，龙虎张口、怒目、侧身卷曲，身躯重点部位饰大乳钉加以突出。龙长角，身饰鳞纹，爪粗壮弯曲，长卷尾；虎曲身，空白处填以小乳钉，外以弦纹为廓。其外环以一周铭文圈带，文"张氏作镜四夷服，多贺君众人民息，胡虏殄灭天下复，风雨时节五谷熟，长保二亲

子孙力"，外环饰栉齿纹一周。宽缘，上饰三角锯齿纹、双线波折纹和三角锯齿纹各一周。

　　此镜龙虎遒劲有力，形象生动。作为神兽的龙，能降妖伏魔，是吉祥、英勇和权贵的象征；虎作为百兽之王，可保安宁。两兽相聚，可谓"生龙活虎"，吉祥、富贵、安宁。（汪茂东）

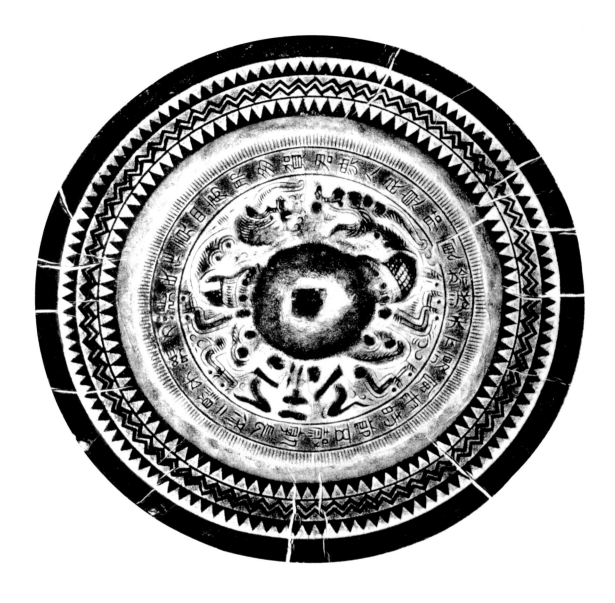

Mirror with inscription of "*Zhang Shi*" and design of dragon and tiger   Eastern Han Dynasty

Diameter: 14.8cm, Thickness of rim: 1.1, Weight: 812gram

Collection of Huainan Museum

The mirror is round in shape. It has a nipple-shaped knob on a round base. Around the base is adorned with dragon and tiger design with nipples which is surrounded with string pattern. Outside the string pattern has a band of inscription "*Zhang Shi Zuo Jing Si Yi Fu, Duo He Jun Zhong Ren Min Xi, Hu Lu Tian Mie Tian Xia Fu, Feng Yu Shi Jie Wu Gu Shu, Chang Bao Er Qin Zi Sun Li*" which is surrounded with a band of fine-toothed pattern. The broad rim is decorated with two bands of saw pattern and a band of wave pattern formed with double lines.

The dragon, as one of mythical animal, keeps away evil and represents the symbol of luck, courage and power. And the tiger, king of animals, keeps peace. The mirror with strong and vivid design of dragon and tiger has a meaning of keeping luck, wealth and peace. (Wang Maodong)

三虎镜 东汉

直径7.9厘米，边厚0.3厘米，重88克
1988年11月于淮南市上窑镇金宝钱处征集

　　圆形，圆钮，圆钮座。座下环绕三虎纹。三虎采用浮雕手法塑造，两虎头右尾左，一虎头左尾右，三虎体态大小相仿：头部硕大，低首而缩颈；尾部粗壮，下垂而后卷；腰身下弓，四肢微曲下蹲，呈待机捕猎状。虎纹外依次饰弦纹、栉齿纹、三角锯齿纹各一周。镜缘坡起，内缓外陡，呈三角状。

　　神兽镜盛行于东汉中后期至三国六朝时期。此镜以虎纹作为主题纹饰，亦属神兽镜范畴。其纹饰采用浮雕技法，环绕式布局，极具鲜明的时代特色。（刘继武）

Mirror with design of three tigers Eastern Han Dynasty

Diameter: 7.9cm, Thickness of rim: 0.3cm, Weight: 88gram
Collected from Jin Baoqian at Shangyao Town in Huainan City in November, 1988

　　The mirror is round in shape. It has a round knob on a round base. Around the base is surrounded with three tigers in relief, among which two have heads on right and tails on left and one head on left and tail on right. Outside the tigers design is adorned with string pattern, fine-toothed pattern and triangle-shaped saw pattern. The rim is sloping and has a surface in triangle shape.

　　The mirror with mythical animal design was popular from middle and late Eastern Han Dynasty to Three Kingdoms and Six Dynasties. The mirror with tiger design is one of mirrors with mythical animal and has distinct features of the time for decoration in relief and layout surrounding. (Liu Jiwu)

三虎镜 东汉
直径9厘米，边厚0.5厘米，重149克
1988年11月于淮南市上窑镇金宝钱处征集

圆形，半球钮，圆钮座。主纹饰有三只浮雕瑞虎，两虎对峙，一虎横卧，虎头硕大，圆目，张口，后足健壮有力，作蹬踏状。外侧饰两周栉齿纹和一周水波纹。宽斜缘。虎纹镜流行于汉魏时期。此镜瑞虎纹饰动感强烈，线条洗练，栩栩如生。（于怀珍）

Mirror with three-tiger design   Eastern Han Dynasty
Diameter: 9cm, Thickness of rim: 0.5cm, Weight: 149gram
Collected from Jin Baoqian at Shangyao Town in Huainan City in November, 1988

The mirror is round in shape. It has a half-sphere-shaped knob on a round base. The major motif is the design of three tigers with big heads, round eyes, opening eyes and strong back legs stretching, among which two are facing each other and one lying. The major design is surrounded with two fine-toothed bands and a wave band. The mirror has a broad and slanting rim. The mirror with tiger design was popular in Han and Wei Dynasties. The tiger design on this mirror is carved with simple lines and has a vivid effect.   (Yu Huaizhen)

盘龙镜 东汉
直径10厘米，边厚0.5厘米，重180克
本馆旧藏

　　圆形，半球钮，圆钮座。绕座饰一盘龙纹，盘龙独角，张口，獠牙，颈部细长，上饰乳钉和短弧线纹，四肢张开，后肢粗壮有力，作屈蹲状，似要推动外侧纹饰转动，尾卷曲。外区饰栉齿纹和三角锯齿纹各一周。缘坡起，内缓外陡，呈三角形。

　　此镜盘龙造型的表现手法与一般高浮雕盘龙纹不同，作浅浮雕线条式样，但纹饰立体感强，由里向外呈阶梯状排列，这种排列方式突出了盘龙纹，使得整个盘龙造型栩栩如生。（单超）

Mirror with coiling dragon design   Eastern Han Dynasty
Diameter: 10cm, Thickness of rim: 0.5cm, Weight: 180gram
Collection of Huainan Museum

The mirror is round in shape. It has a half-sphere-shaped knob on a round base. Around the base has a coiling dragon in shape of single horn, opening mouth, thin and long neck adorned with nipples and short arcs, strong back legs stretching and coiling tail. The dragon design is surrounded with fine-toothed band and saw pattern band. The rim is sloping and has a surface in triangle shape.

Differed from the coiling dragon design in high relief, the dragon design in low relief on this mirror is in stepping layout from outside to inside and appears in vivid and strong shape.   (Shan Chao)

171

神兽镜 东汉

直径9.5厘米，边厚0.3厘米，重129克

2010年8月淮南市谢家集公安分局移交

　　圆形，乳钮，圆钮座。镜背内区重列三段神兽或神人：第一段中间端坐一神人，两侧各饰以神兽，屈肢作伺候状；第二段在镜钮两侧各坐一神人，皆头戴高冠，左侧神人抬头作仰视钮上神人状；第三段在钮下方也端坐一神人，歪头，双手上举，衣着广袖，右衽。外区饰九半圆和九方枚，交错排列，方枚上有铭，铭文漫漶不清，试读为："□作明金幽涑三

□□"，外侧以三角锯齿纹为廓。镜缘坡起，缘上有一周铭文："吾作明镜，幽涑三商，周刻典祀，配象万疆，伯牙举乐，众神见（官）容，天（禽）四孝，福禄正（富）"。此镜布局分段不明显，镜钮的两侧神人还有绕钮趋向，神人神兽造型生动简约，制范精良，是东汉晚期流行的风格。（沈汗青）

Mirror with design of deities and beasts   Eastern Han Dynasty

Diameter: 9.5cm

Transferred by Xiejiaji District Public Security Bureau in Huainan City in August, 2010

The mirror is round in shape. It has a nipple-shaped knob on a round base. The back side of the mirror is decorated with three-layer design of gods and animals from mythology. The top layer is adorned with a god sitting with legendary creatures bending legs and serving on both sides. The middle layer has two gods wearing high crown on both sides of the base, the left one of which is looking up toward the god on the top. The bottom has a god cocking his head and raising his arms below the base. Nine half circles and squares are alternately arranged and surround the major motif. On each square has a character. The inscription shows unclearly "□ *Zuo Ming Jin You Lian San* □□". The saw pattern with triangle shape surrounds the inscription. The sloping rim is carved a band of inscription "*Wu Zuo Ming Jing, You Lian San Shang, Zhou Ke Dian Si, Pei Xiang Wan Jiang, Bo Ya Ju Le, Zhong Shen Jian (Guan) Rong, Tian (Qin) Si Xiao, Fu Lu Zheng (Fu)*". The deities deign tends to surround the base, so the layers are not formed obviously. The design with vivid shape and refined craftsmanship represents the common style of late Eastern Han Dynasty.   (Shen Hanqing)

三段式神兽画像镜 东汉·建安二十年

直径11.6厘米，厚0.3厘米，重187克
本馆旧藏

圆形，圆钮，钮外环绕一周小乳钉纹，主纹分为三段，分段明显：第一段西王母居中，跪坐姿势，身穿宽袖窄衣，头上梳两个隆起的发髻。右侧为东王公，面向西王母笼袖而坐，左侧为一神人，作奏乐侍从状；第二段为两神人，在乳钉钮两侧对称安坐，面部略向内偏；第三段位于乳钉下，为两个昂首神人，呈奏乐状，两神人后各有一侧身神像，左侧神人为老者态，饰冕，身体卷曲成龙形，龙身向上翻卷至东王公，右侧为一神龙，龙首在上，龙身向下卷曲。镜缘铭"吾作明镜，幽涷三商，官克……虎，天皇五帝伯牙单琴，吉羊……白虎青龙，建安二十年"。

此镜属西王母群仙画像镜。西王母神话最早见于《山海经》，传说因周穆王在十三年时到瑶池拜会了西王母。神兽镜主要出土在长江以南地区，淮河以北鲜见，铸造产地主要在浙江会稽和湖北鄂州一带，其纹饰题材基本上是反映道家神仙。铭文建安二十年是公元215年，已至东汉末年。（沈汗青）

Mirror with three-layer portraits of deities and beasts   the 20th year of the Emperor Jian'an of the Eastern Han Dynasty

Diameter: 11.6cm, Thickness: 0.3cm, Weight: 187gram
Collection of Huainan Museum

The mirror is round in shape. It has a round knob on a base adorned with small nipples. The major motif is formed with three layers. On the top layer is the Royal Lady of the West sitting in the middle, the Royal Lord of the East sitting towards the Royal Lady of the West on the right and a god playing the music on the left; on the middle layer is two gods sitting on both sides of the base; on the bottom is two gods looking upward, playing music and accompanying an old man wearing a crown and curving his body in dragon shape on the left and a dragon on the right. The rim has a band of inscription "*Wu Zuo Ming Jing, You Lian San Shang, Guan Ke … Hu, Tian Huang Wu Di Bo Ya Tan Qin, Ji Yang … Bai Hu*

Qing Long, Jian An Er Shi Nian".

The mirror is decorated with portraits of Royal Lady of the West and deities. It is recorded first in *Shan Hai Jing* that the Royal Lady of the West made a visit with King Mu at Jasper Lake in the 13th year of the King Mu of Zhou Dynasty. This kind of mirrors was unearthed mainly in the south of Changjiang River and rarely in north of Huai River. It was cast in the area along Huiji of Zhejiang Province and Ezhou of Hubei Province. The design, in the main, is the gods of Taoism. The 20th year of Jian'an is 215AD and in the period of late Eastern Han Dynasty.   (Shen Hanqing)

吾作明镜铭重列式神兽镜　三国

直径12.1厘米，边厚0.4厘米，重338克
2010年11月淮南市康杰先生捐赠

　　圆形，圆钮，钮顶平。镜背为重列式排列，自上而下分为五段。第一段中间端坐一神人，正面，两侧各列一神鸟；第二段中间直列铭文"宜官"二字，两侧各端坐二神人，神人背后侧立一神鸟；第三段以镜钮为中心，两侧各列坐二神人；第四段中间有直行铭文"宜官"二字，两侧端坐一侧面神人；第五段中间铭文下端坐一正面神人。在四、五段间左侧饰凤，右侧饰龙。镜缘坡起，以双细弦纹为廓，中间环一周铭，试识为："吾作明镜，吉庚马，官吏酉象，五帝□曰天皇，伯乐弹琴，黄帝除凶，未昌玄武，白帝青龙，吏宜高官，四月□"

　　此镜饰有十二个神人，八个神兽禽鸟，镜背布置得十分饱满，繁而不乱。与《中国图镜图典》收录的建安十年重列式神兽镜在布局上基本相似，应是同一时段的作品。（沈汗青）

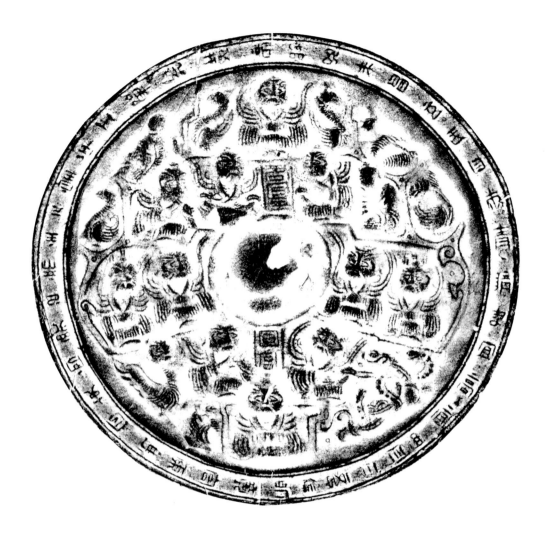

Mirror with inscription of "*Wu Zuo Ming Jing*" and layers of deities and beasts   Three Kingdoms Period

Diameter: 12.1cm, Thickness of rim: 0.4cm, Weight: 338gram

Donated by Mr. Kang Jie in Huainan City in November, 2010

The mirror is round in shape. It has a round knob with flat top. The back side of the mirror is decorated with designs in layers. There are five layers on the back. The top layer is adorned with a god with two birds on sides. The second layer is the inscription of "*Yi Guan*" in the middle and two gods on each side, on the back of which a bird is standing. The third layer is two gods on each side of the base. The forth layer is the inscription of "*Yi Guan*" and a god sitting on each side. The bottom layer is a god sitting below the inscription of the forth layer. Between the forth layer and the bottom is decorated with phoenix on the left and dragon on the right. On the sloping rim is adorned with a band of inscription "*Wu Zuo Ming Jing, Ji Geng Ma, Guan Li You Xiang, Wu Di □ Yue Tian Huang, Bo Le Tan Qin, Huang Di Chu Xiong, Wei Chang Xuan Wu, Bai Di Qing Long, Li Yi Gao Guan, Si Yue □*", both sides of which are arrounded with double-lined string pattern.

The mirror has a rich well-arranged decoration including twelve gods and eight birds. It has the time as early as the mirror with layers of deities and beasts in the 10th year of Jian'an listed in the *A Catalogue of Chinese Bronze Mirrors*.   (Shen Hanqing)

连弧纹半圆方枚镜　南朝

直径10.9厘米，边厚0.2厘米，重147克

本馆旧藏

　　圆形，圆钮，圆钮座。座外由三道宽弦纹组成三个环带，内环带饰有一圈联珠纹，中环带饰有一圈草叶纹，外环带饰有一圈联珠纹。镜中区为主纹饰带，饰有内向十一连弧纹，两弧纹连接处呈叶纹状，在每一个弧纹的下部各有一半圆枚。连弧纹外侧饰一周几何纹。镜背满铺联珠地纹。窄缘。此镜装饰风格较少见，是汉唐铜镜纹饰转化过渡时期的作品。（闫晓娟）

Mirror with design of linked arcs and half circles　Southern Dynasties

Diameter: 10.9cm, Thickness of rim: 0.2cm, Weight: 147gram

Collection of Huainan Museum

　　The mirror is round in shape. It has a round knob on a round base. Outside the base is adorned with bands of continuous beads inside and outside and a grass-leaf band in the middle, which are spaced with string pattern. The major motif is eleven linked arcs. The joint of two arcs is in shape of leaf. Below each arc has a half circle. The geometric pattern surrounds the major motif. The ground motif is design of continuous beads. The decoration style of this mirror is rarely found and represents the features of the bronze mirrors developing in transition period from Han Dynasty to Tang Dynasty.　(Yan Xiaojuan)

环绕式神兽镜 魏晋

直径13.3厘米，边厚0.6厘米，重548克

本馆旧藏

　　圆形，圆钮，圆钮座。纹饰以高圈弦纹分内外二区，内区为十神兽相间环绕，外区为半圆方枚带，半圆方枚错落有致，方枚上有铭文，字迹漫漶不清，无法释读。宽缘，上饰一周变形飞禽云气纹饰。（陶佳）

Mirror circled with deities and beasts　Wei and Jin Dynasties

Diameter: 13.3cm, Thickness of rim: 0.6cm, Weight: 548gram

Collection of Huainan Museum

　　The mirror is round in shape. It has a round knob on a round base. The major motif is divided into two parts by raised string pattern. Inner part is circled with ten beasts. Outer part is alternate designs of half circles and squares. On each square is carved an unclear character. The broad rim is adorned with stylized bird and cloud design.　(Tao Jia)

五月五日铭花卉镜　唐

直径6.8厘米，边厚0.7厘米，重124克
本馆旧藏

圆形，圆钮，圆钮座。一周高圈弦纹将镜背纹饰分为内外两区，高圈内外各饰一周细弦纹。内区围绕镜钮饰缠枝花纹，外区置"五月五日"四字铭文，楷书，阳文，顺时针旋读。每字间以小花朵纹，花朵均为九珠点构成。斜缘，上饰两周锯齿纹。

该镜的造型风格和纹饰还保留有汉魏以来的布局特征，应属唐代早期制镜。镜铭"五月五日"为中国传统的端午节，在唐时又被称为浴兰节。这一天人们要用兰汤沐浴，清洁身体，被除秽气，躲避瘟灾。民间认为悬挂端午日所铸之镜可以达到辟邪驱凶的目的，铭"五月五日"正是这一习俗的体现。（吴琳）

Mirror with inscription of "*Wu Yue Wu Ri*" and flower design　Tang Dynasty

Diameter: 6.8cm, Thickness of rim: 0.7cm, Weight: 124gram
Collection of Huainan Museum

The mirror is round in shape. It has a round knob on a round base. A band of raised string pattern divides the decoration into two parts, each side of which has a band of string pattern. The inner part is adorned with interlocking flowers around the knob. The outer part has a band of inscription "*Wu Yue Wu Ri*" in standard script and relief which are spaced with little flower formed with nine beads. The slanting rim is decorated with two bands of saw pattern.

The shape and design of this mirror keeps the features of the mirrors in Han and Wei Dynasties, so it is inferred that it was produced in early Tang Dynasty. The inscription "*Wu Yue Wu Ri*", which means the 5th day of 5th month, is the Dragon Boat Festival, also called Bath Festival in Tang Dyansty. On this day, people used to have a bath with boiled fragrant thoroughwort water in order to protect against death and devil. It was thought that hanging the mirror cast on Dragon Boat Festival can bring luck and peace, which can be comfirmed with the inscription of "*Wu Yue Wu Ri*". (Wu Lin)

四瑞兽镜　唐

直径9.6厘米，边厚0.9厘米，重213克
本馆旧藏

　　圆形，高圆钮，圆钮座。以一周高凸弦纹带将镜背分为内外两区。内区饰高浮雕四瑞兽，四瑞兽环绕钮同向奔跑，有昂首、侧首、背首、正首四个姿态，身躯饱满富于动感。外区饰一周缠枝花草。镜缘突起成两周弦纹，内弦略低，中间环一周联珠纹。1988年，广西兴安县出土一面与此相同铜镜。此类镜子流行于唐代早期，尚保留汉魏以来镜背分区的特点。
（沈汗青）

Mirror with design of four auspicious beasts　Tang Dynasty

Diameter: 9.6cm, Thickness of rim: 0.9cm, Weight: 213gram
Collection of Huainan Museum

　　The mirror is round in shape. It has a round knob on a round base. Its back side is divided into two parts by a band of raised string pattern. The inner part is adorned with four running auspicious beasts with raising head, turning head, the back of head and the front of head respectively. The ourer part is the design of interlocking flowers. The rim is decorated with a band of continous beads surrounded with string pattern on both sides. The mirror with the same decoration was unearthed in Xing'an County, Guagnxi Province in 1988. The mirror was popular in early Tang Dynasty and keeps the feature having parts on the back in Han and Wei Dynasties.　(Shen Hanqing)

双鸾双瑞兽镜 唐

直径16.9厘米，边厚0.35厘米，重494克

1960年淮南市唐山公社出土

　　圆形，圆钮，八瓣莲花钮座，钮与镜缘间饰双鸾双瑞兽。双鸾体型姿态大致相同，左侧平首，右侧低首，前翅振，后羽高卷。宽平缘。

　　铜镜发展到唐代达到了高峰，尤其是唐高宗至唐德宗的百余年时间里，铜镜制作达到了顶峰，无论是工艺、形制，还是花纹内容皆千变万化。鸾是古代传

说中的神瑞之鸟。《山海经》中记载："其状如翟而五采文，名曰鸾鸟，见则天下安宁。"双瑞兽，上侧瑞兽形如飞马状，但有角、短羽，有的学者识为独角兽，下部瑞兽形如飞狮。此镜纹饰简洁而生动，当属此期的代表作品。（沈汗青）

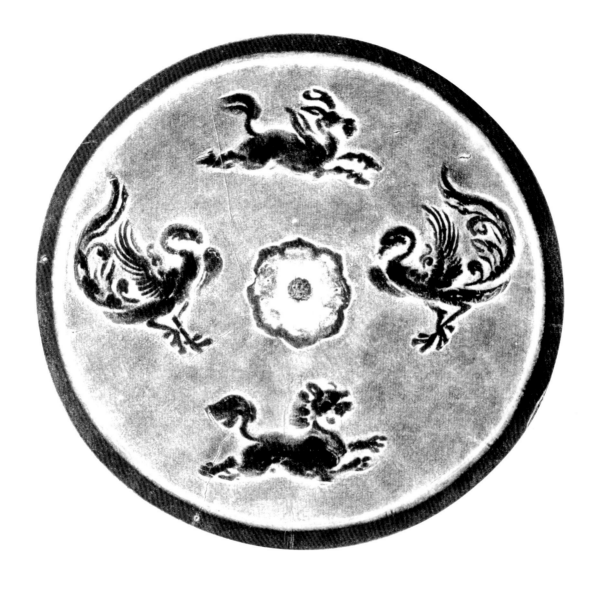

Mirror with design of double phoenixes and double auspicious animals   Tang Dynasty

Diameter: 16.9cm, Thickness of rim: 0.35cm, Weight: 494gram

Unearthed at Tangshan Commune in Huainan City in 1960

The mirror is round in shape. It has a round knob on an eight-petal lotus-shaped base. Between the knob and the rim is adorned with double phoenixes and double auspicious animals. The doubles phoenixes have heads bowing flatly and lowly respectively, wings opening up and tails rolling highly. The mirror has a broad and flat rim.

The Tang Dynasty is a peak period for the development of the bronze mirrors covering craftsmanship, shape and design,

especially over a hundred years from Emperor Gao to Emperor De. Luan, a mythical bird in legend, can be found the records in *Shan Hai Jing*. The auspicious animal on the top is in the shape of flying horse with horn and feathers and is regarded as the unicorn. The animal on the bottom is in the shape of flying lion. This mirror with simple and vivid decoration is the treasure of the Tang mirrors. (Shen Hanqing)

双鸾云鹊葵花镜　唐

直径12.5厘米，边厚0.6厘米，重1261克

本馆旧藏

　　八出葵花形，圆钮。镜背以一周凸弦纹分内外两区：内区钮两侧各置一凤鸟，相对展翅而立，尾羽高高扬起，脚踏如意云纹；钮上饰一衔绶鹊纹，展翅，高冠，作飞行状，钮下饰两朵云纹。外区在八出葵花内饰云纹和鸟纹，相间排列。素缘。

　　此类禽鸟镜是唐代具有代表性的镜式之一。铜镜的制作到唐代时合金比例更加科学，锡的比例加大，使镜背显得亮洁而有光泽，成像清晰，在制作工艺上达到了前所未有的成就。（任胜利）

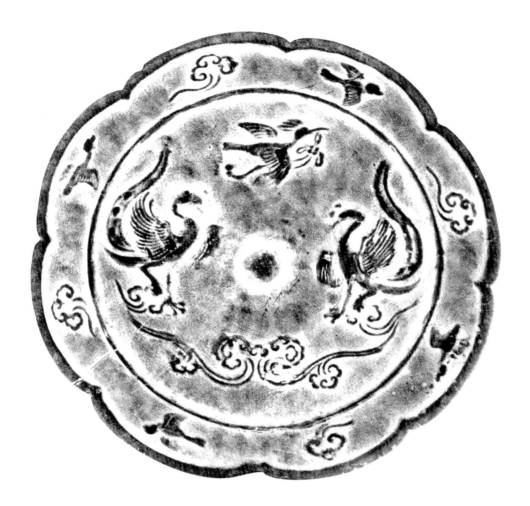

Mallow-shaped Mirror with design of double phoenixes, magpie Tang Dynasty

Diameter: 12.5cm, Thickness of rim: 0.6cm, Weight: 1261gram
Collection of Huainan Museum

The mirror is in shape of eight-petal mallow and has a round knob. Its back is divided into two parts by a band of raised string pattern. Each side of the knob has a phoenix standing on a S-shaped cloud face to face and raising tails. Above the konb is adorned with a magpie flying and holding ribbon. Below the knob have two clouds. Inside each petal of the rim is alternate arranged with clouds and birds. The rim has no design.

The mirror with bird design was one of the typical Tang mirrors. In Tang Dynasty, the mirror was cast with more tin in raw material and has a pleasing cover. The Tang Dynasty was another peak period for casting techniques of the bronze mirrors. (Ren Shengli)

四仙骑镜 唐

直径11.8厘米，边厚0.3厘米，重292克

1984年6月淮南市物资回收公司拣选

　　八出葵花形，圆钮。主纹为浅浮雕的四仙人骑兽跨鹤，兽、鹤皆体态矫健，昂首，绕钮同向飞行；仙人戴冠、披帛，分成两股后向后飘拂。二人骑仙鹤，二人骑瑞兽，作奔腾状。外以一周凸弦纹为廓。在八出葵花内侧近缘处饰四花四蜂蝶，间隔排列。素缘。

　　浙江宁波出土一面同类镜，直径12厘米。此类镜是唐代流行镜式之一，出土较多。（赵永林）

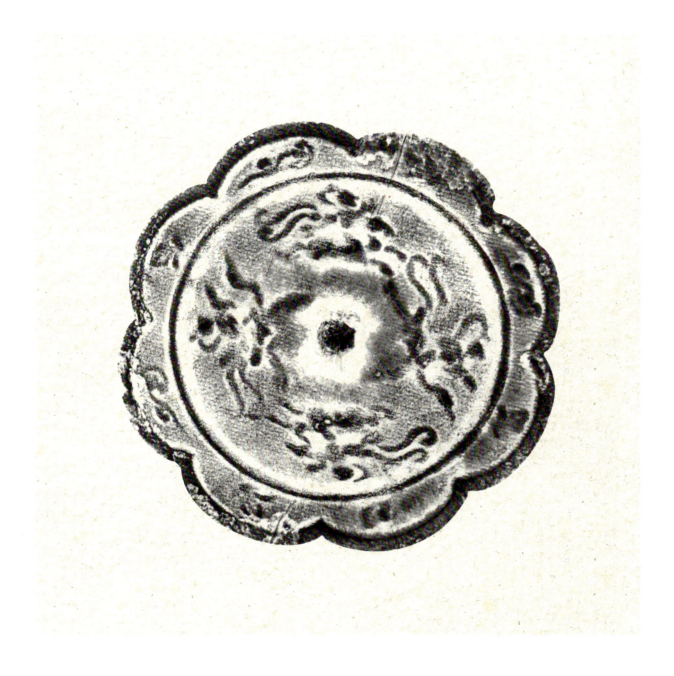

Mirror with design of four gods riding   Tang Dynasty

Diameter: 11.8cm, Thickness of rim: 0.3cm, Weight: 292gram

Got from a material recycling company in Huainan City in June, 1984

The mirror is in shape of eight-petal mallow and has a round knob. The motif design is carved in low relief, including two gods riding cranes and two riding auspicious animals. A band of raised string pattern surrounds the motif design. Inside each petal of the rim are arranged alternately flowers and butterflies. The rim has no design.

The mirror with the same decoration and diameter 12cm was unearthed in Ningbo City, Zhejiang Province. The mirror was popular in Tang Dynasty and was unearthed in a great number. (Zhao Yonglin)

瑞兽葡萄镜 唐

直径11.8厘米，边厚1.1厘米，重499克
1973年淮南市废品收购站拣选

    圆形，伏兽钮。由瑞兽和葡萄蔓枝构成主题纹饰，内区高浮雕四只瑞兽，呈伏卧状，首尾相连，其间绕以葡萄蔓枝叶实；外区为葡萄蔓枝叶和果实、飞禽相间。窄缘，近缘处饰以花草纹。

    瑞兽葡萄镜是将当时常见的葡萄纹样与传统的四神十二辰镜或四神镜等纹样结合起来，并将它们自由组合的产物。葡萄镜的图案是从波斯和拜占庭等地传来的，因而被日本学者称之为"凝结了欧亚大陆文明之镜"。该镜以柔长的枝条、舒展的花叶、丰硕的果实与生动活泼的瑞兽、纷飞的禽鸟构成一幅富有魅力的图案。（吴琳）

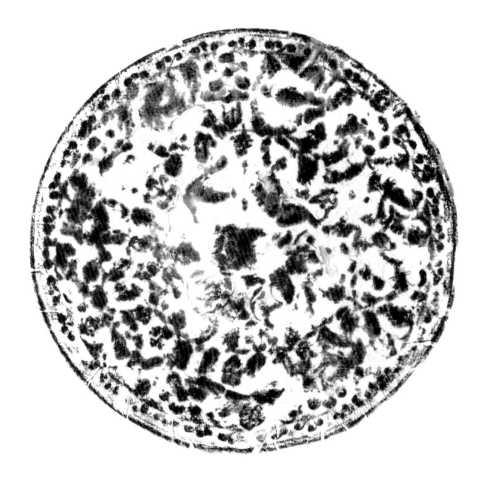

Mirror with design of auspicious animals and grapes   Tang Dynasty

Diameter: 11.8cm, Thickness of rim: 1.1cm, Weight: 499gram
Got from a material recycling company in Huainan City in 1973

The mirror is round in shape and has a squatting beast-shaped knob. The major motif includes auspicious animals and grapes. The inner part is adorned with four squatting auspicious animals in high relief which are surrounded with grapes. The outer part is the design of grapes and birds alternately arranged. Inside the narrow rim is decorated with flowers.

The design of auspicious animals and grapes is the combination of grape pattern with the traditional pattern of four deities and twelve Earthly Branches. The grape pattern was introduced from Persia and Byzantium, so the mirror with grape design is known for the melting civilization of Europe and Asia. This mirror brings a charming picture with long branches, beautiful flowers, rich fruits and vivid animals.   (Wu Lin)

葡萄缠枝花镜 唐

直径9厘米，边厚0.8厘米，重175克
本馆旧藏

　　圆形，圆钮，八花瓣钮座。镜背以高凸弦纹分成内外两区，内区由葡萄蔓枝叶实相间组成，外区为藤蔓相连的花草纹。尖缘。

　　此镜为我国铜镜发展史转型期的典型镜。隋唐时，铜镜出现了巨大的变化，除了形式上突破了圆形、方形的传统以外，还涌现了菱花形、葵花形等花式镜。在镜背的主题纹饰方面则表现为一改早期以灵异瑞兽为主的框框，取材由神话模式转为偏重自由写实，一洗汉式拘谨板滞之态而作流畅华丽之姿。这些变化不是一朝一夕完成的，是由隋和初唐的瑞兽镜、瑞兽葡萄镜、瑞兽鸾鸟镜发展而来的。该镜保留了瑞兽葡萄镜的风格，却将瑞兽省略，而以葡萄蔓枝为主，揭开了唐中期以后以花鸟为主题纹饰的序幕。（吴琳）

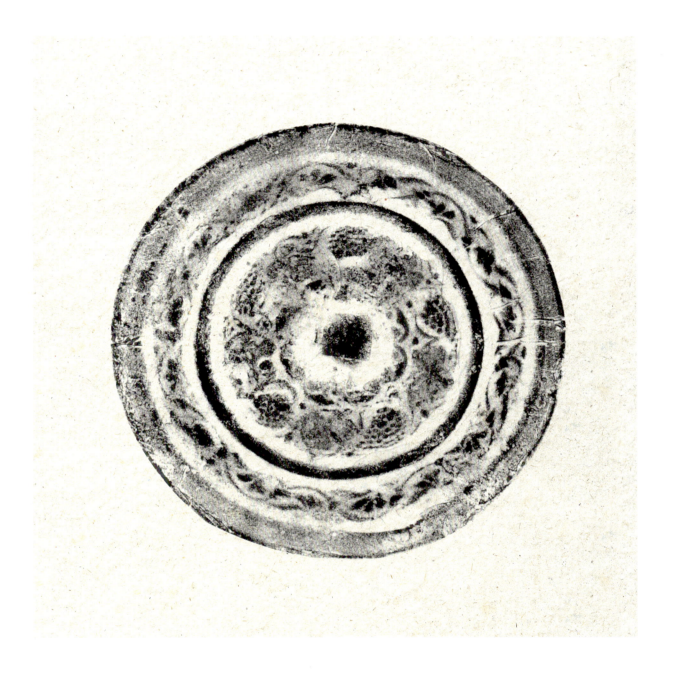

Mirror with design of grapes and interlocking flowers   Tang Dynasty

Diameter: 9cm, Thickness of rim: 0.8cm, Weight: 175gram
Collection of Huainan Museum

The mirror is round in shape. It has a round knob on an eight-petal base. Its back is divided into two parts by a band of raised string pattern. The inner part is adorned with branches and fruits of grape alternately arranged. The outer part is interlocking flowers. The mirror has a sharp rim.

This mirror is the representative style of the transitional period for the development of the bronze mirrors. In Sui and Tang Dynasties, the mirror had been great changes. Besides the round and square shape, there were new shapes like water chestnut shape, mallow shape, etc. The major motif had drawn its material from more real life than mythological beasts and appeared free and delicate decorative effect distinguished from stereotyped effect of Han Dynasty. These changes had developed step by step from mirror with auspicious beasts, mirror with auspicious beasts and grapes and mirror with auspicious animals and phoenixes of Sui and early Tang Dynasties. This mirror holds the style of the mirror with auspicious beasts, but uses the grapes as the major motif, which had opened the design of flower and bird as the major motif since middle and late Tang Dynasty.   (Wu Lin)

双鸾双瑞兽花枝镜 唐

直径11.8厘米，边厚0.6厘米，重401克

2010年9月淮南市谢家集公安分局移交

———

八瓣菱花形，伏兽钮。兽钮的头部写实，眼、鼻、口、耳等十分清晰，双鸾双兽环绕镜钮相间排列，并间隔以花枝和如意云纹。镜缘凸起，每菱花瓣中以流云、蜂蝶相间环置。此镜模铸精良，纹饰造型饱满，细腻清晰，镜背漆黑光亮，是唐镜中的佳品。（沈汗青）

Mirror with design of double phoenixes, double auspicious animals and flowers Tang Dynasty

Diameter: 11.8cm, Thickness of rim: 0.6cm, Weight: 401gram

Transferred by Xiejiaji District Public Security in Huainan City in September, 2010

The mirror is in shape of eight-petal water chestnut and has a squatting beast-shaped knob with realistic head. Around the knob is adorned with alternate arrangement of two phoenixes and two animals which are space with flowers and S-shaped clouds. The mirror has a raised rim. Each petal of the rim is adorned with alternated arrangement of drifting clouds and butterflies. The mirror, as a treasure of the Tang mirrors, boasts exquisite craftsmanship and a black patina all over the body. (Shen Hanqing)

双鸾双鸟镜 唐

直径17.3厘米，边厚0.4厘米，重689克

本馆旧藏

　　八出葵花形，圆钮。镜背以一周凸弦纹分成内外两区:内区在镜钮两侧各饰一系绶鸾鸟，鸾鸟曲颈相对，足踏莲花宝枝，展翅翩翩起舞，绶尾向上飘起;钮上下各饰一飞鸟，同向飞行，上鸟羽翼向上振起，口衔葡萄枝实，下鸟双翼平展，口衔一长绶带。外区在八出葵花内饰相间环绕的带苞花叶和蜂蝶。素缘。该镜是唐代常见的花鸟镜，由花枝和鸟雀相间组合而成。古人把鸾鸟作为一种吉祥的禽鸟，常用于隐喻祥和、夫妻恩爱、健康和长寿等。（单超）

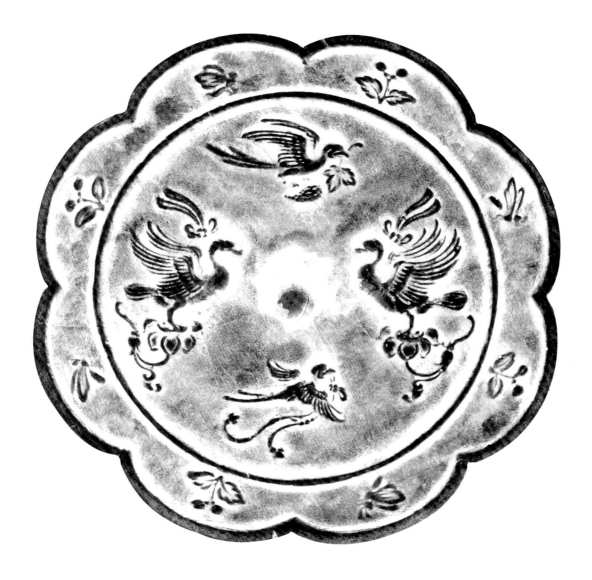

Mirror with design of double phoenixes and double birds Tang Dynasty

Diameter: 17.3cm, Thickness of rim: 0.4cm, Weight: 689gram

Collection of Huainan Museum

The mirror is in shape of eight-petal mallow and has a round knob. The back of the mirror is divided into two parts by a band of raised string pattern. Both sides of the knob are adorned with two phoenixes holding ribbons, facing each other, stepping on lotuses, spreading wings and dancing. The knob is decorated with a bird opening up its wings and holding grapes on the top and a bird opening flatly its wings and holding ribbon, both which are flying toward the same direction. Inside each petal of the rim is decorated with alternate arrangement of flowers and butterflies. The mirror has a rim without design. This mirror is one of the mirrors with flower and bird arranged alternately which are commonly used in Tang Dynasty. Phoenix, as a legendary lucky bird, is given the meaning of peace, deep love of a couple and health. (Shan Chao)

四仙骑兽镜　唐

直径11.6厘米，边厚0.5厘米，重287克

征集品

　　八出葵花形，内切圆形，圆钮。主纹为四仙人骑兽跨鹤，腾空飞翔，同向绕钮。仙人头戴冠，披帛穿过两胁，在背部呈圆弧线后分成两股，顺风飘拂。其中二仙人跨仙鹤，鹤展翅伸颈，作疾飞状；另二仙人骑瑞兽，兽四肢奔腾，作迅跑状。花枝蜂蝶纹缘。此镜是唐代流行镜之一，出土及传世品不少。（陶佳）

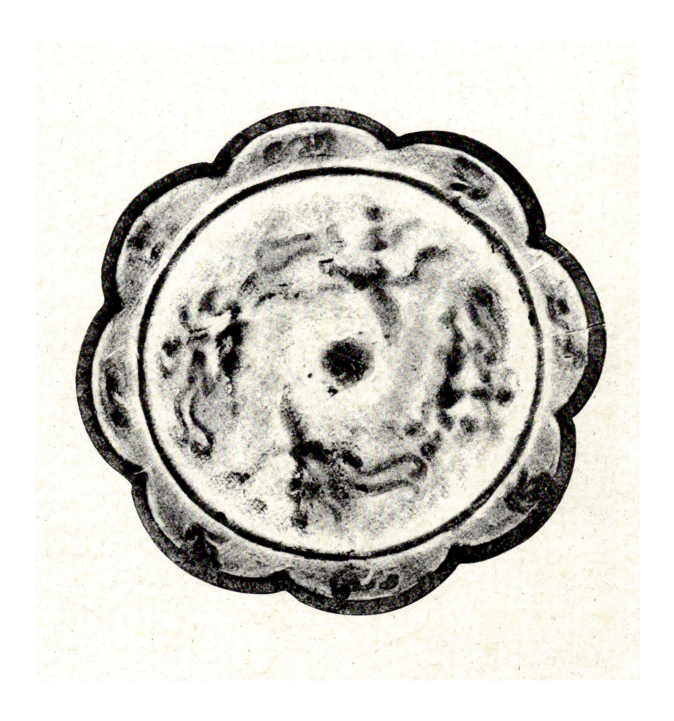

Mirror with design of four gods riding   Tang Dynasty
Diameter: 11.6cm, Thickness of rim: 0.5cm, Weight: 287gram
Collected

The mirror is in shape of eight-petal mallow and has a round knob. The major motif includes two gods riding two flying cranes and tow riding two running auspicious animals. The rim is adorned with flowers and butterflies. The mirror was popular in Tang Dynasty and was unearthed and handed down in a great number. (Tao Jia)

双鸾双瑞兽镜 唐

直径16.5厘米，边厚0.3厘米，重540克

本馆旧藏

　　圆形，圆形钮，莲花钮座。座外分别饰有双鸾双瑞兽，镜钮左右饰两只鸾鸟，展翅翘尾曲颈相对而立，镜钮上下饰双瑞兽，作飞奔状。瑞兽较为写实，鸾鸟多神化形态，禽兽皆栩栩如生。纹饰有浓厚的佛教色彩。镜缘窄，缘面弧。双鸾双瑞兽镜，始于唐代早中期，在中晚期颇为流行，它一改汉镜的刻板形象，镜背装饰趋于生动自然。（文立中）

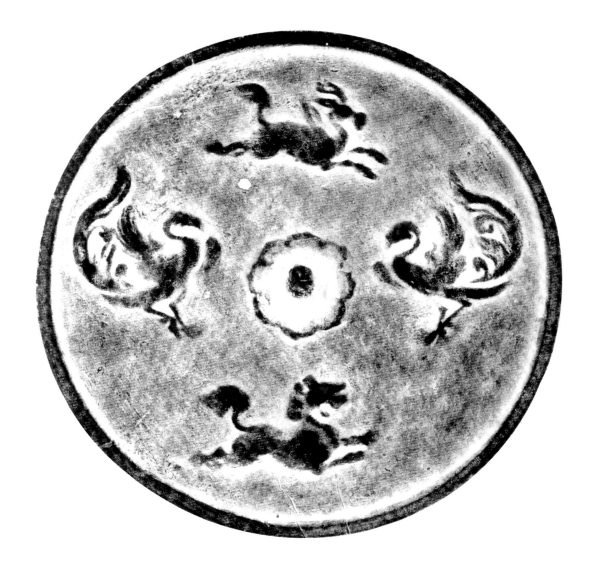

Mirror with design of double phoenixes and double auspicious animals   Tang Dynasty

Diameter: 16.5cm, Thickness of rim: 0.3cm, Weight: 540gram

Collection of Huainan Museum

The mirror is round in shape. It has a round knob on a lotus-shaped base. The major motif is the design of double phoenixes and double auspicious animals. Both sides of the base are adorned with two phoenixes opening up wings, cocking up tails and facing each other. The top and bottom sides are two running animals. The auspicious animal design is in realistic shape and the phoenix design in mythological shape. The decoration has a strong Buddhism color. The mirror has a narrow rim with arc-shaped surface. The mirror with design of double phoenixes and double auspicious animals appeared in early and middle Tang Dynasty and was popular in middle and late Tang Dynasty. Unlike the stereotyped decoration of the Han mirrors, its decoration has a vivid and natural effect.   (Wen Lizhong)

双鸾衔绶镜 唐

直径23.5厘米，边厚0.3厘米，重777克

2010年11月淮南市康杰先生捐赠

　　圆形，圆钮。镜钮两侧对置衔绶鸾鸟，鸾鸟为鹦鹉，口衔绶带，绶带系有二层花结，自口中飘至镜下缘，鹦鹉长尾飘于钮下。二鹦鹉间上下各饰一团花。鹦鹉能言，是忠贞和长寿的象征，是唐人喜爱的宠物之一，有"能言之擅美，冠同类以称奇"的美名。同类镜发现不多，陕西商县博物馆藏有一面，直径21.4厘米，与该镜鹦鹉的造型相似，布局是上下对置，无团花。此镜布局在均衡中富于变化。（沈汗青）

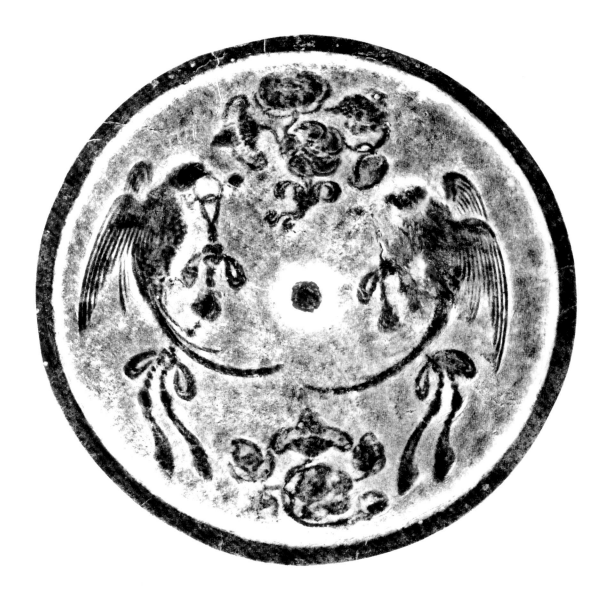

Mirror with double birds holding ribbons   Tang Dynasty

Diameter: 23.5cm, Thickness of rim: 0.3cm, Weight: 777gram

Donated by Mr. Kang Jie in Huainan City in November, 2010

The mirror is round in shape and has a round knob. Both sides of the knob are adorned with two parrots holding ribbons which are tied a two-layer knot and goes toward the rim. Between the parrots have the designs of floral medallion on the top and bottom. Parrot, which is known for its imitating human voices, is regarded as the symbol of loyalty and long life and was one of the favorite pets in Tang Dynasty. Mirror with the same decoration is only collected at Shang County Museum in Shanxi Province, which is 21.4cm diameter and has not the design of floral medallion. This mirror is not only a well-arranged layout but full of changes.   (Shen Hanqing)

双鸾衔绶镜　唐
直径13.3厘米，边厚0.25厘米，重265克
本馆旧藏

　　圆形，圆钮。镜背饰两只衔绶鸾鸟，鸾鸟展翅反向飞翔，姿态飘逸，栩栩如生。宽缘，缘面微弧。双鸾衔绶寓意夫妻幸福长寿，花结表示永结同心。此镜流行于唐代中期，反映了人们的安逸生活，透出一股田园气息。（文立中）

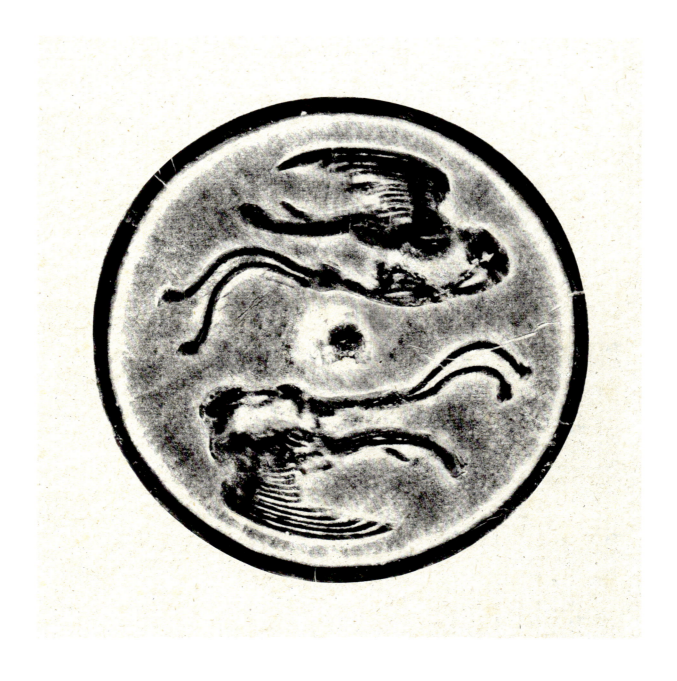

Mirror with double phoenixes holding ribbons   Tang Dynasty

Diameter: 13.3cm, Thickness of rim: 0.25cm, Weight: 265gram

Collection of Huainan Museum

The mirror is round in shape and has a round knob. It is decorated with two vivid phoenixes holding ribbons and flying back to back. It has a broad rim with slightly arc-shaped surface. The design of double phoenixes holding ribbons means happiness and long life of a couple and the knot with floral medallion represents deep love of a couple. This decorative style of the mirror, popular in middle Tang Dynasty, expresses the people's enjoyment for easy life and has an idyllic scene.   (Wen Lizhong)

盘龙镜 *唐*

直径15.6厘米，边厚0.5厘米，重734克

本馆旧藏

　　八出葵花形，圆钮。龙身作"C"形绕钮盘曲，龙头在左，面向中心作吞珠状，双角后翘，张口吐舌，双目圆瞪，龙身粗壮遒劲，背鳍、腹甲、鳞片、肘毛等均刻画细密，四足前伸后蹬，三爪尖锐犀利，呈凶猛矫健之态，纹饰简洁明快，线条丰富饱满，在龙体四周均匀饰有四朵如意云纹。素缘。

　　唐孟浩然诗《同张明府清镜叹》云："妾有盘龙镜，清光常昼发"，反映盘龙镜是唐代较为普遍使用的镜种之一，流行于盛唐时期。（陶治强）

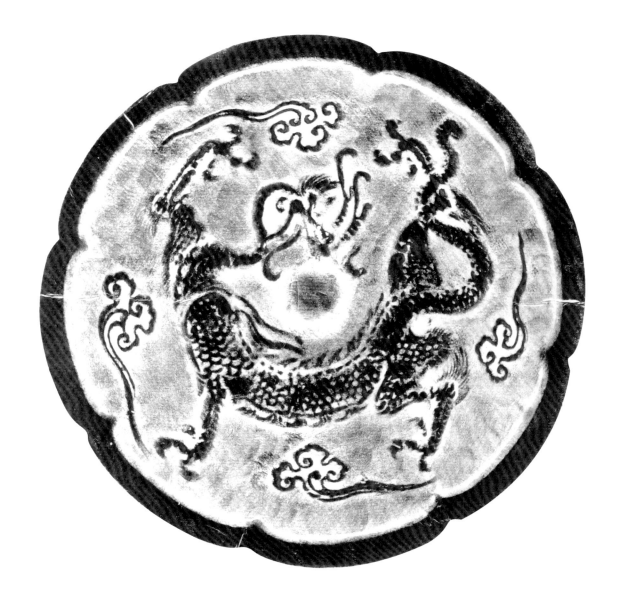

Mirror with coiling dragon design　Tang Dynasty
Diameter: 15.6cm, Thickness of rim: 0.5cm, Weight: 734gram
Collection of Huainan Museum

The mirror is in shape of eight-petal mallow and has a round knob. Around the knob is adorned with a C-shaped dragon design with head in left, mouth swallowing a ball, glaring eyes, scaly body and stretching legs. Four S-shaped clouds surround the dragon. The mirror has a rim without design.

The records of the mirror with coiling dragon design found in poem written by Meng Haoran of Tang Dynasty reflect that it was popular in Tang Dynasty.　(Tao Zhiqiang)

四花枝镜 唐

直径12.2厘米，边厚0.5厘米，重203克

本馆旧藏

　　圆形，圆钮。镜背纹饰以四条联珠纹分为四区，每区内置一折枝牡丹花，花朵怒放，生机盎然。镜缘宽窄不匀，缘中略鼓。花枝镜流行于盛唐时期，纹饰典雅端庄，反映了唐朝国力强盛，文化繁荣，社会欣欣向荣的景象。（文立中）

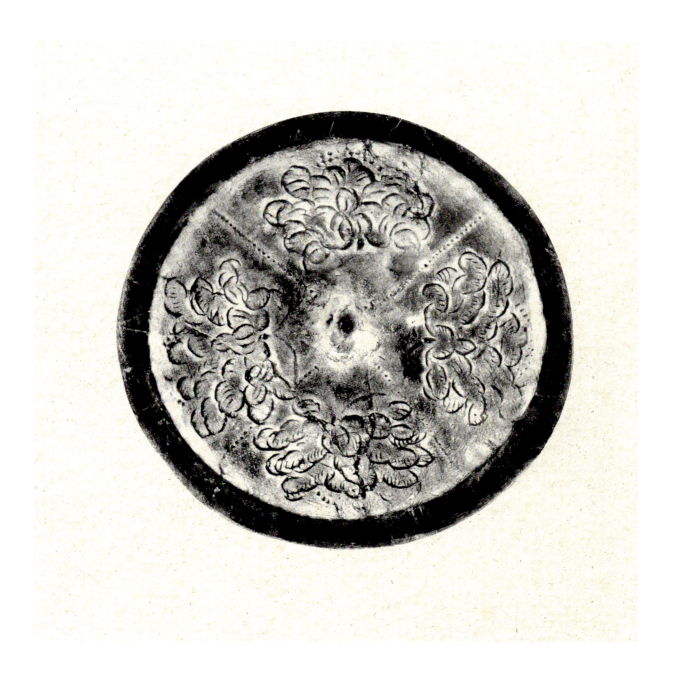

Mirror with design of four flowers　Tang Dynasty

Diameter: 12.2cm, Thickness of rim: 0.5cm, Weight: 203gram

Collection of Huainan Museum

The mirror is round in shape and has a round knob. Its back side is divided into four parts by continuous beads. Each part is adorned with a blooming peony. The mirror has a rim with uneven width. The mirror with flowers was popular in Tang Dynasty. The elegant decoration shows a flourishing society with strong national power and cultural prosperity.　(Wen Lizhong)

折枝花鸟镜　唐

直径21.8厘米，边厚0.4厘米，重1171克

本馆旧藏

　　圆形，圆钮，花瓣纹钮座。镜背纹饰布局系四花枝绕钮同向排列，花枝为有叶有苞的小折枝花，绽蕾怒放，形态一致，每一花枝下饰一鹊，形态或展翅，或作顾首状，间饰一花叶纹，整个镜背简洁清新。素平缘。

　　唐代铜镜以华美著称，其艳丽、明快的风格反映了唐代社会安定富足的景象，成为当时最受人们喜爱的镜类之一。（吴琳）

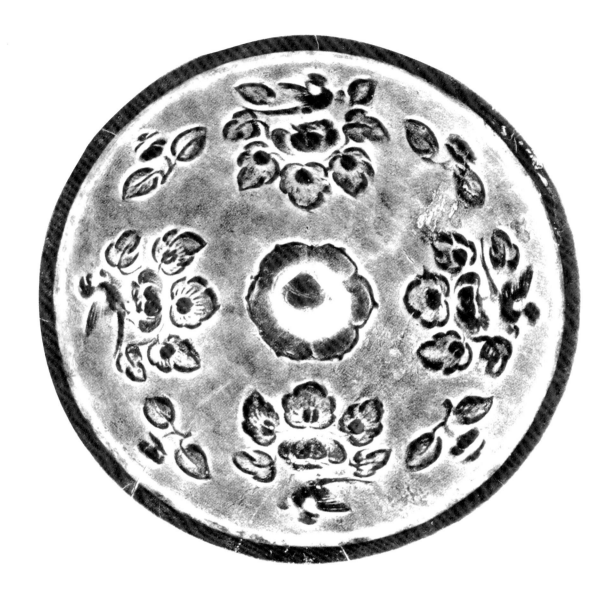

Mirror with design of interlocking flowers and birds   Tang Dynasty

Diameter: 21.8cm, Thickness of rim: 0.4cm, Weight: 1171gram

Collection of Huainan Museum

The mirror is round in shape. It has a round knob on a petal-shaped base. The major motif is the design of four flowers which are spaced with leaves design. Below each flower has a magpie. The decoration is simple and fresh. The mirror has a flat rim without design.

The mirror of Tang Dynasty is known for magnificent decoration and the bright decorative style shows a peaceful and rich scene of the society of Tang Dynasty. This mirror is one of the mirrors commonly used at that time.   (Wu Lin)

六花枝镜 唐

直径21.7厘米，边厚0.5厘米，重1150克

1960年淮南市工农公社出土

镜背主体纹饰为六枝花环绕，花形为二种三组。其一为向外绽开的五瓣形大花，其中两朵大花一小花蕾，下部衬小花叶；其二，三朵上卷的大花朵，两边加以侧开花朵，下部饰花叶。圆钮外置三小鸟、三小花枝相间环列的纹饰。镜背给人以一派繁盛富贵的吉祥景象。唐镜的纹饰风格复杂多变，涉及山水、人物、花鸟等各个方面。此镜纹饰主题纹样突出，间以小花小鸟，增加了变化和韵味，是唐代铜镜工艺制作高峰时期的作品。（沈汗青）

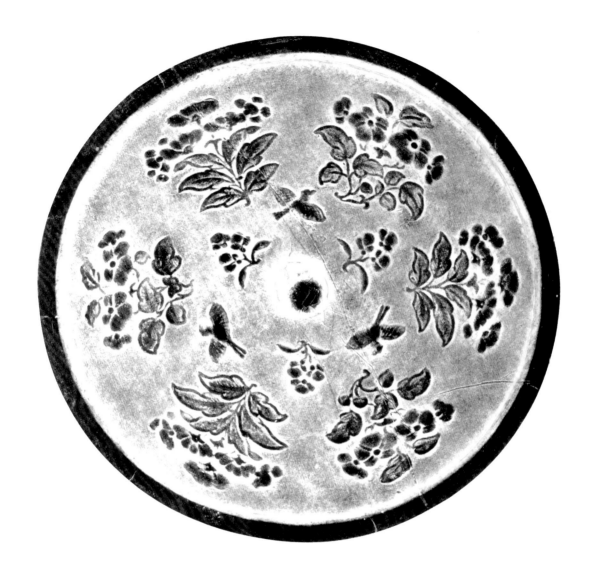

Mirror with design of six flowers Tang Dynasty

Diameter: 21.7cm, Thickness of rim: 0.5cm, Weight: 1150gram

Unearthed at Gongnong Commune in Huainan City in 1960

The major motif is the design of six flowers with two shapes in three groups. One of the flower patterns is formed with two five-petal flowers and a bud above leaves; the other is three flowers rolling up and sides of flowers above leaves. Outside the knob is arranged alternately with three birds and three flowers. The back side of the mirror brings a prosperous and lucky picture. The Tang mirrors were decorated with complicated and varied pattern covering mountains, water, figures, flowers and birds. This mirror with distinct major motif, which is accompanied with flowers and birds and holds a sense of change and rhythm, is the representative of the peak of the casting technology of the Tang mirrors. (Shen Hanqing)

四花四鹊镜 唐

直径18.6厘米，边厚0.3厘米，重738克

本馆旧藏

　　圆形，圆钮。环钮饰对称的四蝶纹，四蝶向外飞舞，主区饰四花枝和四喜鹊相间环绕。四花分两组，一组叶片宽长，一组叶片较短，顶部均饰盛开的花朵，四喜鹊展翅飞舞同向穿越花枝间。凸窄缘。

　　花鸟图案是唐代铜镜常见纹饰。此镜枝繁叶茂，花朵盛开，蝴蝶、喜鹊飞舞其间，刻画细腻，富丽自然，构成一幅繁荣、安宁的吉祥画卷，是盛唐时期人们安居乐业、幸福富足的写照。（汪茂东）

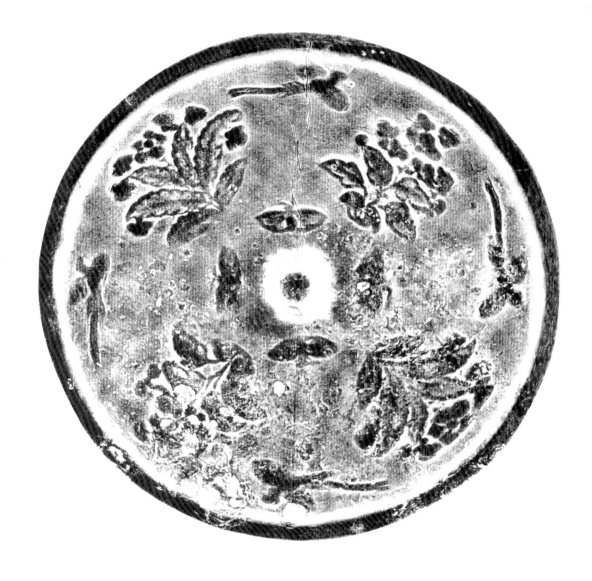

Mirror with design of four flowers and four magpies   Tang Dynasty

Diameter: 18.6cm, Thickness of rim: 0.3cm, Weight: 738gram
Collection of Huainan Museum

The mirror is round in shape and has a round knob. There are four butterflies flying outward around the knob. The major motif is alternately arranged with four magpies and four flowers in two groups, among which there are flowers with long leaves and with short leaves. The mirror has a raised narrow rim.

The pattern of flowers and birds was common decoration on the Tang mirror. This mirror with delicate design of luxuriant leaves, blooming flowers and flying butterflies and magpies, shows a picture of prosperity and peace is a mirror of happy and rich life of the people in Tang Dynasty.   (Wang Maodong)

宝相花镜 唐
直径14厘米，边厚0.25厘米，重270克
本馆旧藏

　　圆形，圆钮，花瓣形钮座。镜背上饰六朵宝相花，呈等距排列，花蕊均为七珠点纹。镜缘较窄，略弧。宝相花镜流行于唐代中晚期，纹饰有浓郁的佛教色彩。此镜纹饰布局匀称，简单中富有变化，显示出唐代社会平和安定的面貌。（文立中）

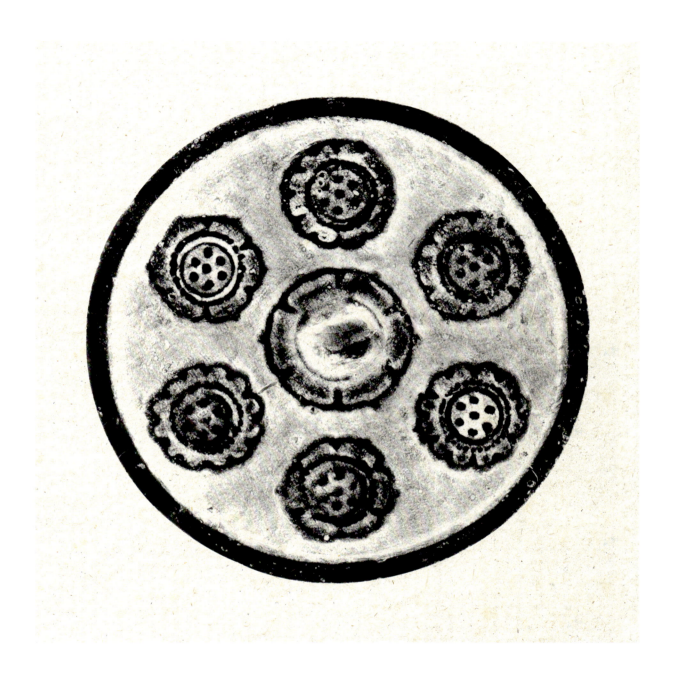

Mirror with rosette design   Tang Dynasty

Diameter: 14cm, Thickness of rim: 0.25cm, Weight: 270gram

Collection of Huainan Museum

The mirror is round in shape. It has a round knob on a petal-shaped base. Its back side is adorned with six rosettes arranging in the same distance, the center of which consist of seven beads. The mirror has a narrow rim with arc-shaped surface. The rosette design was popular in the middle and late Tang Dynasty and has a strong Buddhist color. The mirror with well-balanced layout and simple and rich decoration shows a scene of peace and stable society of the Tang Dynasty.   (Wen Lizhong)

宝相花镜 唐

直径16.8厘米，边厚0.3厘米，重394克

本馆旧藏

　　圆形，圆钮，花瓣形钮座，座外环一周凸弦纹。主题纹饰为两种不同样式的花卉纹各三朵，相间环绕。一组为六瓣莲花，花叶中置花蕊；另一组为旋转式六叶片组成的花瓣内心，外排列三叶片及三弧形花瓣，似一朵绽葩吐芬的大花。素缘。

　　隋唐时期，中国铜镜进入了全盛时期。新形式、新风格、新纹饰层出不穷，特别是纹饰构图不像传统汉式镜那样严格对称，而是采用绘画风格，不求对称，讲究均衡。这面宝相花镜是唐代比较流行的镜式，宝相花象征吉祥幸福，折射出中国封建社会鼎盛时期太平盛世的繁荣景象。（刘继武）

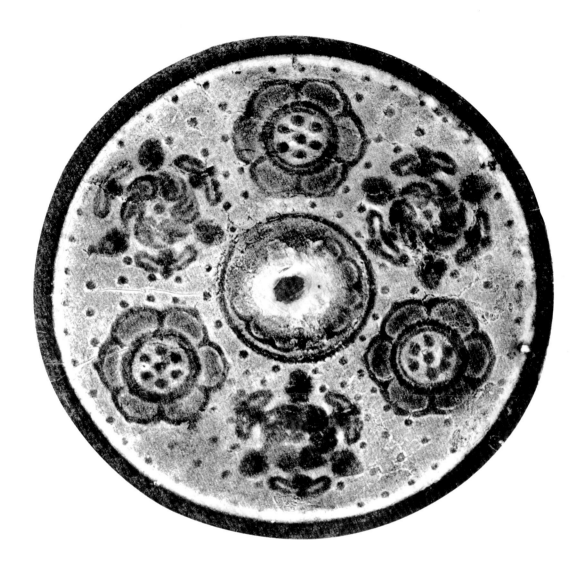

Mirror with rosette design   Tang Dynasty

Diameter: 16.8cm, Thickness of rim: 0.3cm, Weight: 394gram

Collection of Huainan Museum

The mirror is round in shape. It has a round knob on a petal-shaped base. Outside the base has a band of raised string pattern. The major motif includes two types of flower designs arranged alternately. Among them, one is in shape of a lotus with six petals; the other is in shape of a blooming flower consisting of the center with six revolving petals, three leaves and three arc-shaped petals. The mirror has a rim without design.

The bronze mirrors flourished in the Sui and Tang Dynasties.

The new shapes, new decorative styles and new designs sprang up, especially the decorative layout using painting style and showing a balanced picture instead of the symmetrical layout of the Han mirrors. The mirror with rosette design was more popular in the Tang Dynasty, the rosette design, meaning luck and happiness, represents a prosperous scene of the peak of China's feudal society. (Liu Jiwu)

素面镜 唐至五代

直径16.3厘米，边厚0.2厘米，重509克

1984年6月淮南市物资回收公司拣选

圆形，小圆钮。镜背有钮，通体光素无纹。此镜虽无纹饰，但无星点锈蚀，通体黑漆古泛出青光，说明材质优良。镜背宽大，体薄而沉手，体现了铸镜工艺的简约和精湛，虽素面无纹仍不失为佳品。（刘继武）

Mirror without design Tang Dynasty to Five Dynasties

Diameter: 16.3cm, Thickness of rim: 0.2cm, Weight: 509gram

Got from a material recycling company in Huainan City in June, 1984

The mirror is round in shape. It has a round knob and is adorned without design. The mirror, boasting a black patina all over the body, is cast with excellent material. The thin and heavy body shows brief but exquisite craftsmanship. It is regards as a treasure. (Liu Jiwu)

素面镜 唐至宋

直径18.1厘米，边厚0.4厘米，重490克

1984年5月淮南市潘集区架河乡杨集村李长江捐献

　　圆形，圆钮。通体无纹饰。凸窄缘。此镜虽平素无纹，但从其镜面银光看，冶铸精到，其照面效果应当很好，是一件十分注重实用功能的铜镜。（汪茂东）

Mirror without design　Tang Dynasty to Song Dynasty

Diameter: 18.1cm, Thickness of rim: 0.4cm, Weight: 490gram

Denoted by Mr. Li Changjiang in Yangji Village, Jiahe Town, Panji District, Huainan City in May, 1984

　　The mirror is round in shape and has a round knob. It is adorned without design. It has a narrow rim with raised surface. It boasts exquisite craftsmanship, with a shiny reflective side up to now, and is a mirror with practical function.　(Wang Maodong)

连钱锦纹镜 宋
直径14厘米,边厚0.1厘米,重176克
2010年12月淮南市邓宗雨先生捐赠

　　亚字形,半环钮。钮外环一联珠纹菱形框,靠近缘侧随形饰一周联珠纹。两周联珠纹内饰连钱锦纹,锦纹的每个单元图案为五枚钱纹相叠加,形成一个以圆点为中心、十字形四叶展瓣的花卉。但纹饰结合并不严密,多处出现错位现象。素宽缘。

　　连钱锦纹镜,流行于宋神宗至南宋高宗期间,亦称重毯纹、织锦纹、四角朵花纹镜,为五个同等大小的圆与圆相切组成的几何纹饰,有着强烈的图案效果。(吴琳)

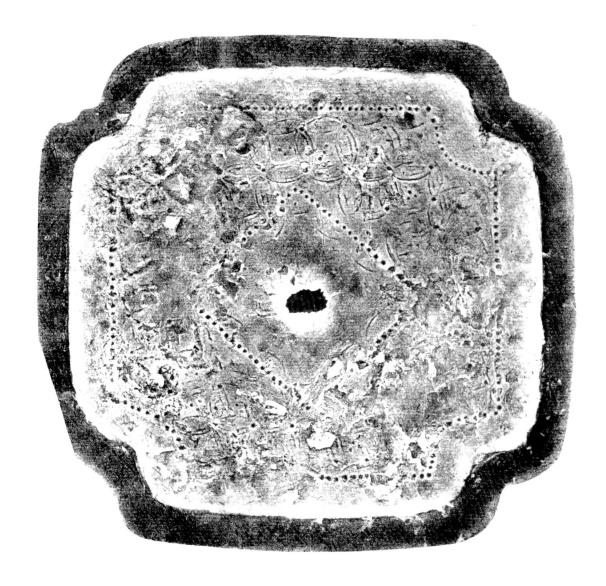

Mirror with design of brocade formed with linked coins Song Dynasty

Diameter: 14cm, Thickness of rim: 0.1cm, Weight: 176gram

Denoted from Deng Zongyu in Huainan City in December, 2010

The mirror is in shape of *Ya* character and has a half-ring-shaped knob. Outside the knob is a rhomboid pattern formed with continuous beads. A band of continuous beads is close to the rim. The major motif is the design of brocade formed with linked coins. Each part of the rough design is a flower formed with five overlapping coins. The mirror has a broad rim without design.

The design of brocade formed with linked coins, prevailing from the Emperor Shenzong to the Emperor Gaozong of the Song, bring us a strong patterned effect. (Wu Lin)

湖州石十五郎铭葵花镜　宋

直径12.7厘米，边厚0.3厘米，重227克
20世纪90年代初安徽省寿县北门建房时出土

六出葵花形，圆钮。素背，钮右侧为长方形框，框内铸铭，竖读两行，铭文："湖州石十五郎真炼铜照子"，楷书，字体不甚工整。素缘。

湖州镜为南宋湖州（今浙江吴兴）铸造的铜镜。湖州是当时著名的铸镜中心，所铸铜镜远销各地。湖州镜多作葵花形、菱花形等，一般素背，背上铸有商号性质的铭记，有的还列有铜镜价格。"青铜照子"、"白铜照子"、"炼铜照子"皆是镜铭中对铜镜本身的称呼。（刘继武）

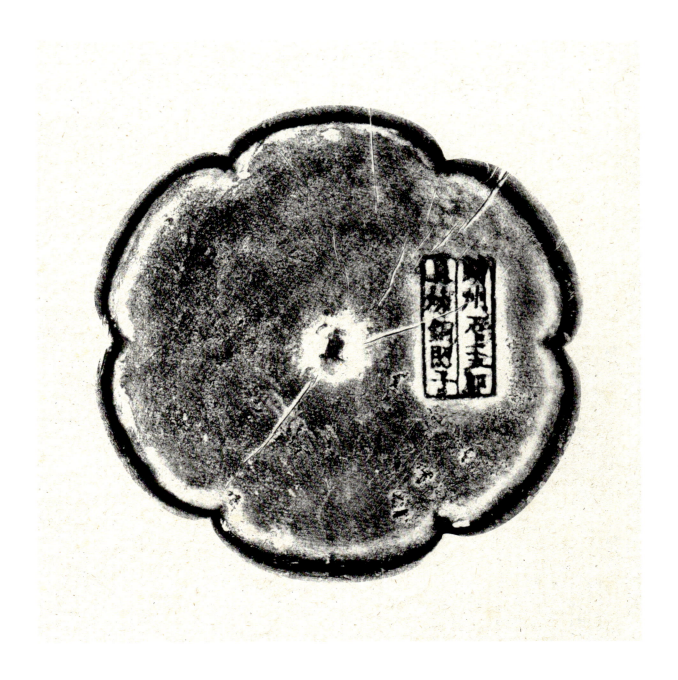

Huzhou Mirror with inscription of "*Shi Shi Wu Lang*" Song Dynasty

Diameter: 12.7cm, Thickness of rim: 0.3cm, Weight: 227gram
Unearthed at a construction site of the north gate, Shou County in 1990's

The mirror is in shape of six-petal mallow and has a round knob. It is adorned without designs. At the right of the knob is a rectangle with inscription "*Hu Zhou Shi Shi Wu Lang Zhen Lian Tong Zhao Zi*" in irregular standard script and two vertical lines inside. It has a rim without design.

The mirror of Huzhou was cast in Huzhou of the Southern Song Dynasty (the present-day Wuxing of Zhejiang), which was a famous center of casting mirrors at that time. The mirrors produced here were exported to all over. The mirrors are generally in shape of mallow, water chestnut and so on and have simple backs with inscription of workshop name and price sometimes. The characters of "*Qing Tong Zhao Zi*", "*Bai Tong Zhao Zi*" and "*Lian Tong Zhao Zi*" show clearly the raw material of the mirror.   (Liu Jiwu)

三凤镜 宋

直径13.8厘米，边厚0.5厘米，重261克

1972年淮南市废品收购站拣选

　　圆形，小圆钮。镜背浅浮雕三只凤鸟纹，拖着长长的尾羽，作展翅飞翔状，其间配以三只雁纹。素缘。

　　宋代铜镜常见以凤鸟为装饰图案，但在表现技巧上多借鉴剪纸、刻纸的手法，有强烈的图案化效果。此镜为浅浮雕，镜背轻微凸起，使凤鸟和大雁形态具体生动，别有趣味。（吴琳）

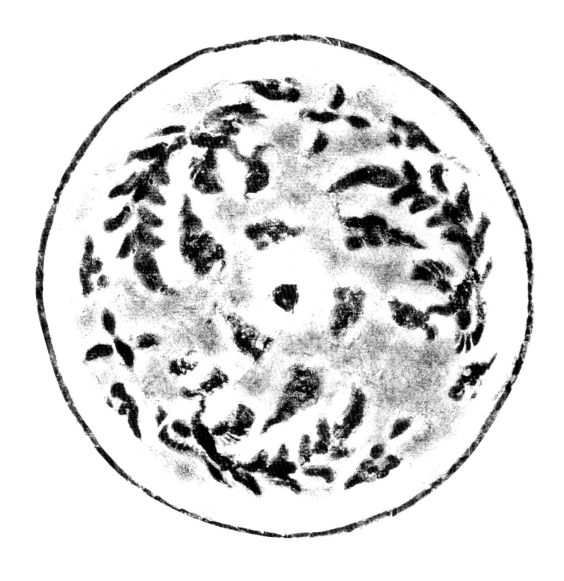

Mirror with design of three phoenixes　Song Dynasty

Diameter: 13.8cm, Thickness of rim: 0.5cm, Weight: 261gram

Got from a material recycling company in Huainan City in 1972

　　The mirror is round and has a round knob. The back side is adorned with three flying phoenixes with long tails which are spaced with three swallows. It has a rim without design.

　　The mirrors of the Song Dynasty often used phoenix as the decorative pattern by means of the paper-cut technique, which brings a strong patterned effect. The design of phoenixes and swallows, showing vivid and natural shapes and an interesting decorative effect, is cast in low relief.　(Wu Lin)

湖州石家铭盾形镜　宋

长10.4，宽8.3厘米，边厚0.4厘米，重161克

1973年7月淮南市废品收购站拣选

　　盾形，鼻钮。钮右侧有长方形框，框内有两行竖排铭文，铭文间有一竖栏，铭"湖州石家法炼青铜照子"。镜缘坡，窄素。广西桂林博物馆藏有一面与此相同铜镜。（赵永林）

Huzhou Shield-shaped Mirror with inscription of "*Shi Jia*"   Song Dynasty

Length: 10.4cm, Width: 8.3cm, Thickness of rim: 0.4cm, Weight: 161gram

Got from a material recycling company in Huainan City in July, 1973

The mirror is in shape of shield and has a nose-shaped knob. At the right side of the knob is a rectangle with inscription "*Hu Zhou Shi Jia Fa Lian Qing Tong Zhao Zi*" in two vertical lines separated with a line. It has a narrow rim slanting. The mirror with the same decoration is collected in Guilin Museum of Guangxi Province.   (Zhao Yonglin)

湖州石家铭葵花镜　宋

直径11.9厘米，边厚0.3厘米，重219克
1974年4月淮南市废品收购站拣选

六出葵花形。素背，在钮的左侧置一长方形框，框内有两列铭文："湖州真石家，念二叔照子"。素平缘。

此镜属纪名号铭镜类，为宋镜中最具特点的镜类，即在镜背素地上标有铸镜字号，字号多为长方形印章式，方框内竖写一行或多行铭文。根据字号内容可以分为湖州镜、建康镜、饶州镜等，其中尤以湖州镜数量最多，而湖州镜中又主要以此种葵瓣形镜为主体。该镜铭"湖州"为铸镜产地，"石家"为铸家的名号，"念二叔"为字号，说明此镜为正宗石家产品。（吴琳）

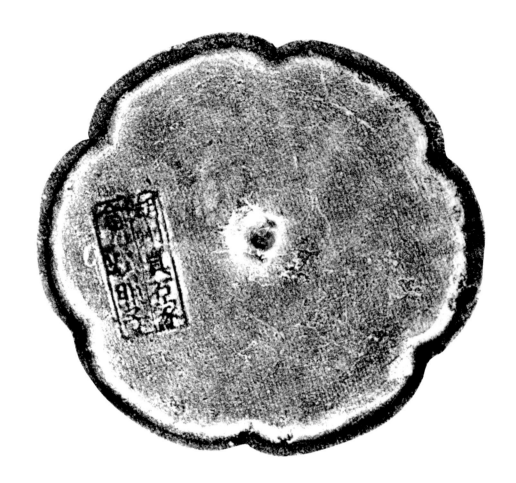

Huzhou Mallow-shaped Mirror with inscription of "*Shi Jia*"   Song Dynasty

Diameter: 11.9cm, Thickness of rim: 0.3cm, Weight: 219gram

Got from a material recycling company in Huainan City in April, 1974

The mirror is in shape of six-petal mallow and a back side without design. At the left side of the knob is a rectangle with inscription "*Hu Zhou Zhen Shi Jia, Nian Er Shu Zhao Zi*" in vertical lines. The rim is flat and has no design.

The mirror with inscription of name is the most characteristic one of the Song mirrors, which was carved with one or several vertical lines in seal-shaped rectangle. Base on the inscription, the mirrors can be divided into several categories: mirrors of Huzhou,

mirrors of Jiankang, mirrors of Raozhou and so on, among which the mirrors of Huzhou were found in a great number. The mirrors of Huzhou are generally in shape of mallow. The characters "*Huzhou*" of the inscription refers to the casting area, "*Shi Jia*" is the caster's surname and "*Nian Er Shu*" is his name. So the inscription tells clearly that this mirror was cast by Shi's Family workshop.   (Wu lin)

观星望月桃形镜 宋

高12.5厘米，宽9.3厘米，边厚0.7厘米，重179克

本馆旧藏

　　桃形，圆钮，花瓣钮座。钮座上端饰有祥云、弦月、星辰，下侧饰有弯曲的松枝及成簇的松枝四组，左侧立一人，对月而立，全神贯注，作观星望月练气功状。素缘。此镜纹饰布局疏朗，人物造型简练传神。（程东雯）

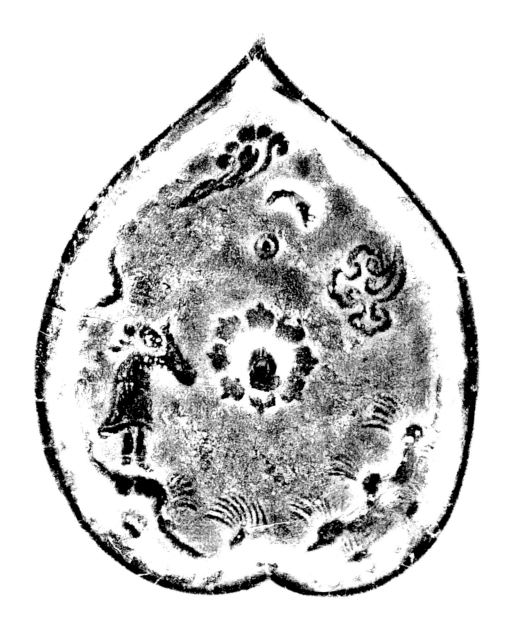

Peach-shaped Mirror with pattern of astronomical observation Song Dynasty

Height: 12.5cm, Width: 9.3cm, Thickness of rim: 0.7cm, Weight: 179gram

Collection of Huainan Museum

The mirror is in shape of a peach and has a round knob on a petal-shaped base. Above the base are the patterns of clouds, crescent and stars. Below the base are the patterns of pine branches and a figure observing stars and playing Qigong. The mirror has a rim without design. This mirror is decorated with a pithy layout and vivid patterns.   (Chen Dongwen)

菊花镜 宋

直径12.2厘米，边厚0.2厘米，重120克
1988年5月淮南市唐山乡双古堆砂场墓葬出土

圆形，圆钮，内向七连弧纹钮座。座外以两周联珠纹勾框，主区纹饰为一朵硕大的菊花纹，钮及钮座即为其花蕊，层层叠叠，呈叠压旋转状，极富动感。

镜缘较窄。菊花纹镜始于唐代晚期至五代。此镜当为北宋产品，纹饰气氛浓烈，造型优雅大方，工艺精湛，为宋镜中的佳品。（文立中）

Mirror with chrysanthemum desig Song Dynasty
Diameter: 12.2cm, Thickness of rim: 0.2cm, Weight: 120gram
Unearthed from the tombs at a sand works in Shuanggudui, Tangshan Town, Huainan City in May, 1988

The mirror is round and has a round knob on a base with seven linked arcs inside. The base is surrounded with continuous beads. The major motif is a large chrysanthemum with the knob and the base as the center and the petals overlapping and revolving, which shows a vivid decorative effect. The mirrors with chrysanthemum design were used from the late Tang Dynasty to Five Dynasties. This mirror was cast in the Song Dynasty and was a treasure of the Song mirrors, boasting an elegant shape and exquisite craftsmanship. (Wen Lizhong)

方格纹镜　宋

直径15.5厘米，边厚0.4厘米，重318克
本馆旧藏

　　圆形，小桥钮，长方形钮座。镜背满布方格纹。方格纹形似"四出五铢"钱的穿缘状。镜缘宽窄不一，当是模范所致，有明显的北宋风格。方格纹镜，与钱纹镜、锦地纹镜在北宋较流行，镜纹由单一的几何纹构成，它反映了当时人们渴求安定，追寻平淡自然生活的心理状态。（文立中）

Mirror with check design　Song Dynasty

Diameter: 15.5cm, Thickness of rim: 0.4cm, Weight: 318gram
Collection of Huainan Museum

　　The mirror is round in shape. It has a bridge-shaped knob on a rectangle base. Its back side is adorned with check design. The width of the rim varies. This mirror shows a distinct feature of the Northern Song Dynasty. The check design with cask design and brocade ground was popular in the Northern Song Dynasty. The decoration, only formed with geometric patterns, represented the people's expectation of the peaceful and natural life. (Wen Lizhong)

祥云纹菱花镜 宋

直径11.5厘米，边厚0.5厘米，重234克

本馆旧藏

　　六出菱花形，桥钮，钮孔较大。钮上下对称饰一祥云纹。素缘。

　　此镜采用宋镜中常见的菱花形造型，纹饰简洁。

铜镜业发展至宋代，所铸铜镜无论质量、纹饰变化都远不如唐代，铜镜制作开始走向衰落。（刘继武）

Water-chestnut-shaped mirror with cloud design Song Dynasty
Diameter: 11.5cm, Thickness of rim: 0.5cm, Weight: 234gram
Collection of Huainan Museum

The mirror is in shape of a six-petal water chestnut and has a bridge-shaped knob with a big hole. Above and below the knob is a cloud arranged respectively. The mirror has a rim without design.

This mirror is in shape of a water chestnut which was often seen in the Song mirrors. It is adorned with pithy patterns. In the Song Dynasty, the mirrors with quality and variety of designs did not equate with the mirrors of the Tang Dynasty. The production of the mirrors had declined since the Song Dynasty.   (Liu Jiwu)

双凤纹方形镜 宋

长9.1厘米，宽8.9厘米，厚0.1厘米，重60克
2010年10月安徽省黄山市太平区征集

　　方形，半环钮，钮两侧细线浅雕双凤纹，双凤对飞，四角饰花草纹。凤头呈三角形，尖喙，双翅伸展，尾羽曲曲弯弯，缓缓舒展。宽素平缘。

　　该镜胎质较薄，采用细致入微的细线浅雕，这是宋代铜镜的一个重要表现技法。线条纤巧、精致美观，特别是那长长的尾羽，轻松浪漫，体现了宋代匠师的卓越技艺。（吴琳）

Rectangular Mirror with design of double phoenixes　Song Dynasty

Length: 9.1cm, Width: 8.9cm, Thickness: 0.1cm, Weight: 60gram

Collected in Taiping District, Huangshan City, Anhui Province in October, 2010

The mirror is rectangle in shape. It has a half-ring-shaped knob. There are two flying phoenixes with triangle head, sharp beam, spreading wings and rolling tails. Each corner of the square is adorned with pattern of flower and leaf. The mirror has a broad and flat rim without design.

The mirror with thin body is decorated with low relief, which was an important decorative technique of the Song mirrors. The delicate and perfect lines, especially the long tails which express an easy and romantic beauty, reflect the distinguished technique of the casters in the Song Dynasty.　(Wu Lin)

任敬轩铭镜 宋

直径8.4厘米，边厚0.2厘米，重126克

1993年10月淮南市唐山乡打击盗墓收缴

　　圆形，圆钮。素面无纹，仅钮右侧铸"任敬轩"三字铭，楷书。无缘。此镜流行于南宋时期，多见湖州镜，属作坊名号铭镜，即在镜背铸上制镜的产地、作场等标记。该镜虽无纹饰，但铸造工艺讲究。（文立中）

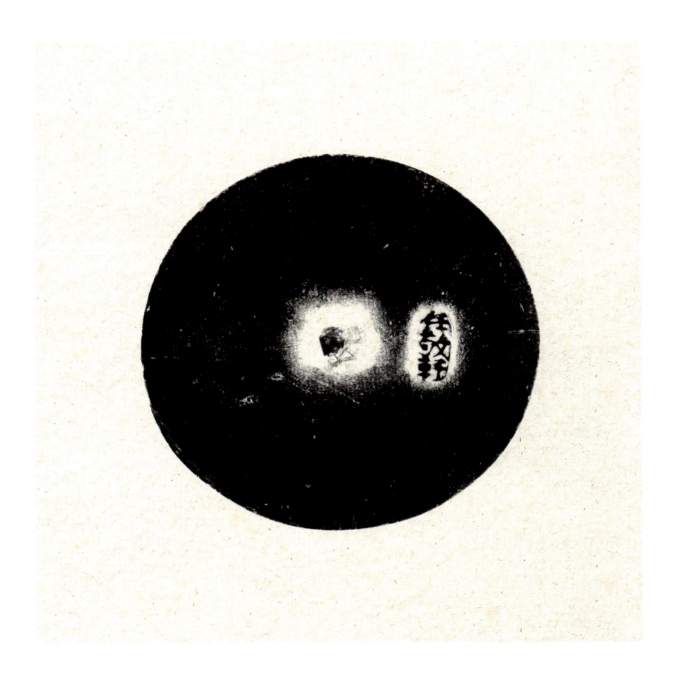

Mirror with inscription of "*Ren Jing Xuan*"   Song Dynasty

Diameter: 8.4cm, Thickness of rim: 0.2cm, Weight: 126gram

Got from an operation against tomb robbers in Tangshan Town, Huainan City in October, 1993

The mirror is round in shape and has a round knob. It is only adorned with the inscription "*Ren Jing Xuan*" in standard script at the right of the knob. The mirror has no rim. The mirrors with this decorative style were popular in the Southern Song Dynasty, especially in the mirrors of Huzhou which belong to the mirrors with inscription of name. The mirrors with inscription of name are cast with inscription about producing area, workshop on the back side. This mirror without design is cast with refined craftsmanship. (Wen Lizhong)

双鱼镜 宋

直径12.6厘米，边厚0.5厘米，重148克
1972年11月淮南市物资回收公司拣选

镜体薄。镜背小圆钮。钮左右各饰一翘首张口、展鳍甩尾、作腾跃状的鲤鱼纹。两鱼形态一致，头尾相接，以圆钮为中心呈对称布局，镜钮两侧各饰一云纹。外置凸弦纹一周。窄缘。在中国传统的图案中，鱼具有生殖繁盛、子孙兴旺的祝福含义，同时鲤鱼跃龙门又有祈求登仕高升的寓意。（刘继武）

Mirror with design of double fish   Song Dynasty

Diameter: 12.6cm, Thickness of rim: 0.5cm, Weight: 148gram

Got from a material recycling company in Huainan City in November, 1972

The mirror has a thin body and a round knob. There are two fish, which are raising heads, opening mouths, spreading fins and swinging tails, at both sides of the knob. The fish are spaced with clouds. A band of raised string pattern surrounds the major motif.

The mirror has a narrow rim. In the Chinese tradition, the fish is the symbol of numerous offspring and the carp leaping over the Dragon Gate has a meaning to succeed in civil service examination in former times.   (Liu Jiwu)

许由巢父故事镜　金

直径13.5厘米，边厚0.45厘米，重299克
1984年6月淮南市物资回收公司拣选

　　圆形，圆钮。钮上方近缘处置一单线方框，框下峰峦起伏，空中云彩缭绕，山上山下点缀树林。镜下方较模糊，隐约可见河水奔流，左侧坐一人，手抬至耳边，作洗耳状。右侧下游有一人牵牛，一手指向上游坐者。外以一周弦纹为界。高素缘。

　　该镜纹饰内容与吉林德惠"许由巢父故事镜"如出一辙，唯缺少方框内铭文。史载尧让天下于许由，许由不愿，遁去；尧又召其为九州长，由听了此语后认为脏了耳朵，于颍水旁洗耳。正好被许由的朋友巢父看见，得知原委后，巢父指责许由为何不去高岸深谷而到处游荡，实际上还是想沽名钓誉，并且认为其洗耳之水污染了它的牛口，故牵牛离开，此镜纹饰即生动传神地展现了这一传说故事。（吴琳）

Mirror with pattern of legendary incident of Xu You and Chao Fu Jin Dynasty

Diameter: 13.5cm, Thickness of rim: 0.45cm, Weight: 299gram

Got from a material recycling company in Huainan City in June, 1984

The mirror is round in shape and has a round knob. Above the knob is a rectangle formed with single line. Below the rectangle are mountains, clouds and trees. At the bottom of the mirror is a picture of flowing river, a figure sitting and washing out his ears on the left and a figure leading a cattle and pointing at the sitting figure on the right. The major motif is surrounded with a band of string pattern. The mirror has a high rim without design.

The mirror has the same decoration with the one found in Dehui, Jiliin, on which the rectangle is carved with characters. According to the records, Emperor Yao tried to demise the throne to Xu You but was declined. Emperor Yao asked Xu You to be official. Unwilling to hear such words, Xu You ran to the stream nearby to wash out his ears. Chao Fu happened to pass by with his cattle. Chao Fu blamed him for his roving the streets to make him known instead of living in the trackless wilderness. He got cross because the mouth of his cattle was smeared by washing out ears here. So Chao Fu went for the upper reach of the stream to water his cattle. The pattern of this mirror vividly shows the scene of the legendary incident.   (Wu Lin)

高山流水人物镜　金

直径16.3厘米，边厚0.5厘米，重566克

1977年8月淮南市物资回收公司拣选。

　　圆形，圆钮，钮顶平。镜钮上方为山峰、树木，右侧山石间一瀑布直泻而下，下方为潭水溪流。镜钮左下方山坳之中，一人倚石临溪而坐，抬头侧目远望瀑布，左臂附于左腿之上，右腿盘屈，左腿弓膝，神情悠然自得。外围一圈凸棱勾廓。宽素平缘。此镜布局结构、装饰风格与金代许由巢父故事镜相类似，是金代铜镜中的典型器。（刘继武）

Mirror with patterns of high mountains, flowing water and figure Jin Dynasty

Diameter: 16.3cm, Thickness of rim: 0.5cm, Weight: 566gram

Got from a material recycling company in Huainan City in August, 1977

The mirror is round in shape and has a round knob with a flat top. Above the knob are mountains and trees. A waterfall between rocks is on the right, which is flowing down. A river is on the bottom. A man by the river is sitting and enjoying the scene of waterfall. The major motif is surrounded with a band of raised string pattern. The mirror has a broad and flat rim without design. This mirror, as the representative of the Jin mirrors, has the same layout and decorative style with the mirror with patterns of Xu You and Chao Fu. (Liu Jiwu)

双童采莲镜 金

直径8.9厘米，边厚0.35厘米，重132克
淮南市废品收购站拣选

　　圆形，圆钮。钮左右各饰一童，皆梳髻，双手上举，一手攀枝，一手举藤，右童略仰望左童。二童头上有朵盛开的莲花，脚下一片硕大的荷叶，周围为水波纹。素缘。

　　此镜构图简洁，但装饰手法流畅，为金代比较流行的镜式。其纹饰取自中原地区流行的婴戏纹样，加以佛教标志的莲花，寓意吉祥，又暗合了古诗"江南可采莲"的意蕴。这是汉族与女真族人民在经济、文化、思想等方面互相学习、互相渗透的结果。（吴琳）

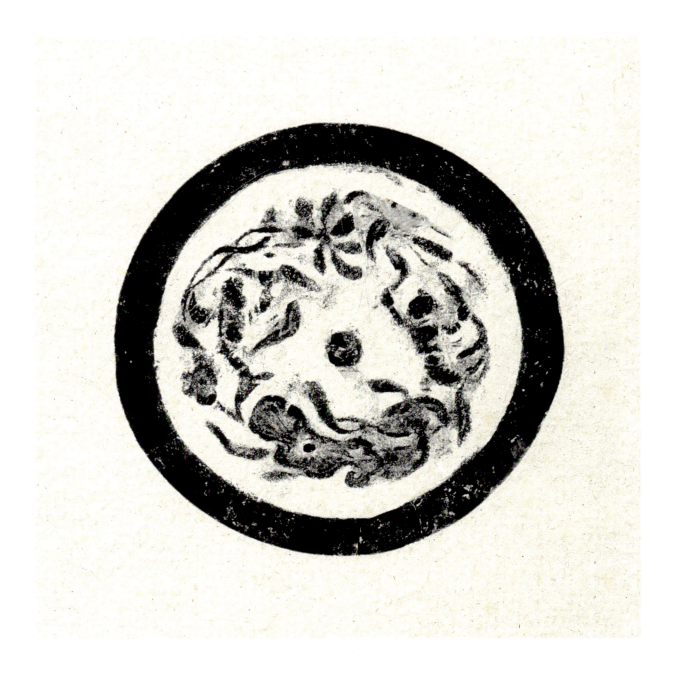

Mirror with pattern of two boys collecting lotus   Jin Dynasty

Diameter: 8.9cm, Thickness of rim: 0.35cm, Weight: 132gram

Got from a material recycling company in Huainan City

The mirror is round in shape and has a round knob. At both sides of the knob are two boys with the hair worn in a bun and hands climbing up or raising the branches. The child on the right is looking up at the other child. A blooming lotus is above the children and a large lotus leaf is below them. The wave design surrounds them. The mirror has a rim without design.

This mirror with pithy pattern and smooth decoration was popular in Jin Dynasty. The pattern was derived from the design of playing boys that prevailed in the Central Plain. The picture of boys with lotus that is the symbol of Buddhism, which stands for the luck and implies the meaning of "collecting lotuses in the south of the Yangtze River" in ancient poem, reflects the effect of learning and permeating each other between the Han nationality and the Nuchen on economy, culture, thought and so on.   (Wu Lin)

童子骑马镜　金

直径11厘米，边厚0.4厘米，重174克

1984年6月淮南市废品收购站拣选

　　圆形，弓形小钮，花式钮座。绕钮座一周联珠纹，中区饰浮雕八骑马童子，同向环绕，八童均侧身骑木偶状木马上，外以一周联珠纹与外区纹饰间隔。外区饰一周花枝纹。在镜钮的右上方有一方框，框内有铭，漫漶不清。1958年5月河北省完县出土一面同类镜，布局结构似同，其右上的方框内铭文"镜子局造"四字。（赵永林）

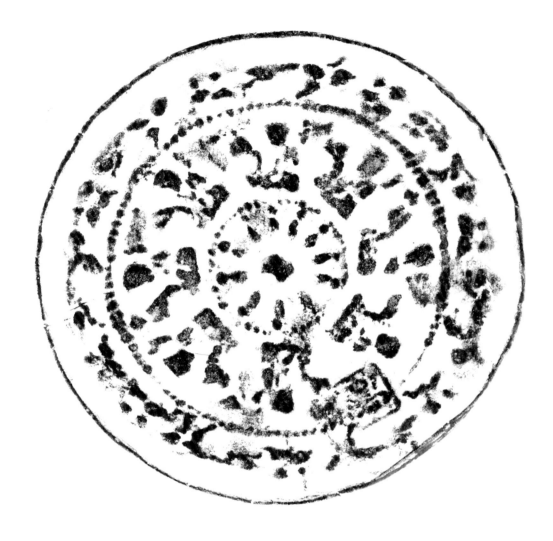

Mirror with pattern of boys riding   Jin Dynasty

Diameter: 11cm, Thickness of rim: 0.4cm, Weight: 174gram

Got from a material recycling company in Huainan City in June, 1984

The mirror is round in shape. It has a bow-shaped knob on a flower-shaped base. Around the base is surrounded with continuous beads. The middle part is adorned with the pattern of eight circling boys in the same direction, which are riding wooden horses. The middle part and the outer part are divided with continuous beads.

The outer part is adorned with flowers. At the right top of the knob is a rectangle with unclear inscription. The mirror with the same decoration was unearthed in Wan County, Hebei Province in May, 1958. At the right top of the mirror is the inscription of "*Jing Zi Ju Zao*".   (Zhao Yonglin)

莲花纹有柄镜　金
直径8厘米，执柄长6.5厘米，宽1.4厘米，边厚0.2厘米，重45克
本馆旧藏

　　圆形，长柄。镜背用单线装饰有一朵盛开的莲花，下部装饰一荷叶，荷叶叶面下垂，下侧为简线水波纹，两侧分别有一外撇莲茎。窄素凸缘。此镜莲花古拙不拘泥，呈自然态，有写意画之感。（于怀珍）

Mirror with handle and lotus design   Jin Dynasty

Diameter: 8cm, Length of handle: 6.5cm, Width: 1.4cm, Thickness of rim: 0.2cm, Weight: 45gram

Collection of Huainan Museum

The mirror is round in shape and has a handle. The back side of the mirror is adorned with design of a blooming lotus, a lotus leaf, wave and stem going outside, which are formed with single line. The mirror has a narrow and raised rim without design. The lotus design with unsophisticated and natural shape brings us a sense of spontaneous expression.   (Yu Huaizhen)

莲花纹有柄镜 金

直径8.1厘米，柄长6.9厘米，宽1.3厘米，边厚0.15厘米，重58克
本馆旧藏

　　圆形带柄。镜背阳线勾勒出一朵盛开的荷花，下为一片张开的荷叶，左侧饰有荷花花蕾，纹饰简约。窄缘。宋金时期的花草图案，注重写意，造型简约，恬淡自然。（陶治强）

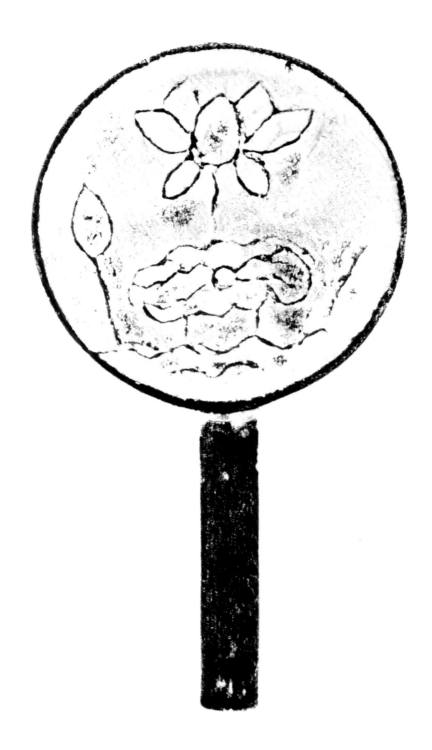

Mirror with handle and lotus design   Jin Dynasty

Diameter: 8.1cm, Length of handle: 6.9cm, Width: 1.3cm, Thickness of rim: 0.15cm, Weight: 58gram

Collection of Huainan Museum

The mirror is round in shape and has a handle. The back side of the mirror is adorned with a blooming lotus, an opening leaf and a bud on the left. The mirror has a narrow rim. In Song and Jin Dynasties, the design of flowers and leaves with vivid and simple shape has a sense of spontaneous expression.   (Tao Zhiqiang)

人物仙鹤多宝镜 明

直径7.6厘米，边厚0.7厘米，重69克

1985年6月淮南市园艺场砖厂征集

　　圆形，小圆钮。镜钮上下各有一个如意云头纹饰，上方为一展翅回首的仙鹤，两侧饰交叉的犀角与书卷；钮左右各置一插花宝瓶，宝瓶外侧各饰一人物，直立而稍侧身，双手横捧一琵琶形乐器；钮下的如意云头纹饰下方饰双犀牛角，两侧对称饰银锭。窄缘，高卷。

　　明代铜镜纹饰的最大特点是"图必有意，意必吉祥"，多宝镜图案的内容虽有差异，但它们都是象征吉祥如意、财亨福洪、平安长寿，生活气息浓郁。而且多宝镜是明代独具特色的一个镜种，内容丰富，繁而不乱，且大多做工精美，可谓铜镜铸造史上最后的光芒。（刘继武）

Mirror with design of figures, crane and treasures   Ming Dynasty

Diameter: 7.6cm, Thickness of rim: 0.7cm, Weight: 69gram

Collected from a brick workshop at a horticultural market in Huainan City in June, 1985

The mirror is round in shape and has a round knob. At each of the top and bottom sides of the knob is an S-shaped cloud, above which is a crane spreading wings and looking back, on both sides of which are the rhinoceros horn and the book crossing. At each of the right and left sides of the knob is a vase filled with flowers, at each side of which are a figure standing, leaning slightly to a side and holding a pipa. Below the S-shaped cloud at the bottom are two rhinoceros horns crossing, on each side of which is the silver ingot. The rim is narrow and raising highly.

The decoration of the Ming Dynasty has the major feature of patterns with lucky meanings. The patterns of treasures, as the symbols of good luck, big wealth, peace and long life, have a strong sense of life, varying slightly. The patterns of treasures with rich and symmetrical contents and refined craftsmanship are peculiar to the Ming Dynasty, which is the last highlight of the casting history of the bronze mirrors.   (Liu Jiwu)

仿汉四神博局镜 明
直径10.3厘米，边厚0.4厘米，重95克
淮南市物资回收公司拣选

　　圆形，银锭形钮，圆钮座。座外围一双线方框，内作简单装饰。主题纹饰位于方框外，为四神博局纹，四个带座乳钉将纹饰分为四区，四区各置一对神兽，分别为青龙配羽人、白虎配羊、朱雀配瑞兽、玄武配蟾蜍，外以一周斜向栉齿纹带和一周凸弦纹为栏。窄缘。

　　银锭钮为明代特有的形制，此镜仿汉代博局纹样后稍加演变而成。铜色泛黄，制作较规整，纹饰比较清晰，四神栩栩如生，是明代仿镜中的佳品。
（孙梅）

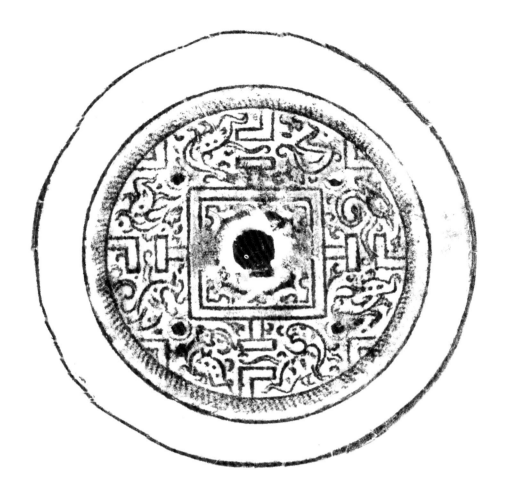

Imitation of Han Mirror with design of four deities and gambling Ming Dynasty

Diameter: 10.3cm, Thickness of rim: 0.4cm, Weight: 95gram

Got from a material recycling company in Huainan City

The mirror is round in shape and has an ingot-shaped knob on a round base. Outside the knob is a square formed with two lines, which is adorned with simple patterns. Outside the square is the major motif, which is the design of four deities and gambling. The decoration is divided into four parts by four nipples with bases, at each part of which is a pair of auspicious animals, including Green Dragon with winged figure, White Tiger with ram, Scarlet Bird with auspicious animal and Somber Warrior with toad. The

bands of fine-toothed pattern and raised string pattern surround the decoration. The mirror has a narrow rim.

The ingot-shaped knob was peculiar to the Ming Dynasty. This mirror is decorated with the evolved design of gambling. The mirror with yellow cover, refined craftsmanship and clear design is a treasure of the imitations of the mirrors of the Ming Dynasty. (Sun Mei)

仿汉四乳禽鸟镜 明

直径8.1厘米，边厚0.4厘米，重134克

本馆旧藏

　　圆形，半球钮，圆钮座。两周栉齿纹将纹饰分为两区，主纹为四乳钉，将主区纹饰分为四段，每段内饰以一组禽鸟，禽鸟相对而立，形似鸳鸯，造型简约。宽平素缘。缘上对称两侧各铸有铭文，应为仿照汉镜翻模制成。（陶治强）

Imitation of Han Mirror with design of four nipples and birds   Ming Dynasty

Diameter: 8.1cm, Thickness of rim: 0.4cm, Weight: 134gram

Collection of Huainan Museum

The mirror is round in shape and has a half-sphere-shaped knob on a round base. Two bands of fine-toothed pattern divide the decoration into two parts. The major motif is the design of four nipples, which spaces the major motif into four areas. Each area is adorned with a pair of birds facing each other, which is in the shape of mandarin duck. The mirror has a broad and flat rim without design, which is arranged symmetrically with two inscriptions. The mirror was cast with the copied mould of the Han mirror.　(Tao Zhiqiang)

仿汉四神博局镜 明

直径12.4厘米，边厚0.4厘米，重245克

本馆旧藏

　　圆形，半球形钮，柿蒂纹钮座。座外饰一周双线方格纹，方格外以"TLV"格式博局纹装饰，在方格四角和"V"形尖角相对处各置一带座小乳钉，将镜背分为四区，每一区除饰博局纹外，还填饰四神和瑞兽纹饰，其外以一周栉齿纹为廓。宽缘，缘上饰两周三角锯齿纹，且外侧锯齿间添饰一周小联珠纹。该镜纹饰不清晰，镜面呈色有别于汉镜，是明代翻模铸造。

（王莉）

Imitation of Han Mirror with design of four deities and gambling   Ming Dynasty

Diameter: 12.4cm, Thickness of rim: 0.4cm, Weight: 245gram

Collection of Huainan Museum

The mirror is round in shape and has a half-sphere-shaped knob on a base with kaki calyx design. Outside the base is a square formed with double lines. Outside the square is TLV-shaped gambling design. Between each corner of the square and each closed angle of the V-shaped design is a nipple with a base which spaces the back side of the mirror into four parts. Each part is adorns with gambling design, four deities and auspicious animals. The band of fine-toothed pattern surrounds the major motif. The broad rim is adorned with two bands of saw pattern, the outer band of which is filled with beads. The mirror with unclear design and the color different from the Han mirror was cast with the copied mould.   (Wang Li)

仿汉四神博局镜 明

直径10.9厘米，边厚0.5厘米，重327克

2010年9月淮南市谢家集公安分局移交

　　圆形，半球钮，柿蒂钮座。座外是一双线方框，方框外各边中间饰双线"T"形纹，其外与双线"L"纹相对，"V"形纹和方框四角相对，中间夹一圈点珠纹。在博局纹外饰四神，兽昂首、张口，作爬行状，朱雀曲颈、展翅、卷尾，造型栩栩如生。外以一周斜向栉齿纹为栏。宽素缘。

　　该镜面泛银光，合金比例有别于汉镜，为明代翻铸品。（孙梅）

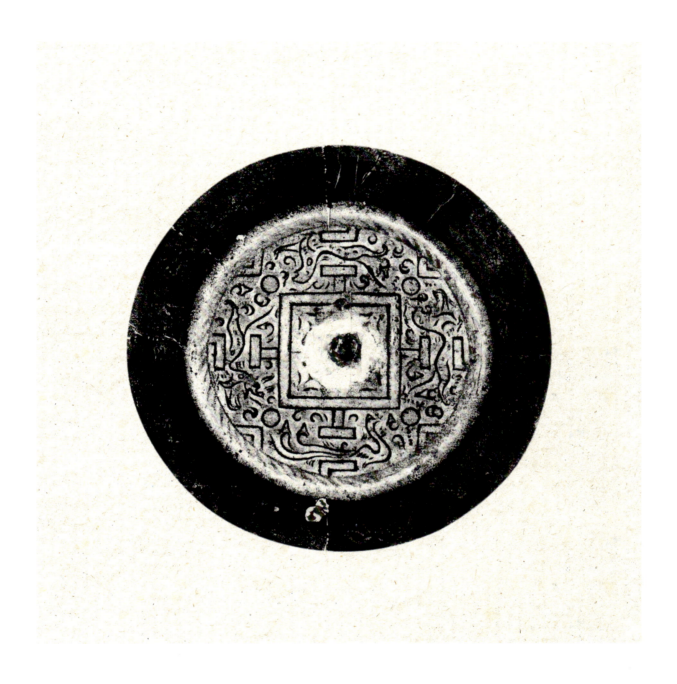

Imitation of Han Mirror with design of four deities and gambling   Ming Dynasty

Diameter: 10.9cm, Thickness of rim: 0.5cm, Weight: 327gram

Transferred by the Xiejiaji District Public Security Bureau in Huainan City in September, 2010

The mirror is round in shape and has a half-sphere-shaped knob on a base with kaki calyx. Outside the base is a square formed with double lines. T-shaped pattern formed with double lines adorns the middle of each side of the square, which's opposite the L-shaped pattern formed with double lines. Each corner of the square and a V-shaped pattern are facing each other and space with bead. Outside the gambling design is the design of four deities. The band of fine-toothed pattern surrounds them. The mirror has a broad rim without design.

The mirror, which has a cover of silver light and a proportion of annoy different from the Han mirrors, was cast in the Ming Dynasty.   (Sun Mei)

许字铭人物杂宝镜 明

直径9厘米，边厚0.7厘米，重139克
1973年3月淮南市物资回收公司拣选

　　圆形，银铤形钮。纹饰虽然由上至下多层次排列，但层次界限并不严格。镜最上方饰如意云纹，两侧各一对犀牛角，其下各饰一铜钱；钮上方为三方胜纹；钮两侧自内向外分别饰有梅花、宝瓶、侍者人物，宝瓶内插花枝；钮下饰一方胜。镜下方饰银锭、人物，其间还置一阳文字号铭"许"。窄缘。（吴琳）

Mirror with inscription of "*Xu*" and design of figures and treasures   Ming Dynasty

Diameter: 9cm, Thickness of rim: 0.7cm, Weight: 139gram

Got from a material recycling company in Huainan City in March, 1973

The mirror is round in shape and has an ingot-shaped knob. The patterns were arranged into several layers with unclear limits from the top to the bottom. At the top is an S-shaped cloud, on each side of which is a pair of rhinoceros horns, below each is a copper coin. Above the knob is a design of three intersecting lozenges. At both sides of the knob are plum blossoms, vases with flowers and figures. Below the knob is an intersecting lozenge design. The design of sliver ingots, figures and a character "*Xu*" in relief adorns the bottom of the mirror. The mirror has a narrow rim.   (Wu Lin)

□泉□造铭素镜 明

直径8.7厘米，边厚0.15厘米，重148克

本馆旧藏

　　圆形，柱状钮，钮顶平。镜背通体素面无纹，唯钮面铸铭，内有两列四字，阳文楷书，文"□泉□造"。镜平直无廓。此镜虽素面无纹，但铸造精良。

（陶治强）

Simple Mirror with inscription of "□ *Quan* □ *Zao*" Ming Dynasty

Diameter: 8.7cm, Thickness of rim: 0.15cm, Weight: 148gram

Collection of Huainan Museum

The mirror is round in shape and has a column-shaped knob with a flat top. Its back side is adorned with a simple surface. The knob surface is adorned with inscription "□ *Quan* □ *Zao*" arranged in two vertical lines and cast in relief and standard script. The mirror has no rim but refined craftsmanship.   (Tao Zhiqiang)

仙阁人物多宝镜 明

直径10.7厘米，边厚0.9厘米，重158克
1984年6月淮南市物资回收公司拣选

　　圆形，银锭形钮。镜背纹饰分三层：上层中间为一座二层琼阁，琼阁下钮上为一对犀牛角，两侧各置一飞鹤，作侧身展翅状，鹤下分别有宝钱和花叶；中层纹饰在钮的两侧饰四人物纹，手托食盘作行走状；下层纹饰中间为一几案，上置一宝鼎，两侧为宝瓶，内插花束，其外有方胜、宝钱、双犀牛角及画卷。窄缘。（吴琳）

Mirror with design of pavilion, figures and treasures   Ming Dynasty

Diameter: 10.7cm, Thickness of rim: 0.9cm, Weight: 158gram

Got from a material recycling company in Huainan City in June, 1984

The mirror is round in shape and has a ingot-shaped knob. The decoration of its back side can be divided into three layers: at the top are a two-story pavilion and a pair of rhinoceros horns with a flying crane on each side, coins and leaves below; at the middle is four figures holding food containers on both sides of the knob; at the bottom is a table with Ding, vases with flowers, intersecting lozenge, coins, two rhinoceros horns crossing and painting scroll. The mirror has a narrow rim.   (Wu Lin)

人物杂宝方镜 明

长6.8厘米，宽6.8厘米，边厚0.6厘米，重88克
1991年12月安徽省长丰县张池乡赵村谢道坤捐赠

　　方形，银铤形钮。镜背以凸起方框分为内外两区，内区在钮两侧饰两人物纹，作捧盒状；钮上置一对犀牛角，下置一张口瑞兽，翘尾伏于地上；外区素面无纹。窄缘。

　　该镜为简化人物多宝镜，明代以杂宝、仙人、瑞兽等象征吉祥如意。（吴琳）

Mirror with design of figures and treasures Ming Dynasty

Length: 6.8cm, Width: 6.8cm, Thickness of rim: 0.6cm, Weight: 88gram

Denoted from Mr. Xie Daokun in Zhangchi Town, Changfeng County, Anhui Province in December, 1991

The mirror is round in shape and has an ingot-shaped knob. Its back side is divided into two parts by the raised rectangle. The inner part is adorned with two figures holding food containers on both sides of the knob. Above the knob is a pair of rhinoceros horns and below the knob is an auspicious animal opening mouth, squatting and raising tail. The outer part has no decoration. The mirror has a narrow rim.

The mirror is decorated with simplified figures and treasures. In the Ming Dynasty, the treasures, gods and auspicious animals were regarded as the symbols of good luck and wish. (Wu Lin)

五子登科铭镜　明

直径9.3厘米，边厚0.6厘米，重252克

1984年5月淮南市古沟乡陶圩村孟庆早捐献

圆形，小圆钮，钮顶平。钮四周各有一方框，方框内各铸有一字，依上下右左为"五子登科"，楷书，方框与字体均不够端正规整，且"登"、"科"二字模糊，外饰一圈凸棱。窄缘。

在铜镜上以大字楷书分上下左右而列吉祥语铭文

属明代最为常见。相传宋代窦禹钧的五子：仪、伊、侃、偁、僖相继及第，故称"五子登科"。《三字经》中有"窦燕山，有义方；教五子，名俱扬"，镜铭寄托了联袂获取功名的美好愿望。（刘继武）

Mirror with inscription of "*Wu Zi Deng Ke*"　**Ming Dynasty**

Diameter: 9.3cm, Thickness of rim: 0.6cm, Weight: 252gram

Denoted from Mr. Meng Qing in Taowei Village, Gugou Town, Huainan City in May, 1984

The mirror is round in shape and has a round knob with a flat top. At the four sides of the knob are the irregular squares with characters of "*Wu Zi Deng Ke*" arranged in succession and carved in standard script, which were not carved rightly and clearly. A raised band surrounds the inscription.

The mirrors with inscription arranged from top, bottom, right to left and carved in standard script, which means luck and happiness, were generally cast in the Ming Dynasty. According to the record in *Shan Hai Jing*, in the Song Dynasty, the five sons of Dou Yujun succeeded in the civil examinations and became high officials, hence the name of "*Wu Zi Deng Ke*" that refers to the good wish for the high official.　(Liu Jiwu)

八卦镜　明
直径5.2厘米，边厚0.5厘米，重55克
1985年10月淮南市贺疃乡古路岗大队谭庄征集

　　圆形，圆钮。纹饰以一周凸起高圈的弦纹为廓，内饰八卦纹。窄缘。

　　八卦，传说是伏羲氏所作，《易·系辞传》说："易有太极，是生两仪，两仪生四象，四象生八卦。"八卦符号在明代后期，尤其是嘉靖以后受到推崇，因明帝笃信道教，追求长生不老，使得八卦符号广泛用于各种装饰上。（陶治强）

Mirror with design of the Eight Diagrams　Ming Dynasty
Diameter: 5.2cm, Thickness of rim: 0.5cm, Weight: 55gram
Collected from Tan Zhuang in Gulugang Brigade, Hetuan Town, Huainan City in October, 1985

　　The mirror is round in shape and has a round knob. The decoration surrounded with raised string pattern is the pattern of the Eight Diagrams. The mirror has a narrow rim.

　　The Eight Diagrams were invented by Fu Xi in the legend. The *Yi·Xi Ci Zhuan* records: "The Yi produces the Taiji. The Taiji produces the Two Forms, named Yin and Yang. The Two Forms produce the Four Phenomena. The four phenomena act on the Eight Diagrams." The Eight Diagrams had prevailed since the Emperor Jiajing of Ming. In the Ming Dynasty, the emperors believed in Taoism and pursued living forever, so the Eight Diagrams, as one of the symbols of the Taoism, were used widely.　(Tao Zhiqiang)

富贵双全铭镜　明

直径40厘米，厚1.5厘米，重6934克

1965年淮南市废品收购站拣选

　　圆形，圆钮，钮顶平，动物纹钮座，外环一周凸弦纹。其外一周饰四只展翅飞翔的大雁，间饰四花枝纹；中区四周各饰一宽带方框，框内有铭，楷书"富贵双全"，铭文周围饰人物、动物、花卉、云朵和八宝等纹饰，皆左右对称布局。其中有14位人物纹，形态各异，构成一幅其乐融融、恬静富足的生活画面。宽卷缘。此镜镜体硕大、厚重，纹饰美观，模铸精良，是明代铜镜的代表作品，弥足珍贵。（汪茂东）

Mirror with inscription of "*Fu Gui Shuang Quan*"   Ming Dynasty

Diameter: 40cm, Thickness: 1.5cm, Weight: 6934gram

Got from a material recycling company in Huainan City in 1965

The mirror is round in shape and has a round knob with a flat top on a animal-shaped base, which is surrounded with a band of raised string. Four flying cranes spaced with four flowers surrounds the band. At each side of the middle part is a square with inscription "*Fu Gui Shuang Quan*" in standard script. The inscription is symmetrically surrounded with the design of figures, animals, flowers, clouds and Eight Emblems. The design of 14 figures shows a scene of happy and wealthy life. The mirror has a broad rim rolling. The mirror with heavy body, beautiful and refined craftsmanship, is a rare treasure of the Ming mirrors.   (Wang Maodong)

彦和铭镜　明

直径8.5厘米，边厚0.4厘米，重29克

1986年安徽省长丰县埠里乡土段埂村出土，1987年淮南市潘集区袁庄工商银行李文濂捐赠

圆形，银锭形钮。镜钮上下各有一楷书大字，上"彦"下"和"。字体端正有力，近缘一圈凸棱，宽素边。窄缘。据《尔雅·释训》："美士为彦"。"彦"是指古代有才学、德行的人。而镜铸"彦和"是以示心愿，寓意自己的形象可与古代"美士"相比。（刘继武）

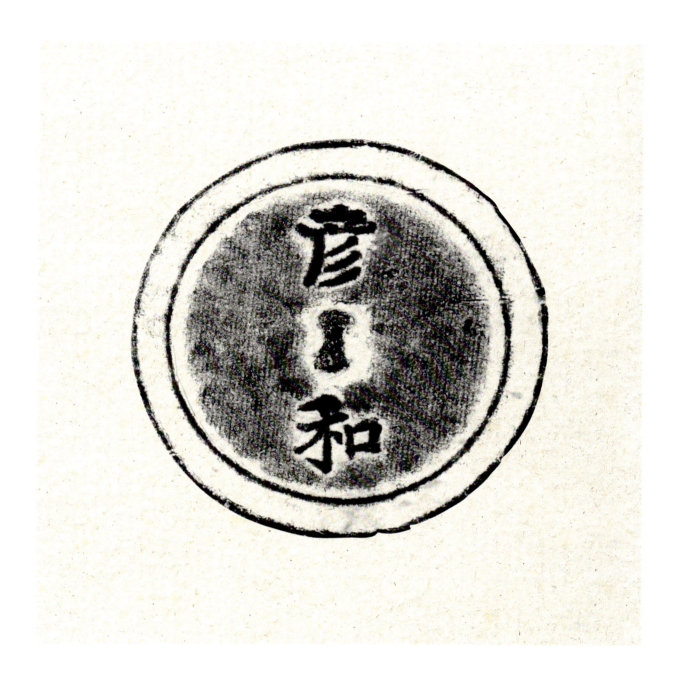

Mirror with inscription of "*Yan He*"   Ming Dynasty

Diameter: 8.5cm, Thickness of rim: 0.4cm, Weight: 29gram

Unearthed at Tuduangeng Village, Buli Town, Changfeng County, Anhui Province in 1986

Denoted from Mr. Li Wenlian working in Yuanzhuang ICBC, Panji District, Huainan City in 1987

The mirror is round in shaped and has an ingot-shaped knob. Above the knob is the character "*Yan*" and below the knob is "*He*". A raised band is close to the rim. Between the band and the narrow rim is a broad and simple band. According to the record in *Er Ya·Shi Xun*, Yan refers to the people with intelligence and moral integrity. The inscription of "*Yan He*" means good wish for being a man with intelligence and moral integrity.   (Liu Jiwu)

喜报三元铭镜 明

直径20.4厘米，边厚0.6厘米，重556克

淮南市废品收购站拣选

圆形，圆钮，钮顶平。钮上下左右各有一双重方框，框内楷书阳文"喜报三元"四个大字，字形端正工整，美观大方，笔画粗壮有力，外置一圈凸棱。素边窄缘。

"三元"指的是乡试的"解元"、会试的"会元"、殿试的"状元"，在科举时代乡试、会试、殿试三级都是第一名方称"连中三元"。然而科场竞争激烈，能够榜上有名已属不易，而连中三元更是凤毛麟角，历史上获此殊荣者仅17人。"喜报三元"只是体现了父母望子成龙、登科及第的美好愿望。（刘继武）

Mirror with inscription of "*Xi Bao San Yuan*"   Ming Dynasty

Diameter: 20.4cm, Thickness of rim: 0.6cm, Weight: 556gram

Got from a material recycling company in Huainan City

The mirror is round in shape and has a round knob with a flat top. At four sides of the knob are a square formed with double lines. The characters "*Xi Bao San Yuan*" with regular and powerful strokes are respectively at each square, which are carved in standard script and in relief. A raised band surrounds them. The mirror has a narrow rim without design.

"*San Yuan*" refers to the extremely man who was the first on the pass lists of each of three levels of civil service recruitment examinations, including Provincial Examination, Metropolitan Examination and Palace Examination. There were only 17 men who got "*San Yuan*" in the history. The inscription of "*Xi Bao San Yuan*" expresses the good wish of getting promotions step by step. (Liu Jiwu)

大宣年制铭镜 明

直径4厘米，边厚0.12厘米，重10克

本馆旧藏

　　圆形，桥形钮。钮周饰四字楷书铭"大宣年制"，外以弦纹一周为廓。窄缘。"大宣"有人释为"大明宣德"的简称，尚待考证。此镜直径仅4厘米，应为随身携带用镜。（汪茂东）

Mirror with inscription of "*Da Xuan Nian Zhi*"　Ming Dynasty

Diameter: 4cm, Thickness of rim: 0.12cm, Weight: 10gram

Collection of Huainan Museum

　　The mirror is round in shape and has a bridge-shaped knob. The inscription "*Da Xuan Nian Zhi*", which was carved in standard script, is around the knob and surrounded with a band of string pattern. The mirror has a narrow rim. Some experts thought that the characters of "*Da Xuan*" are the "*Da Ming Xuan De*" (Emperor Xuande of the Ming dynasty) for short. This mirror with diameter 4cm was carried with the ancient people.　(Wang Maodong)

戊子年置铭镜　明

直径9.5厘米，边厚0.25厘米，重138克
1984年6月淮南市物资回收公司拣选

　　圆形，圆乳钮。钮周饰"戊子年置"，通体无纹饰。平缘。

　　明代铜镜，官府和民间都有铸造。铜镜多有铭文，大致分为两类：一是纪年铭文，二是商标铭记或使用铭记，与宋镜有些相似，但明镜的商标铭记后常常加"造"、"铸造"、"记"等，或仅有铸造者的姓名。此镜铭文属制作纪年。（汪茂东）

Mirror with inscription of "*Wu Zi Nian Zhi*"　Ming Dynasty

Diameter: 9.5cm, Thickness of rim: 0.25cm, Weight: 138gram
Got from a material recycling company in Huainan City in June, 1984

　　The mirrors of the Ming Dynasty were cast by the imperial workshops and civil workshops. The mirrors have the similar inscriptions with the mirrors of the Song Dynasty, including inscriptions of year and inscriptions of workshop name. The inscriptions in the Ming mirrors have the characters of "*Zao*", "*Zhu Zao*", "*Ji*" or the maker's name. The inscription of this mirror belongs to the inscriptions of year.　(Wang Maodong)

厚德荣贵铭镜 清

直径4厘米，边厚0.04厘米，重8克

本馆旧藏

　　圆形。镜体薄，上铸有阳文四字，为"厚德荣贵"，楷书字体。缘低平，素面。此镜直径仅4厘米，当为随身携带所用。（陶治强）

Mirror with inscription of "*Hou De Rong Gui*"　Qing Dynasty

Diameter: 4cm, Thickness of rim: 0.04cm, Weight: 8gram

Collection of Huainan Museum

　　The mirror is round in shape and has a thin body. The mirror was carved the inscription of "*Hou De Rong Gui*" in standard script and relief. It has a flat rim without design. The mirror with diameter 4cm was carried with the ancient people. (Tao Zhiqiang)

菱花纹有柄镜 *清*

直径13.3厘米，柄长10.2，宽2.3厘米，边厚0.4厘米，重429克

本馆旧藏

　　圆形带柄。在锦纹地上开菱形花窗，主纹为变形　　一对条形叶分隔；镜背满铺锦纹地。窄缘。此镜制作
菱纹，大菱形纹的上下对角变形为一相连的小菱形图　　规整，主纹与地纹模范清晰，是清代铜镜中的佳品。
案。内饰一上下对称的扇形花朵，花中有蕊，中间以　　（陶治强）

Mirror with handle and rhomboid pattern   Qing Dynasty

Diameter: 13.3cm, Length of handle: 10.2cm, Width: 2.3cm, Thickness of rim: 0.4cm, weight: 429gram

Collection of Huainan Museum

The mirror is round in shape and has a handle. The mirror is adorned with rhomboid pattern as the major motif and the brocade pattern as the ground motif. Inside the rhomboid pattern is a pair of fan-shaped flowers spaced with a pair of leaves. The mirror has a narrow rim. The mirror with regular layout and clear decoration is a treasure of the Qing mirrors.   (Tao Zhiqiang)

礼字铭有柄镜　*清*

直径17.3厘米，柄长10.9厘米，宽3.2厘米，边厚0.4厘米，重510克
淮南市废品收购站拣选

　　圆形，长柄。镜背中心有一繁体楷书"礼"字，外置宽带形圆框，其上有重圈圆框围绕的竖读阳文楷书"张九锡造"四字，其下为单方框围绕竖读阳文楷书"上上青铜"四字，两侧依镜形饰长条花枝纹。窄素缘。镜下接柄，素面，长条形。在镜背上端及柄下端各有一圆形小穿孔。

　　有柄镜大量出现时代较晚。此类镜因有柄而无需固定，方便使用，可从各角度理容照面。此镜铭文端正，纹饰规整，制作精细。（刘继武）

Mirror with handle and inscription of "*Li*"   Qing Dynasty

Diameter: 17.3cm, Length of handle: 10.9cm, Width: 3.2cm, Thickness of rim: 0.4cm, Weight: 510gram

Got from a material recycling company in Huainan City

The mirror is round in shape and has a handle. In the middle of the mirror is the character "Li" in standard script, which is surrounded with a circle. Above the character is a circle with inscription "*Zhang Jiu Xi Zao*" in standard script. Below the character is a rectangle with inscription "*Shang Shang Qing Tong*".

The flowers adorn both sides of the character. The mirror has a narrow rim without design and a rectangle-shaped handle without design. At the top of the mirror and the bottom of the handle is a hole.   (Liu Jiwu)

后 记

新中国成立以来，淮南市博物馆通过考古发掘、征集、接受捐赠、公安部门移交和20世纪80年代从市物资回收公司拣选等方式，入藏了一批铜镜。将这批资料进行梳理并公开出版是我们多年的心愿。为此，我们把这项工作列入了今年的工作任务。

经过认真筛选、反复斟酌，本书收录了150面铜镜。考虑到时代延续性，也兼顾了早期铜镜的珍贵性，对重复较多、品相不佳者没有收录。为了把一些残缺的铜镜能够完整地展现出来，我们邀请了国内著名的青铜器修复专家金学刚、金春刚两位先生予以修复。在此，我们表示诚挚的谢意。

对这批资料的整理过程，也是全馆同志学习业务知识的过程。全馆同志分别承担了数量不等的铜镜说明和赏析文章的撰写，为了能够写好文章，大家查找资料，请教老师，数易其稿，在馆内形成了良好的学习氛围。实践证明，这种方法是提高业务知识水平的有效途径。

本书在内容和形式上力求图文并茂、雅俗共赏，对重要的铜镜做到既有照片，也有拓本，目的是将文物所包含的信息量最大限度地传达给广大研究者和社会各界读者。

以一家博物馆的铜镜收藏，出版一本反映历代铜镜面貌的专门书籍，本身就是一件不容易的事情。加上我们的专业能力和认知水平有限，本书一定存在诸多不足，恳请读者批评指正。

《淮南市博物馆藏镜》的出版，得到了淮南市文化广电新闻出版局、淮南市财政局的大力支持，安徽省鉴定站的专家周京京、李广宁、王刚、傅慧娟等同志，在工作十分繁忙的情况下，认真对书稿予以审校。刘继武同志为资料整理付出了艰苦的努力。吴琳同志牺牲休息时间，不辞辛劳承担了书稿全部文字的录入工作。冯伟女士为本书提供了英文翻译。于怀珍、汪茂东承担了大量的编务工作。沈汗青、刘继武同志承担了铜镜拍摄工作。全书最后由沈汗青同志承担了统稿工作。对以上付出辛勤劳动的同志们，我们在此一并表示衷心的感谢！

编 者

2010年12月18日